Party Discipline and Parliamentary Politics

One of the chief tasks facing political leaders is to build and maintain unity within their parties. *Party Discipline and Parliamentary Politics* examines the relationship between party leaders and Members of Parliament in Britain, Canada, Australia, and New Zealand, showing how the two sides interact and sometimes clash. Christopher J. Kam demonstrates how incentives for MPs to dissent from their parties have been amplified by a process of partisan dealignment that has created electorates of non-partisan voters who reward shows of political independence. Party leaders therefore rely on a mixture of strategies to offset these electoral pressures, from offering MPs advancement to threatening discipline, and ultimately relying on a long-run process of socialization to temper their MPs' dissension. Kam reveals the underlying structure of party unity in modern Westminster parliamentary politics, and drives home the point that social norms and socialization reinforce rather than displace appeals to MPs' self-interest.

CHRISTOPHER J. KAM is an Assistant Professor of Political Science at the University of British Columbia in Vancouver, Canada. He has received major research grants from the US National Science Foundation and the Social Sciences and Humanities Research Council of Canada and his work on political parties and parliamentary government has appeared in the *British Journal of Political Science*, *Legislative Studies Quarterly*, and *Governance*.

Party Discipline and Parliamentary Politics

CHRISTOPHER J. KAM
University of British Columbia

CAMBRIDGE
UNIVERSITY PRESS

CAMBRIDGE UNIVERSITY PRESS
Cambridge, New York, Melbourne, Madrid, Cape Town, Singapore, São Paulo, Delhi

Cambridge University Press
The Edinburgh Building, Cambridge CB2 8RU, UK

Published in the United States of America by Cambridge University Press, New York

www.cambridge.org
Information on this title: www.cambridge.org/9780521518291

© Christopher J. Kam 2009

First published 2009

Printed in the United Kingdom at the University Press, Cambridge

A catalogue record for this publication is available from the British Library

ISBN 978-0-521-51829-1 hardback

Contents

Figures

vi

Tables

Acknowledgements

The number of people who have assisted my research for this project is quite staggering. Pippa Norris, Jack Vowles, Ian McAllister, Lynda Erickson, Joseph Wearing, Philip Norton, Philip Cowley, and Brian Gaines generously donated data without which this project could not have been started, let alone finished. Renee Smith, John Carey, Randy Calvert, Richard Johnston, Paul Warwick, Tony Sayers, Lanny Martin, Aaron Wicks, Georg Vanberg, Gail McElroy, Campbell Sharman, Ben Nyeblade, and Patrick Francois provided advice and commentary on chapters and grant applications. Bing Powell and Indridi Indridason deserve special mention in this regard. The fieldwork for this project also depended heavily on many people: Wayne Hooper of the Australian Senate Research Office, Brian Hallett of the Australian Electoral Commission, Doug Eckhoff of the New Zealand Electoral Commission, Sandra Smugler at Robarts Library, and Don Curtin of the Canadian Parliamentary Library are just a few. Adam Barrett, Peter Regenstrief, Raymond Miller, and Ian McAllister helped me arrange interviews with Canadian, Australian, and New Zealand MPs. Raymond Miller and Ian McAllister also made sure that I had access to the libraries at the University of Auckland and ANU, respectively. Cathy Job of the ABC provided insight into the personalities and politics in Canberra. Confidentiality precludes me from listing the MPs who generously shared their time and thoughts with me, but they were, of course, critical to this project. Finally, I would like to thank Carla Hudson Kam for her patience and support.

Chapter 4 was previously published as 'Do Ideological Preferences Explain Parliamentary Behaviour: Evidence from Great Britain and Canada', *Journal of Legislative Studies*, 7 (2001): 89–126. Chapter 7 was previously published as 'Demotion and Dissent in the Canadian Liberal Party', *British Journal of Political Science*, 36 (2006): 561–74. The US National Science Foundation, the Social Sciences and Humanities Research Council of Canada, and the Department of Political Science at the University of Rochester provided funding. I hope the final product is sufficient return on their investment.

1 | *Introduction*

Yet day after day with a Prussian discipline [British MPs] trooped into the division lobbies at the signals of their Whips and in the service of the authoritarian decisions of their parliamentary parties ... We are so familiar with this fact that we are in danger of losing our sense of wonder over them (*sic*).

(Beer 1965, pp. 350–1)

Beyond the party-as-unitary-actor assumption

On 9 November 2005, Tony Blair's government lost two successive votes on its Terrorism Bill. The government's sixty-five-seat majority in the Commons was entirely undercut by the rebellion of forty-nine Labour Members of Parliament who voted with opposition MPs, first to reject the government's recommendation of a ninety-day detention period for terrorist suspects, and then to force on the government an amendment limiting the detention period to twenty-eight days (Cowley and Stuart 2005). Immediately after the defeats, British odds-makers lowered the odds of Blair leaving office before the end of the year from three to one to seven to four (*Guardian*, 10 November 2005). This was a rare event inasmuch as it was the first government defeat at Westminster in ten years, but it was hardly novel or trend-setting. Blair's predecessor, John Major, had suffered four parliamentary defeats during his term of office, being forced on one occasion to use a confidence motion to force rebellious Eurosceptic Conservative MPs to support the Social Chapter of the Maastricht Treaty, the measure the rebels had helped to defeat the previous day. This, too, was the continuation of a trend rather than a break with the past. On 14 April 1986, for example, the open rebellion of seventy-two Conservative MPs and the purposeful absence of a further twenty led to the defeat of the Thatcher government's Shops Bill (Bown 1990). James Callaghan's Labour government was undone in a similar fashion, when some of its own MPs allied with the

Conservatives to impose threshold restrictions on the Scottish and Welsh devolution referendums. Unable to surpass the mandated 40 per cent threshold, the Callaghan government lost the 1979 referendum in Scotland, and shortly thereafter, with its chief constitutional reform in tatters, succumbed to a Conservative non-confidence motion.

Parliamentary events of this sort – backbench MPs acting against their own parties – are hardly unique to the United Kingdom. On 24 February 2004, thirty Canadian Liberal MPs voted in favour of a Bloc Quebecois motion condemning American efforts to develop a continental missile defence system and demanding that Paul Martin's Liberal government refuse to participate in the programme. With Conservative support, the Liberal front bench saw off the motion – but consequences would still follow. Almost exactly a year later, with the Liberals now controlling just a minority government, the Americans brought the issue back to the fore: Would the Canadian government participate in the missile defence system or not? A definite answer was required, and a presidential visit by George Bush left no doubt as to the preferred reply. To refuse the American request would further damage Canada's already strained relations with its most important ally, and this after Martin had campaigned as the man to improve those relations. Martin had little room to manoeuvre, however. The election had not fundamentally altered the division of opinion over missile defence within the parliamentary Liberal Party. With a majority, Martin might have withstood the defection of thirty MPs; with just a minority, he would have had to rely on the Conservatives to pass the necessary legislation and to maintain the government.[1] This was too great a risk to take, and so on 24 February 2005, Martin formally rebuffed the Americans, in essence accepting the position outlined in the opposition motion that his government had defeated exactly one year before.

The orthodox view of parliamentary parties is that they are so highly cohesive that they can be considered unitary actors, MPs' deviations from the party line being so infrequent and inconsequential that they can safely be ignored (Franks 1987; Jackson 1987; Laver and Schofield 1990; Jaensch 1992, pp. 126–7). This view has its merits: across

---

[1] The talk in the parliamentary corridors was that Martin could expect approximately thirty MPs to vote against missile defence (personal communication, John Ibbitson, parliamentary correspondent for the *Globe and Mail*, 12 February 2004).

parliamentary systems, MPs overwhelmingly vote with, not against, their parties (Powell 2000, p. 60). Correspondingly, parliamentary leaders can typically rely on a modicum of party cohesion, and when it is not forthcoming, employ a variety of institutional tools to impose discipline. Nevertheless, as the examples above suggest, the orthodox view is overstated. Parliamentary parties are not perfectly monolithic entities: MPs can and do vote against their parties, sometimes to great effect. The more nuanced reality is that MPs' loyalty is not automatic, but must be constantly elicited.

The puzzle of backbench dissent

Students of British parliamentary politics are well aware of this nuanced reality. Prior to the 1970s, party cohesion in the House of Commons was so regularly close to 100 per cent that there seemed little point in using the division lists (i.e., roll-calls) to study or understand parliamentary politics or behaviour (Beer 1965, p. 350). However, extensive work by Philip Norton (1975, 1978, 1980) showed that the frequency with which British MPs voted against their own parties increased dramatically from 1970 onward. Whereas in the 1950s under one division in fifty saw a British MP vote against his or her party, in the 1970s almost one out of every five divisions witnessed this sort of dissent. Government defeats increased in lockstep, British governments suffering sixty-five defeats between 1970 and 1979 compared to just five over the previous twenty-five years (Schwarz 1980, p. 36; Norton 1985, p. 27; Cowley and Norton 1996).[2] The internal difficulties of the British Conservative Party over the issue of European integration, especially during John Major's tenure, and Tony Blair's battles with the left wing of the Labour Party over the invasion of Iraq, university tuition fees, foundation hospitals, and the prevention of terrorism indicate that this pattern has not abated (Cowley 2002, 2005).

Norton's work presented a provocative puzzle: why did backbench dissent in the British Commons surge in the 1970s? Authors have approached Norton's puzzle in a variety of ways. Some conceive of it as a purely British phenomenon, to be explained in terms of British

---

[2] Norton (1980, p. 336) records ten defeats between 1950 and 1966 and Norton (1981, p. 227) counts eleven between 1945 and 1970. Note that 45 per cent of the government defeats between 1970 and 1979 were due to backbench rebellions.

political personalities, issues, or history. Matthew Sowemimo (1996), for example, explains dissent in the British Conservative Party over European integration as a legacy of historically ingrained ideological tendencies in the Tory camp. Other authors offer more general explanations for the rise in dissent. For his part, Schwarz (1980) argues that the demise of the 'parliamentary rule' of governmental resignation upon a parliamentary defeat was the key to the increased dissension in the 1974–9 Parliament, backbench logic being that if the government did not collapse upon defeat, then cross-voting was less risky. Alt (1984) and King (1981), on the other hand, identify social rather than institutional changes as the cause of the dissent. Alt, in passing, casts the upswing in parliamentary dissent as symptomatic of a broader de-alignment of the British party system. King focuses more closely on Parliament itself, arguing that the increasing domination of Parliament by career politicians infused parliamentary politics with a volatile combination of professional pride, restless ambition and ideological extremism that is difficult for leaders to control and which is frequently unsupportive of party cohesion (King 1981, p. 283). These dynamics are, in fact, reflected in Norton's argument that the surge in dissent was sparked by the abrasive leadership style of Edward Heath. Norton's depiction of Heath is that of a leader who dealt poorly with the new social reality of Parliament, who tried to run the Conservative Party in a rigidly hierarchical fashion, who sought to set policy unilaterally, and who failed to use his powers of appointment wisely (Norton 1980, p. 341; 1987, p. 146).

There is, in short, a variety of plausible hypotheses for the surge in backbench dissent in Britain – so many in fact that they overwhelm the available data. If, for example, institutional changes (the easing of the confidence convention – Schwarz's explanation) and social changes (the growing professionalism of British MPs – King's explanation) occur simultaneously, then it is difficult to establish which explanation is the right one – especially when particularistic explanations like Heath's poor leadership are always on hand as alternative hypotheses.

A comparative approach

There is no need to confine one's attention to Britain; as the example of the Martin government indicates, the experiences of other parliamentary systems are also germane. Once these comparative cases are considered, one is pushed away from trying to explain why backbench dissent in Britain surged in the 1970s and toward considering parliamentary behaviour and intra-party politics in a more general light. Consequently, this book examines party discipline and parliamentary politics in four Westminster parliamentary democracies: Great Britain, Canada, Australia, and New Zealand. The focus is on a single political act, the decision by an MP either to toe the party line or to break ranks and dissent.[3] Of course, MPs not only make this decision repeatedly throughout their careers, they do so alongside other MPs who belong to the same parliamentary party and in response to the decisions and actions of their leaders. Collectively, their decisions determine the degree to which their party is cohesive or disunited, and in this respect the focus is on party cohesion as well as the individual MP's decision to dissent.

Party cohesion and parliamentary behaviour have received a good deal of scholarly attention (e.g., Rice 1925; Duverger 1962; Cox 1987; Morgenstern 2004), but truly comparative work on the topic is rare (Patterson 1989; Mezey 1993), largely because the wide variation in national parliamentary practices and conventions poses a serious obstacle to valid comparison. Simply put, one cannot just run around collecting data on the assumption that all legislators everywhere are governed by the same rules, have the same preferences, face the same strategic choices, and therefore behave in the same way. In Great Britain, for example, voting in a division (i.e., a roll-call vote) involves having one's name checked off a list as one passes through a doorway to a lobby. The procedure is similar in the German Bundestag, save for the crucial difference that legislators' names are not recorded. This means that in Westminster voting is a public act while in the Bundestag it is an anonymous one (Saalfeld 1986, p. 533). For an MP to vote against his or her party is, therefore, a qualitatively different activity in Great

---

[3] *Dissent* occurs when a party member acts against his or her party. Dissent may take a range of forms, from speaking out publicly against one's own party to voting against one's party whip. *Cohesion* refers to the degree to which members of the same party can be observed to work together in pursuance of the party's goals (Ozbudun 1970, p. 305). In so far as legislative behaviour is concerned, this refers the extent to which members of the same party vote together. Party *discipline* is cohesion achieved by the application of sanctions or inducements. Studying discipline properly requires noting not only the degree of party cohesion but also the means by which it is achieved (Jackson 1968, p. 6).

Britain from what it is in Germany and to compare them as if they were equivalent would involve an undesirable degree of 'conceptual stretching' (Sartori 1991). In contrast, there is (for historical reasons) an extensive overlap in parliamentary practice, convention, language, and ethos between Britain, Canada, Australia, and New Zealand. Importantly, even if Canadian, Australian, and New Zealand MPs do not file into lobbies to record their votes exactly as British MPs do at Westminster (they rise from their seats and declare their votes), voting in these Parliaments remains a public act.[4] Restricting attention to these four countries, taking what Lijphart (1975) terms a similar systems approach, is thus one way to facilitate valid cross-national comparison.

There are other reasons to limit the sample to Westminster-style parliamentary systems. Westminster parliamentary government is characterized by a double monopoly of power: first, the cabinet's near monopoly of executive and legislative power and second, a single party's monopoly of the cabinet itself (Palmer 1995, pp. 168–70). This double monopoly is generated initially by an electoral system that tends to manufacture legislative majorities, but it is sustained thereafter by cohesive party behaviour. In other words, a single party can form, control, and maintain the cabinet, and through it the content and timing of the legislative agenda – providing that it votes cohesively in Parliament. Party cohesion is, therefore, the central strategic problem of Westminster government.

Coalition government, on the other hand, presents parties with additional strategic challenges, most notably government formation and survival. Party cohesion remains a concern, of course, because undisciplined and fractious parties are not attractive coalition partners. What is important to realize, however, is that these strategic problems – coalition bargaining and party cohesion – are not independent of one another (Laver 1999). Unlike leaders of single-party governments, party leaders in multiparty governments have incentives to turn a blind eye to dissent in order to increase their leverage vis-à-vis their coalition partners. In simple terms,

---

[4] The New Zealand practice changed substantially when the New Zealand House of Representatives overhauled its standing orders in anticipation of the adoption of proportional representation in 1996. The new standing orders empowered the party whips to cast 'party votes' on behalf of all the MPs in the party. In effect, New Zealand MPs who wish to vote against the party position now have to reclaim their proxies from their party whips (S. O. 155, *Standing Orders of the House of Representatives*, 2005). In consequence of these important institutional changes, I limit my attention to New Zealand prior to 1996.

party leaders can use backbench dissent to make credible the plea that they cannot possibly get their MPs to go along with what their coalition partners are asking. This dynamic could occur outside the confines of a multi-party government, as when, for example, a single-party minority government bargains with non-government parties for legislative support – and these situations do occur in the Parliaments studied here (in Canada most frequently). Generally speaking, however, the prevalence of single-party majority governments in these Westminster systems allows one to study backbench dissent and party cohesion free from the additional complications of coalition formation and survival.[5]

A similar systems approach does have drawbacks, the chief one being a loss of variance on key variables. This turns out not to be a serious problem in this case. Table 1.1 shows the percentage of dissenting divisions – Norton's measure of dissent – for major parties in each country from 1950 onward.[6] In other words, these are the percentage of whipped divisions in which at least one MP voted against his or her party. Variance in the frequency of these dissenting divisions is evident, and it raises a host of interesting questions: why do Canadian and British MPs dissent so much more frequently than Australian and New Zealand MPs; why do Australian Coalition senators dissent more than Coalition representatives? Even this cursory look at the data should convince the reader that the raw material for extensive and rewarding research – interesting questions and variance in the dependent variable – is at hand.

The significance of backbench dissent

Of course, much is hidden by Table 1.1, such as the average number of MPs who engage in dissent in each parliament, the degree to which dissent is a government or opposition preserve, the use of alternative methods of dissent, and how often it translates into government defeats.

---

[5] The inclusion of the Australian Liberal–National Coalition in the study does provide variance on this front, however, and evidence (see Chapter 8) suggests that the contrast between single-party and coalition government should not be overdrawn. At the end of the day, parliamentary government, whatever its precise form, requires a high degree of party unity.

[6] A division is said to be *whipped* when the party has given its MPs express instructions on how to vote. A division is *free*, on the other hand, whenever party leaders allow their backbenchers to vote as they wish.

Table 1.1. *The percentage of dissenting divisions by party in Britain,*
Canada, Australia, and New Zealand, 1950–2004

Country	Party	Percentage dissenting divisions*
Britain	Labour	8.81
	Conservative	9.72
Canada	Liberal	8.77
	Progressive Conservative	15.11
	Bloc Quebecois	3.30
	Reform / Alliance	6.89
Australia	Coalition (House)	1.72
	Coalition (Senate)	2.85
	Australian Labor Party (House)	0.03
	Australian Labor Party (Senate)	0.47
New Zealand	National	1.57
	Labour	0.27

* Percentages are computed by dividing the total number of divisions witnessing dissent across all parliaments in the sampling frame by the total number of divisions. So, for example, the British Conservatives participated in 16,848 divisions between 1945 and 2004 and experienced dissent on 1,602 of those divisions.

Sources: Britain: Norton (1975, 1980), Cowley (1999, 2005); Canada: *Parliamentary Debates of the House of Commons of Canada*; New Zealand: *Parliamentary Debates (Hansard)*; Australia: Lucy (1985), *Parliamentary Debates of the Commonwealth of Australia (House of Representatives)*; *Parliamentary Debates of the Commonwealth of Australia (Senate)*. See also: Hobby (1987); Cowley and Norton (1996); Cowley *et al.* (1996); Wearing (1998, and personal communication).The Australian statistics have been estimated to some extent by sampling (3,020 Senate divisions and 1,897 House divisions). The same is true of the Canadian figures for the period 1997–2004, for which I sampled 392 divisions.

This last aspect is worthy of immediate attention because it might be assumed that dissent is trivial unless it actually results in the government falling. This position ignores a number of facts and deserves a strong rebuttal. First, dissent may result in the defeat of specific government bills or policies without the government losing the House's confidence and collapsing. Indeed, the Blair government's defeat on its Terrorism Bill illustrates exactly this point. Second, dissension can have pernicious electoral effects on a party even if it does not immediately alter legislative outcomes (Franks 1987, p. 109). Backbench dissent hampers a party's internal operations by setting MPs against one another in the attempt to distance themselves from unpopular party policies. In this sense, it ignites a simmering collective action problem in the party (Docherty 1997, pp. 169–70), one that undermines the electoral prospects of loyal MPs (who are stuck supporting an unpopular or contentious party policy) and sends a signal of disunity and disorganization to voters. Indeed, John Major himself worried that his government's policy initiatives were drowned out by his party's internecine squabbles (Major 1999, p. 610). There is empirical support for this effect: regressing the percentage of dissenting divisions that the parties in Table 1.1 experience during a parliament on their vote shares in the subsequent elections returns a coefficient of –0.2. In other words, a 1 per cent increase in dissenting divisions is associated with a 0.2 per cent decrease in the party's vote share. Questions can be raised about cause and effect here, but those questions recommend further study rather than dismissal of the topic as trivial.

Dissent can also destabilize a party's leadership. The rebellion by British Conservative MPs against the party's then leader, Iain Duncan Smith, over the Blair government's Adoption and Children Bill in November 2002 provides one example. The bill sought to permit adoptions by homosexual couples, and wishing to present the Conservative Party as the defender of the traditional family, Duncan Smith ordered Conservative MPs to oppose it. (The Labour government's more cautious strategy was to allow its MPs a free vote on the bill.) A number of Conservative MPs refused, and in the face of this pressure Duncan Smith half-relented, granting permission for Conservative MPs to absent themselves from the House should they not wish to vote against the bill (*Daily Telegraph*, 2 November 2002). The climb-down was widely interpreted as a sign of weakness and incompetence (*The Times*, 5 November 2002), and when several prominent Conservatives, including heavyweights such as John Bercow, Michael Portillo, and Kenneth Clarke, nevertheless ignored the party whip and voted for the bill, it was also seen as the beginning of the end for Duncan Smith (*The Economist*, 7 November 2002).[7] Canadian Alliance MPs went a step

---

[7] Duncan Smith managed to hang on to the leadership until 29 October 2003, when a scandal involving his wife finally pushed Conservative MPs to pass a non-confidence vote against their leader. (There were hints that the scandal was, in fact, manufactured as an excuse to dump Duncan Smith, and he was cleared of any impropriety (see http://news.bbc.co.uk/1/hi/uk_politics/3578323.stm). Without doubt, however, the rebellion on the Adoption and Children Bill was the turning-point in his leadership.)

further to depose their leader, Stockwell Day.[8] Dismayed by Day's lacklustre performance at the 2000 election and embarrassed by his repeated political gaffes, fourteen Alliance MPs, including Chuck Strahl and Deborah Grey, the party's chief whip and deputy leader, respectively, split from the party to sit as independents.[9] The tactic succeeded in forcing Day from the leadership despite the fact that party rules did not empower the parliamentary party to sack the Alliance leader. A more general if less dramatic result is provided by Kam and Indridason (2005), who show that surges in parliamentary dissent among governing parties is a leading indicator of cabinet reshuffles. Indeed, sometimes the mere appearance of dissent is sufficient to create instability. Several Canadian, Australian, and New Zealand MPs with whom I spoke talked of a tip-of-the-iceberg phenomenon where for every MP who votes against the party or speaks out in the media, ten more unhappy MPs are believed to exist.[10] This creates a perception that the party leadership is unpopular, that a 'spill' is imminent, and that some change in policy or personnel is required to avert a crisis. Perhaps because of these effects, the threat of dissent sometimes leads party leaders to compromise on policy (Butt 1967, chapters 6–8). Dissent is important, then, because it may lead to organizational tension, the amendment of government bills, electoral misfortune, or the replacement of one set of leaders with another.

The above arguments are quite valid, but they should not be taken to extremes. The vast majority of the time, parliamentary parties are highly cohesive, and the intention here is not to suggest that leaders are constantly being toppled, legislation altered, or elections lost because of dissent. To see the book this way is to mistake its purpose. The aim is to examine how parliamentary parties come to be so cohesive. This is a central puzzle of intra-party politics, but a difficult one to investigate because parliamentary parties go to great lengths to maintain façades of unity, airing internal grievances and hammering out

---

[8] The Canadian Alliance was simply a relabelled Reform Party. The Reform Party changed its name prior to the 2000 election as part of an attempt to rebrand the party and encourage a merger with the Progressive Conservative Party. The two parties merged formally into the Conservative Party of Canada in 2003.

[9] The defectors eventually organized themselves as a party to secure access to parliamentary resources and later coalesced with the Progressive Conservatives.

[10] I interviewed twenty-five Australian, eleven New Zealand, and thirteen Canadian MPs between July and November 1999.

compromises only behind the closed doors of the party rooms. Observed dissent, however, provides some insight into what is going on in the privacy of the party rooms. Thus, another way to justify a study of backbench dissent is to think of it as an instrument for studying intra-party politics, politics that are generally seen to be a vital aspect of parliamentary government, but for the most part go unobserved.

Theoretical approaches to parliamentary behaviour

I have found it helpful when thinking about the causes of backbench dissent to think in terms of three approaches or perspectives on parliamentary behaviour: preference-driven, institutional, and sociological. What separates these approaches are the answers that each gives to the question: 'What goals do MPs desire and what, if anything, constrains how they pursue and achieve these goals?' This question is at the core of any theory of parliamentary behaviour, and the answer that each approach provides to the question deserves careful attention.

The preference-driven approach

A preference-driven approach to parliamentary behaviour takes the view that legislative outcomes (e.g., the result of a parliamentary vote) are determined directly by the aggregation of preferences in the chamber.[11] That is, MPs have certain policy preferences, and they simply vote in a way that optimises these preferences. Thus, the only things that one needs to know to predict parliamentary behaviour are MPs' preferences over the legislative options before them. The best example of a preference-driven model of legislative behaviour is due to Krehbiel (1993, 1999). Krehbiel asks us to consider the possibility that when casting their votes legislators simply vote for the party advocating the position closest to their own. Almost always this will be the party to which the legislator belongs, but it need not be. (Presumably, legislators do not join parties espousing policy positions with which they completely disagree.) If one takes this view, then it is not clear a priori whether parties force their members to vote together in spite of their disagreements about policy, or whether they vote together simply because they already agree over

---

[11] Of course, a variety of social choice theories suggests that the link between individual preferences and the group choice may be a complicated matter.

policy (Krehbiel 1999). If the latter is true, then cohesion is entirely and simply a function of the distribution of MPs' electorally induced policy preferences within and between parliamentary parties.

Krehbiel's model is a very parsimonious – one might even say spare – explanation of legislative behaviour and party cohesion. Nevertheless, it does tell one what conditions are necessary and sufficient for party cohesion (a certain distribution of preferences within and between parties) and which others (party rules on seniority, for example) are unnecessary. In this regard, Krehbiel's theory is quite complete, and indeed its combination of parsimony and completeness makes it an excellent starting-point for more complicated models of legislative behaviour and party cohesion.

The institutional approach

Krehbiel's model is driven by MPs' unconstrained policy preferences. In contrast, the general idea behind the institutional approach to parliamentary behaviour is that formal rules and organizations (e.g., the vote of confidence, the electoral system, the internal rules of political parties, etc.) alter the manner in which MPs pursue their preferences. In other words, institutions constrain behaviour. In Cox's (1987) *Efficient Secret*, for example, the changes to the franchise and voting brought about by the Reform Acts were central in pushing British MPs away from a politics based on the delivery of particularistic goods to constituents and loose parliamentary alliances toward one dominated by cohesive electoral and legislative parties that offered competing policy programmes. More recent work by John Huber (1996a) has emphasized how rules surrounding the vote of confidence procedure and time allocation have strengthened party cohesion in the French Fifth Republic. In institutional models, politicians' actions do not follow directly from their preferences, but from a combination of preferences and institutional constraints. As a matter of course, then, predicting MPs' behaviour requires knowledge of their preferences and their institutional environment.

Agenda-setting models (e.g., Tsebelis 2002; Cox and McCubbins 2005) are an important way-station between preference-driven and institutional approaches to parliamentary behaviour. The central idea of agenda-setting models is that parliamentary rules provide some actors with control over the parliamentary agenda, who can then use this agenda control to channel the preferences in the chamber toward the outcomes they desire (Cox 2000). Agenda-setting opens the door to the possibility that party leaders manipulate the parliamentary agenda to conceal disunity within their parties. Leaders might, for example, broker policy compromises, grant free votes on especially divisive issues (e.g., as the Blair government did on the Adoption and Children Bill described above), or avoid having votes on such issues altogether. In a way agenda-setting models pose the same theoretical challenge as preference-driven models: is agenda control by itself sufficient to generate party unity?

The sociological approach

Both the preference-driven and institutional approaches to parliamentary behaviour are rational choice approaches, that is, they assume MPs are strategic utility maximizers. Those who adopt a sociological approach to parliamentary behaviour do not see MPs' actions as being guided by consciously strategic cost-benefit calculations and they do not see the behaviour that follows these decisions as being constrained primarily by formal rules. Instead, the backbencher's decision to toe the line flows (not necessarily consciously) from internalized norms of party solidarity and loyalty (Kornberg 1967; Crowe 1983, 1986).[12] Keith Jackson (1987, p. 55) sums up the position nicely:

MPs are socialised into the practice of parliamentary parties informally. The legally structured nature of parliamentary proceedings with its emphasis on competing teams, the frequent meetings of caucus and the constant emphasis on the contributions of MPs to the overall good of the party means that, with or without formal rules, this is a highly disciplined existence. To become an MP in New Zealand is not unlike joining the army, with less security of tenure. The difference is that MPs are more self-disciplined. Once MPs accept the framework within which they work, they are less conscious of formal discipline.

It has been suggested, half-jokingly, that if economics is all about how people make choices, then sociology is about how they do not have choices to make. Recognize, though, that modern sociological perspectives on parliamentary behaviour are not entirely rigid and they do not

---

[12] See also: Hobby (1987).

view MPs as automatons. MPs' behaviour is constrained – but not determined – by norms (i.e., shared expectations about what constitutes appropriate and inappropriate behaviour (Kornberg 1967, p. 5)). Moreover, parliamentary and party norms are not completely divorced from formal sanctions and rewards. It is just that these formal institutions are decidedly secondary in significance. The parallel here is with a written (i.e., formal) employment contract and a company's corporate culture (i.e., the informal, unwritten part of the contract): IBM executives are not contractually obligated to wear dark blue suits, but thanks to the company's culture few do otherwise.

A synthetic model

There are certainly sharp differences between these three approaches. The divide is especially pronounced between the preference-driven and institutional approaches on one hand and the sociological approach, on the other; the former are rooted in rational choice theory, the latter is diametrically opposed to rational choice theory. However, even the institutional and preference-driven approaches have their differences, as to whether institutions generate real behavioural effects or are just epiphenomenal, for example. The temptation – in light of these differences – is to cast the approaches as contending theories and engage in a 'race of the variables' in which one approach is designated as 'correct' because a variable that is designated as its proxy is more strongly associated with dissent than variables representing the other approaches. To some extent, this is how several previous studies of backbench dissent have proceeded (e.g., Franklin *et al.* 1986; Mughan 1990; Pattie *et al.* 1994; Benedetto and Hix 2007). This is a worthy task in light of the many conflicting hypotheses about the causes of backbench dissent, but the combined effect of this literature is to generate a fairly fragmented understanding of backbench dissent rather than a general theory of parliamentary behaviour or intra-party politics.

A more useful strategy begins by recognizing that these three approaches are not mutually exclusive. Dissent, for example, could be curbed by institutional incentives as well as by sociological forces. Clearly, party leaders rely on shared ideological preferences to provide them with a modicum of cohesion – but beyond that they may have to use institutional carrots and sticks to bring their MPs into line. Indeed, I intend to argue – and demonstrate – that these approaches to parliamentary behaviour hang together empirically in a particular fashion. My argument is as follows: ideological disagreement and electoral pressures (e.g., differences in electoral environments and incentives across constituencies) set the stage for dissent to occur. Agenda control on its own tends not to be able to offset these divisive forces, and leaders have to rely on other institutional rules of Westminster parliamentary government work to contain them. The confidence convention is the most imposing of these rules, but it is a heavy-handed instrument, ill-suited for securing members' loyalty on an on-going basis (and of no use whatsoever to leaders of opposition parties). Consequently, leaders prefer to take advantage of their MPs' progressive ambitions (Schlesinger 1961) and use their monopoly control of the recruitment channels that lead to the party front bench to secure unity.

The weakness in the leaders' strategy is that there comes a point when an MP can no longer be promoted (because, for example, there are not enough places at higher levels of the parliamentary hierarchy). At this point, additional forces must be harnessed to prevent ideological disagreement and electoral tensions from breaking out into open dissension. Formal discipline is one option, but it can be politically costly. Consequently, leaders tend to fall back on informal measures (e.g., threats, insults, peer pressure) and socialization, that is, the long-term inculcation of norms of loyalty, solidarity, and the like. In this fashion, sociological forces reinforce rather than displace self-interest. Note the divergence between this model and a purely preference-driven model: on this view, ideological differences within the party are necessary *but not sufficient* to incite dissent, whereas in Krehbiel's model, such differences are necessary *and* sufficient for disunity. This statement can be inverted to provide the ingredients of party unity or loyalty, to wit, ideological agreement within the party *or* a combination of advancement, discipline, and socialization sufficient to offset any ideological or electoral disagreements. I label this the LEADS model of parliamentary behaviour, the MP's Loyalty Elicited through Advancement, Discipline, and Socialization.

The level of analysis

In developing and setting out my argument I have wrestled with the issue of whether explanation and testing should proceed at the level of the individual MP or at some higher level of aggregation, the party, the

parliament, or country perhaps. My preference is to privilege the individual level of analysis. In the first place, aggregate-level concepts are
typically rooted in the actions of individuals. The frequency of dissent
that the party experiences, for example, flows directly from individual
MPs' decisions to toe the party line or dissent. In addition, aggregate
relationships may gloss over collective action problems or puzzles that
come through more clearly when an individual-level perspective is
undertaken. Indeed, one of my complaints is that the system-level
observation that parliamentary parties are highly cohesive obscures
the fact that such cohesion must be constructed one MP at a time –
and that MPs may well face incentives *not* to toe the party line. Leaders
of parliamentary parties are successful (or, perhaps, simply lucky)
at counteracting these incentives to disloyalty and generating high
levels of party cohesion, but that does not mean that unity is, in some
Aristotelian sense, the natural state of parliamentary parties. Both of
these concerns lead me to the view that causal relationships are best
enunciated and explored at the individual level of analysis.

That said, I am not blind to the fact that broad environmental differences across systems can affect the choices and behaviours of individuals.
Moreover, large-N, aggregate-level analyses are required to establish the
external validity of individual-level relationships that one may happen to
find in more focused country- and time-specific studies. The question is
how best to combine individual and system-level relationships in a single
study. Przeworski and Teune (1970) advocate theorizing and testing in
terms of the individual and bringing in system-level variables only when a
hypothesized individual-level relationship breaks down for some subset of
individuals. The advantage of Przeworksi and Teune's strategy is that it
allows the researcher to isolate the explanatory effects of system-level
variables from those of individual characteristics. My initial intent was
to execute Przeworski and Teune's strategy. In other words, the plan was
to include British, Australian, Canadian, and New Zealand legislators in
every statistical model in every chapter, using system-level variables only
as required for satisfactory explanation. Conceptual stretching and measurement error are certainly major problems in comparative politics, but
as I found out, the availability of the requisite data is often the biggest
obstacle to comparison; very frequently the data required to replicate
analyses in all four countries are simply not available.

My alternative strategy is to combine individual and aggregate-level
analyses. Theorizing takes place predominantly at the individual-level.

In particular, I assume that all parliamentarians, regardless of party affiliation and nationality, are strategic actors concerned with policy-making, career advancement, and re-election, with – in Müller and Strøm's (1999) terms – policy, office, and votes. Testing takes place at multiple levels of analysis: country- and time-specific individual-level analyses are used to establish the internal validity of the model, aggregate-level cross-national analyses to establish its external validity. The book's various chapters, then, shift from country to country, and from considering the individual MP to the parliamentary party.

The plan of the book

The book follows in ten chapters. The second chapter develops the LEADS model more fully, drawing on a variety of qualitative evidence gleaned from primary sources and interviews for support and illustration. I then set out the model more formally, arguing that the two basic mechanisms of intra-party politics are, first, changes in the intensity of MPs' incentives to dissent, and second, in the relative costs to the leader of offering advancement versus discipline (formal or informal) or policy compromise, on the other. These mechanisms appear in various guises throughout the book. The discounting of office benefits by MPs and their increasing socialization, for example, alters the relative costs to leaders of offering advancement or imposing discipline, and explains why leaders shift from advancement to discipline over the course of MPs' careers. Electoral de-alignment, on the other hand, intensifies MPs' incentives to dissent, helping to explain the cross-national differences in dissent observed in Table 1.1.

The empirical implications of the LEADS model are first followed up at the aggregate level. The third chapter begins by tracing out the broad patterns in parliamentary dissent across these countries over the post-war period. It then develops a multivariate model to account for the cross-national and cross-temporal variation in dissent. Environmental and institutional forces shape the contours of dissent. At the environmental level, the decline in party identification among voters that accompanies dealignment is a critical variable. Institutionally, there is evidence that the confidence convention exerts some pressure on the ebb and flow of dissent within parties, but the relative availability of career advancement opportunities is actually a better predictor of the degree of dissent that a party experiences. Where these opportunities are scarce dissent is both more frequent and more severe.

These results do not falsify the preference-driven argument, because the aggregate-level analysis cannot control for the distribution of ideological preferences in these parliaments. It is entirely possible that these aggregate results are spurious, the relative availability of advancement opportunities, for example, simply mirroring the push and pull of ideological forces within and between parties. The fourth chapter is therefore given over to an empirical investigation of Krehbiel's preference-driven theory of legislative behaviour. The chapter demonstrates that MPs' parliamentary behaviour is not solely due to their ideological positions; other variables are required to adequately explain party unity.

One of the main assumptions of the LEADS model is that MPs reap electoral rewards for taking a stand against their parties. The fifth chapter puts this assumption to an empirical test. Using data from British and New Zealand election surveys, I show that MPs who voted against their party lines in the House or who spoke out against their parties' policies or leaders in the media enjoyed higher levels of name recognition and popularity than their more loyal colleagues, especially among weakly partisan voters. In New Zealand, these effects translated into a personal vote of about 2 to 3 per cent, about the same amount as generated by constituency service. These results not only demonstrate that dissent wins MPs votes, they draw a causal connection between electoral dealignment and dissent, showing how dealignment allows MPs to use non-partisan cues to appeal to a growing pool of non-partisan voters.

The sixth chapter looks at the other side of this political equation, that is, at the cost of dissension and disunity to the party generally. In theory, party discipline is a prisoner's dilemma in which MPs, left to their own devices, look out for their individual interests at the expense of the party's collective efforts. Is this in fact the case? Do the gains that accrue to dissenting MPs necessarily come at the party's expense? The cross-national data on this front are not straightforward, but an examination of the British electorate's reaction to the country's participation in the invasion of Iraq, a decision on which the Labour government openly split, suggests that Labour's disunity on Iraq sent voters mixed signals about where the party stood on the issue. These mixed signals had a disproportionate impact on Labour Party identifiers, leaving poorly informed Labour supporters confused and highly informed Labour supporters sceptical. These results contrast sharply with those of the previous chapter: whereas Chapter 5 showed that dissent earns the MP votes primarily from non-partisan voters, Chapter 6 drives home the point that the broader effect of disunity is to undercut the party's core electoral constituency.

The seventh chapter looks at backbench dissent in the Canadian Liberal Party, linking dissent directly to the personnel decisions that Prime Minister Jean Chrétien made after assuming the party leadership. The analysis has the form of a natural experiment: at the start of the 1993–7 Canadian Parliament, Chrétien promoted some MPs and demoted others. The demoted MPs proceeded to dissent at a higher rate than their more fortunate colleagues – with no suggestion that their dissent was due to a lack of socialization, ideological disaffection, or a prior history of rebellion. This chapter provides a nice causal linkage between the party leader's domination of career advancement, the MPs' discounting of future promotion, and the dissent that follows.

The eighth chapter analyses party discipline in Australia and Canada, showing how leaders shift from using advancement to discipline to control their parties. The tactic works: discipline reduces the rate at which dissent in the media is translated into dissent on the floor of the House. This is an important result as it suggests why party leaders – who, I assume, care deeply about presenting a united front to the voting public – sometimes engage in highly public battles to discipline rebels.

The ninth chapter follows several cohorts of British MPs over the course of their parliamentary careers. A two-stage model is used to show how MPs' career expectations influence their parliamentary behaviour and further how their subsequent behaviour modifies their future career expectations. The statistical results of this chapter confirm that advancement is the main determinant of MPs' loyalty: when advancement cannot be maintained, MPs dissent. The data also suggest, however, that the longer an MP is in the House, the more strongly the MP's attachments to norms of party loyalty constrain his or her voting behaviour. Hence even MPs who are demoted later in their parliamentary careers, and who have little hope of further advancement, rein in their dissent over time. The evidence suggests, then, that a process of socialization occurs alongside the rational pursuit of higher office, helping to temper the incentives to dissent generated by declining career prospects.

The tenth chapter offers a conclusion that ties together the theoretical model set out in Chapter 2 with the aggregate- and individual-level analyses of the previous chapters. Two things stand out at this point of the analysis, the connection between electoral dealignment and parliamentary behaviour, on the one hand, and the centrality of career advancement incentives to intra-party politics, on the other.

2 | *A model of intra-party politics*

Introduction

MPs might benefit collectively from maintaining a united front, but individually they face incentives to act independently. Party leaders use a variety of strategies to counteract these incentives: screening out the uncongenial, distributing office perks to the loyal, and disciplining the recalcitrant. Judging by the high level of cohesion exhibited by parliamentary parties, leaders apply these methods skilfully. Unity is not preordained, however: MPs can and do dissent from the party line. In this chapter I explore the strategic interaction between MPs and party leaders, asking what motivates MPs to toe the line or dissent and in light of these motives, how party leaders forge unity. My argument, broadly speaking, is that leaders elicit loyalty in the short and medium term by judiciously distributing career advancement to MPs. In the long term, however, these direct appeals to MPs' career ambitions lose their force and leaders have to rely on discipline and social pressure to limit dissent.

MPs' preferences: policy, office, and votes

The consensus in the legislative behaviour literature is that politicians desire a combination of policy influence, office perks, and votes (i.e., re-election) (Müller and Strøm 1999). The drive for re-election is certainly a powerful one. As Michael Laws, a New Zealand National MP, noted in his memoirs, 'Having been elected an MP, I wished to be re-elected. All my actions over the next three years would accumulate merit or demerit points toward that objective' (Laws 1998, p. 185). The high incumbency return rates for these countries suggest that Law's sentiments are widely shared. In Australia, the UK, and New Zealand, between 70 and 80 per cent of incumbent MPs seek and secure re-election (Matland and Studlar 2004, p. 93). The corresponding figure is lower for Canada (53.1 per cent), but only because Canada's volatile electoral environment makes it harder to get re-elected. Tellingly, 95.2 per cent of the 271 Canadian Liberal and Conservative MPs elected between 1972 and 1980 presented themselves for re-election.

For most politicians, re-election is a means to an end. Often, that end is a diffuse desire to serve their communities or to make a difference, but it may also involve securing a particular policy outcome. This sort of focused policy-seeking behaviour is particularly evident in the US Congress (Fenno 1973), but it is also visible in Westminster systems despite the fact that backbench MPs have little direct impact on policy in comparison with American Congress members. The 1993 *Canadian Candidate Study*, for example, reported that 15.3 per cent of candidates had run for office out of a desire to promote a particular policy agenda. (By comparison, 14 per cent ran 'to make a difference', and 11 per cent to serve their communities.) A New Zealand cabinet minister with whom I spoke exemplified this commitment to policy. The minister told me how he had run for re-election and accepted a cabinet post only because he had long wanted to implement a new unemployment insurance scheme. When that was done, he said, he would retire.

Policy-seeking can be justified as serving a broader social purpose, office-seeking cannot; it is an activity that benefits the MP alone. In consequence, few MPs admit to being motivated by the perks of office. Tell-tale signs of office-seeking are not hard to spot, however. King (1981, pp. 262–3), for example, shows that the average age at which British MPs enter the House has steadily declined over the post-war period, whilst the average age at which they retire has increased. In other words, British MPs are getting into politics earlier and staying longer, evidence that implies that they are approaching politics as a profession rather than a sideline. Anecdotal evidence points in the same direction. John Major, for example, was critical of how obvious office-seeking had become at Westminster:

Most of the newcomers wanted, and in some cases expected, to become ministers within months of arriving at Westminster. Four of the 1992 intake met with the Chief Whip in 1993 to ask when they would be made ministers – unthinkable behaviour in previous generations. (Major 1999, p. 347)

Office-seeking is hardly unique to the UK. Why, for example, did an Australian Parliamentary Secretary interrupt our interview to point out to me the picture of his swearing-in ceremony, noting the presence of the governor-general and senior members of the cabinet? Clearly, he was proud of his appointment and considered it the high point of his political career.

Electoral pressures

MPs pursue policy, office, and votes within the confines of a particular institutional environment. The electoral system is a critical part of this institutional environment. All of these countries employ majoritarian electoral systems that operate across a large number of single-member districts.[1] The aggregate effects of these majoritarian systems are familiar: a tendency to support just two major parties and to generate single-party majority governments (Duverger 1962; Cox 1999). In so far as these electoral arrangements provide party leaders and MPs with incentives to cater to different electoral audiences, they may also generate tensions within parties. Party leaders have strong incentives to move their parties' policies toward the position of the median voter *in the national electorate* (Downs 1957). This is the strategy most likely to deliver the party an overall electoral victory (i.e., a majority of seats in parliament), but not necessarily one that is in the best interests of each of the party's MPs. Elected to represent a constituency that may be socially and economically quite unlike any other, the overriding incentive for the individual MP is to cater to the median voter *in her constituency*.[2]

The incentive to cater to local sentiment is amplified when party rules dictate that MPs have to be reselected by local party associations as the parties' official candidates. In these situations, MPs have to respond to local party activists, a group that is even less representative of the national electorate than local voters. To the extent that the candidate selection process is beyond the control of the national party leadership, the door opens for local activists to select MPs who do not share the

---

[1] In the UK, Canada, and New Zealand (up to the 1996 election) a plurality formula is used. Australia uses an alternative vote for House of Representatives elections. The exception here is the Australian Senate, which is elected by a version of the single transferable vote, with each state serving as a multi-member electoral district.

[2] The median voter equilibrium falls away in multi-dimensional policy environments. My point, however, is not so much that median-seeking behaviour is optimal, but that the party leadership and MP are likely to disagree as to what policy is optimal irrespective of the dimensionality of the policy space.

leadership's policy preferences. There is the potential, then, for the candidate selection process to inject ideological tensions into intra-party politics. These ideological tensions exist alongside and reinforce the electoral tensions discussed above, the whole process of reselection and re-election reflecting the fact that, as a New Zealand MP put it, 'Local areas throw up local candidates.' It is precisely because MPs are produced by, reflective of, and responsive to local rather than national concerns that what is good electoral politics for the party leadership is not always good for the individual MP (Gaines and Garrett 1993, pp. 117–19).

How MPs respond to electoral pressure: constituency service and dissent

Friction between MPs and the party is not inevitable. Nevertheless, should an unpopular party policy endanger an MP's re-election pro-spects, the MP can take two courses of action to protect her electoral interests. First, the MP can engage in constituency service to build up a personal vote that is independent of the MP's party and its policies. Alternatively, the MP can dissent to distance herself from the party's position.[3]

The constituency service efforts of MPs in Westminster parliamen-tary systems are well documented (e.g., Irvine 1982; Anagnoson 1987; Cain *et al.* 1987; Bean 1990; Ferejohn and Gaines 1991; Norton and Wood 1993, Heitshusen *et al.* 2005). Certainly, MPs in these systems feel a normative commitment to serving their constituents (Searing 1994), but a desire for electoral security also fuels their efforts. Party leaders view constituency service as an anodyne activity and they encourage it. An anecdote related to me by a Canadian Liberal MP illustrates the point. The MP had discovered the unmarked and untended grave of a former prime minister in his constituency. The MP decided to press the civil servants at the Heritage Ministry to declare the site a historical landmark. This was a classic bit of constituency service, the local MP tackling the bureaucracy to obtain recognition and

---

[3] This argument is purposely overdrawn for analytic purposes. MPs are likely to lobby party leaders within the confines of the party room, and only if these efforts fail is the MP confronted with the hard choice of dissenting or toeing the line on an unpopular policy.

funding for the area. The bureaucracy was not initially helpful, but somehow the prime minister heard of the affair, stopped the MP in the parliamentary lobby one day, muttering that it was important to protect the country's history and that he would make a phone call. The project was approved within days. The MP noted the effects: 'Now the site's fenced in with flags and plaques. Every year there's a dedication ceremony – and the press contacts me because I started this.' This is not an isolated example: Denmark (2000) shows that Australian parties systematically funnel political pork into marginal constituencies, allowing the local MP to engage in credit-claiming while simultaneously shoring up the party's (and the MP's) electoral prospects in the district.

As important as constituency service may be to MPs, it hardly renders dissent obsolete. Indeed, when I asked the Canadian MP above why MPs did not stick to these safe vote-winning strategies, the reply was short and to the point: 'Because there's not enough of them.' At some point, the MP's demand for votes outstrips what constituency service can deliver, and dissent becomes a viable option. In theory, dissenting from party policy insulates the MP from the negative consequences of unpopular party policies. MPs certainly operate under this belief. A Canadian Liberal MP, and sometime rebel, stated as much when he said to me:

You know, I got some advice from Warren Allmand [a long-serving former Liberal MP], and he said to me: 'You have to be prepared for the day that the party's fortunes change. You have to be able to swim against the stream. You know what lets you do that? It's the air of independence.'

An interview with another Canadian Liberal rebel underscored the electoral incentive behind dissent. I had asked him to tell me what he thought about John Nunziata, an MP who had just been expelled from the party for dissenting:

I understand where John was coming from. He campaigned publicly on the GST [the Liberal's promise to repeal the Goods and Services Tax] and then he was hung out to dry ... I was in a different situation than John, *but I do what I do* [rebel] *because I'm in a right-of-centre riding* [my emphasis].

Question: And your independence helps you win there?

Yes. My independence creates a high profile [showing me that day's *Toronto Star* newspaper with his name in it] and it gets me a margin of around 10 per cent.

The MP went on to tell me that he knew that he had a substantial personal vote because at election time about 700 ballots had been spoiled by people who ticked his name while simultaneously crossing out the adjacent Liberal Party label.

A similar story was told to me by an Australian Liberal rebel. John Howard's (the PM) stance on Aboriginal matters, the MP told me, reflected an insensitivity that he could not support, not ethically and – as he freely admitted – not politically, either:

This isn't Queensland. That sort of stuff is not on in Victoria, particularly around this area [suburban Melbourne]. My electorate is full of young, upwardly mobile people starting their families and buying their first homes. These people are rate-payers, they're worried about their mortgage. They are economically conservative, but they aren't socially conservative and the prime minister's treatment of Aboriginal people was unpopular here.

Did his show of dissent pay off at the polls? The rebel was sure that it had. He said that he was the only MP in the area to improve his margin at the 1998 election. He also noted that he had received several hundred more votes than a neighbouring colleague at a polling location shared by both electorates.

Party leaders and backbench dissent

The cost of dissent to the party

Party leaders are sensitive to the electoral pressures faced by their MPs, but they are equally aware of the costs of disunity to the party. The negative effects of dissent are both internal, that is, damaging to the party in parliament, and external, that is, damaging to the party in the electorate. An Australian chief whip described the internal effects of dissent:

I see the temptation for members to put their electorate before the party. The great risk is that if one person does it, if they start thinking that way and you let them get away with it, then another person says, 'Well, why can't I do it?' So you've got to hold the line at the very beginning … and if you don't it eventually destabilizes the leadership.

Similar sentiments were voiced by a Canadian Liberal MP, but he focused less on the effects of dissent on the leadership and more on how dissent, if left unchecked, would lead to a serious collective action problem within the party:

The problem with what John [Nunziata, a dissident MP] was doing was he was putting his neighbouring MPs in a lot of difficulty. Imagine two Liberal MPs in ridings that are next door to one another where one stands up against a bill and the other doesn't. All the people in the neighbouring riding will point at their MP and say, 'Why aren't you doing what that guy is doing?' We've got to ensure that people don't take all the good from being in government without taking any of the bad. The problem with poking holes in the ship is that everyone sinks with it.

An Australian ALP senator concentrated instead on the external effects of dissent, bluntly declaring, 'Disunity is death. It's about the media and people's perceptions, and it [disunity] leads directly to unpopularity.' These sentiments were echoed by an ALP shadow minister: 'There's a perception out there that if you can't run your party, you can't run the country.' These opinions are not without foundation. Examining survey data from the 1990 New Zealand election, Vowles and Aimer (1992) show that New Zealand voters, even staunch Labour Party supporters, were repelled by the feud between the Labour prime minister, David Lange, and his finance minister, Roger Douglas. Disunity costs votes, and left unchecked it can lose elections.

Using candidate selection and policy compromise to avoid dissent

Ideally, party leaders can head off dissent before it becomes a problem. One option is for leaders to use the party's candidate selection rules to weed out uncongenial candidates before they get to parliament. Certainly, unity would be easier to achieve and maintain if all that party leaders had to contend with were party loyalists or, barring that, pragmatic MPs with whom deals might be reached. Party leaders, however, do not always control candidate selection at the local level, and even when they do, practical politics (e.g., a lack of local knowledge, a shortage of candidates, and fear of a backlash) can make leaders unwilling to select or veto candidates directly (e.g., Webb 1994; Sayers 1999; Katz 2001, p. 285; Carty 2002).

Agenda control offers leaders another chance to defuse dissent pre-emptively. By declaring free votes or brokering policy compromises that all MPs can tolerate, leaders can at least partially conceal internal divisions. These strategies have limits, however. Opposition parties in Westminster systems have little control over the parliamentary agenda, and while governing parties might formally possess agenda control, they cannot indefinitely avoid tackling pressing and perhaps divisive issues. Governing parties also have a constitutional obligation to maintain confidence and collective responsibility; public divergence on the issues of the day is a luxury that Westminster governments cannot afford. Finally, as a discussion with a New Zealand National MP on the transition to coalition government revealed, policy compromises may just as often spark dissent as quell it.

Q. Was there resentment on the back bench at having to share cabinet posts with a coalition partner?

A. Yes, but not only at having to share cabinet seats, *but also at having to water down policy proposals* [my emphasis].

Linking loyalty to career advancement

The New Zealand MP's continued commentary on the transition from single-party to multi-party government revealed an especially important dynamic in the intra-party politics of Westminster parliamentary government:

In the old two-party system the accommodation [on policy] was made in caucus, and people could structure caucus decisions so that people had a collective stake in them. The tensions were contained within the party and the caucus *and you kept quiet because you had an eye on your chances to advance in the party* [my emphasis]. But now the tensions are between parties, and leaders have to bargain for everything, leaving the backbenchers grasping at straws.

Two ideas come to the fore in this quote. First, there is the notion that party leaders use the promise of advancement to secure the loyalty of wavering MPs. Second, there is an implicit suggestion that this exchange between party leaders and MPs is institutionally reinforced by traditional Westminster parliamentary rules (and commensurately weakened by the more fluid bargaining environment inherent in multi-party government).

At the centre of Westminster parliamentary government is a double monopoly of power: the system (1) concentrates office perks and policy influence in a single body, the cabinet, and then (2) provides one set of party leaders with exclusive control of the cabinet and the recruitment channels that lead to the cabinet (Palmer 1995, pp. 168–9). This double monopoly of power fuses professional advancement and policy influence into a single indivisible good controlled by the party leadership. In the purest form of Westminster parliamentary government, there are no alternative centres of perks or policy influence. Unlike many continental European legislatures there are no powerful committees through which a backbencher could wield some degree of policy influence (Strøm 1986; Dalton 1993; Döring 1995). Moreover, one does not observe a division between positions of legislative power and party leadership (as is sometimes the case in the United States or the Netherlands, for example). Nor is there a seniority system such as exists in the US Congress (Epstein *et al.* 1997); re-election, while necessary for career advancement and policy influence, *is not sufficient* to secure these things. Quite the opposite; in a Westminster system *promotion is necessary for policy influence* (Norton 2000).

The implications of the system are straightforward: an MP who wishes to exercise policy influence or enjoy the fruits of higher office must attain a cabinet post. Party leaders control advancement to the cabinet (or, in opposition, to the shadow cabinet); the MP's advancement depends, therefore, on maintaining good relations with party leaders. Inevitably, this involves supporting the party leadership. Indeed, should the MP secure a ministerial position, the relationship is expressed formally in a constitutional convention of collective responsibility.[4] Thus even as an MP gains access to the perks of office and policy influence, she loses the ability to distance herself from party policy. As Frank Allaun, a British Labour MP who resigned from the Wilson government, remarked, 'As a backbencher you can say what you like, take up whatever issue you like, mix with unpopular trade unionists, MPs or journalists – and the whips can't touch you. *It is only when you are tempted by ambition for office that you are no longer free* [my emphasis]' (quoted in McSmith 1996, p. 19).

The broad appeal of advancement provides party leaders with a powerful lever over MPs, but it is not without weaknesses. The logistical problem of having enough places in the parliamentary hierarchy to

---

[4] Opposition parties also tend to observe a convention of collective responsibility.

satisfy members' ambitions is not trivial. Elections, for example, either place the party in government and provide it with abundant resources or condemn it to opposition, where resources are scarce. Representational demands (of gender, region, faction, etc.) also soak up a portion of available positions. In addition, there is little public tolerance for politicians showering office perks upon themselves; the cabinet can be expanded, and salaries and staff increased, but only gradually and at a cost. This means that winning a large majority is a mixed blessing: it ensures that the party forms the government, but it leaves a large pool of potentially frustrated members on the back bench. The Canadian Liberal Party found itself in precisely this situation after the 1993 election. A Liberal MP noted the consequences:

Q. Did people get frustrated because of the small size of the ministry in the first term?

A. Many people didn't get in [to the ministry], and certainly what's happened is that the parliamentary secretaryships were used to spread patronage around in the first parliament, but what's happened as they've [the secretaryships] been rotated again and again and not many people have made it from parliamentary secretary to become a minister, is that there's increasing frustration because people realize that they [parliamentary secretaryships] aren't stepping-stones.

Party leaders consequently find themselves in control of a powerful but limited resource that must be carefully distributed to maximize its effectiveness. The difficulty that leaders face is that the mathematics of parliamentary politics dictate that the bulk of MPs reach a point where it is evident that they are no longer on an upward career trajectory. There are, in the first place, fewer spots on the party front bench than there are caucus members. Amplifying the problem is the fact that parliamentary politics is a young person's game. Those who do not get into parliament early and move quickly up the parliamentary career ladder have little chance of achieving a cabinet position (Buck 1963; MacDonald 1987). Finally, even frontbench careers are finite, with scandals, poor performance, and failing health pushing ministers and shadow ministers to the back bench. Backbench MPs are as familiar with these realities as party leaders are and as a result hope cannot be sustained for ever. Once MPs know that they will not be promoted (at all or beyond some point in their careers), they have little incentive to toe the party line. In this respect, using career advancement to secure the MP's loyalty is an effective but temporary strategy.

Discipline and social pressure

Eventually, a point is reached where an MP realizes that promotion is not forthcoming and that little is to be gained by obediently toeing the party line. At this point, frequent dissent becomes a real possibility and the party leadership must ensure the MP's loyalty by other means. Formal sanctions (e.g., withdrawal of the party whip or expulsion) can make dissent costly to MPs, but too heavy a reliance on formal discipline can be counter-productive. The ALP, for example, makes its MPs pledge their loyalty to the party under pain of expulsion. Expelling an MP is, however, a messy, public process. As an ALP shadow minister conceded:

You'll 'carpet' a member and give them a warning. I remember doing this several times when I was on the national executive. But you can't really do too much more. If a member's done something only once or twice, it's counter-productive to expel them because it makes rifts in the party even more public.

Consequently, it is more common for leaders to resort to informal discipline, such as threats, to keep backbenchers in line. An Australian Liberal MP, for example, recounted to me how his public criticism of John Howard invited a telephone call from the party leadership pointedly reminding him that reselection meetings were looming and that the leadership would not shield him from challenges.

Discipline, whether formal or informal, is a last resort. Party leaders prefer to use social pressure to head off dissension. An Australian chief whip described how he approaches dissatisfied MPs:

I prefer to rely on social influence. I try to appeal to their better nature. I tell them, 'You lost on this one, but you'll get the next one.' Sometimes I have to go to the leader and say, 'You have to give this fellow something.' The question that I always ask these people is, 'Why aren't you dealing honourably with me?'

Ideally, MPs come to view party loyalty as normatively desirable, that is, they become socialized and internalize the costs of violating these norms. Once MPs are socialized in this way, party unity is far easier for leaders to achieve and maintain.

A formal model of intra-party politics

The preceding discussion highlights three aspects of intra-party politics that might serve as the building-blocks of a model of intra-party politics, to wit:

1. Party leaders and MPs play to different electoral audiences. Both sides know that this situation generates incentives for MPs to distance themselves from unpopular party policies.
2. Indeed, MPs believe that dissent may win them votes (or at least protect them from losing votes), though they also recognize that dissenting limits their advancement and invites discipline.
3. Leaders, equally aware of the damage that dissent can inflict on the party, counter with a variety of tactics, sometimes compromising on policy, but more often using their monopoly on advancement to elicit loyalty, and when that fails resorting to formal discipline and social pressure.

To help explain how these three aspects of intra-party politics can come together to explain variation in dissent, I construct a game-theoretic model of intra-party politics in which an MP and a party leader disagree about the direction of party policy. (Appendix 1 provides a formal treatment of the model.) The leader in the model can alter party policy, offer the MP advancement or impose discipline to elicit the MP's support. The MP reacts by supporting or opposing the leader's policy, in whole or in part. The model suggests three things about parliamentary dissent that are neither obvious from the qualitative discussion above nor intuitive in and of themselves. First, dissent becomes visible only when the electoral returns of dissent to the MP pass some critical threshold. Second, advancement and discipline are not perfect substitutes for one another. Third, party leaders tend to rely on advancement and discipline rather than policy compromise to maintain unity.

The structure of the game

The game starts with a disagreement between a party leader and an MP over what policy is electorally optimal on some issue. The disagreement between the leader and the MP is modelled by placing the ideal points of a party leader and an MP at opposite ends of a unidimensional policy space.[5] The party's policy can be located anywhere in this policy space, and both the MP and leader prefer the party's policy to be as close as possible to their own ideal point.

The leader has the privilege of setting the party's policy position, and her ideal outcome is to place the party's policy at her own ideal point. However, the leader also prefers to have the MP support her policy so that the party presents a united front to voters. The leader has three means of obtaining the MP's support. First, the leader can place the policy at some point between the MP's ideal point and their own, in effect, compromising with the MP on the party's policy. Second, the leader can offer advancement to the MP in exchange for the MP's support. Third, the leader can discipline the MP to get the MP to support the policy. These strategies are not mutually exclusive, and the leader may combine policy compromise, advancement, and discipline to elicit the MP's support. All of these options are costly to the leader, however, with the delivery of advancement and imposition of discipline characterized by increasing marginal costs.[6] If the MP dissents from the leader's policy despite these efforts, the leader incurs two additional costs. First, the MP's dissent imposes a direct cost on the leader (and the greater the MP's dissension, the greater this direct cost). Second, the MP's dissent reduces the value of any policy gains that the leader obtains from moving policy toward her own ideal point. These dynamics proxy the internal (parliamentary) and external (electoral) effects of dissent discussed above.

Confronted with the party leader's decision over policy, advancement, and discipline, the MP can support the leader's policy or dissent more or less extensively from it.[7] Dissent shelters the MP from the

---

[5] One might, for example, think of the MP's ideal point as the position of the median voter in the MP's constituency, whereas the leader's ideal point might be the position of the median voter in the national electorate. This construction is not meant to imply, however, that the leader and MP hold diametrically opposed policy positions at the very extremes of the party, only that the MP and leader disagree to some extent on what policy is electorally optimal.

[6] Compromising on policy is costly to the leader in the sense that the leader gives up her preferred policy. Increasing marginal costs to advancement and discipline might result if, for example, voters begin to view the disciplining of MPs or the distribution of patronage to MPs as indicative of the leader's arrogance or lack of probity (as the case may be).

[7] The model is silent on how the MP goes about dissenting, simply allowing the MP to choose a higher or lower level of dissent in response to the leader. In a series of

electoral consequences of the party's policy. Specifically, while the MP's re-election prospects (and utility) decline as the party's policy moves away from the MP's ideal point, dissent partially offsets this decline.[8] There are, however, diminishing (and possibly negative) returns to the MP from dissenting – as might be expected if dissent beyond some level is interpreted by voters as a sign of the MP's unreliability or opportunism. Dissent also exposes the MP to disciplinary sanctions and closes off advancement in the party, and the greater the MP's dissension, the stiffer the disciplinary sanctions and the less valuable the office rewards.[9]

Comparative statics

The game, then, involves the party leader setting a party policy along with some level of advancement and discipline and the MP responding with some level of dissension. The main comparative statics of the game's Nash equilibrium are straightforward: the more policy compromise, advancement, and discipline the leader offers, the less the MP dissents. Three other results are not so obvious, however:

1. The MP does not dissent until the electoral returns of dissent to the MP pass a threshold.[10] Up to this threshold, a variety of levels of advancement, discipline, and policy compromise are compatible with the MP's complete loyalty.

divisions on the policy, for example, the MP may dissent on substantive motions but vote the party line on procedural matters. Alternatively, the MP may exercise 'exit' rather than 'voice' (Hirschman 1970) and leave the party to sit as an independent or a member of another party. The model also abstracts from the possibility that the MP's opposition or defection leads to a policy reversal on the parliamentary floor or brings down the government.

[8] The term 're-election prospects' can be interpreted as a quantitative measure such as the MP's expected vote share or number of votes at the next election, but it might simply be the MP's subjective estimate of their probability of securing re-election given the party's policy position. Note also that re-election in this context includes the preselection process, should incumbent MPs not be automatically reselected as their party's candidate.

[9] Constructing the model in this fashion accords with Piper's (1991) work showing that British prime ministers did not completely shut rebellious MPs out of higher office.

[10] The threshold effect is more a function of the electoral returns to dissent than of advancement, discipline, or policy compromise. When the electoral return to dissent is low, the point at which the returns to dissent begin to diminish is also very low. Consequently, low levels of advancement and discipline (and no policy compromise whatsoever) are sufficient to keep dissent at the point where it provides no benefit to the MP.

2. As the cost to the leader of providing advancement to the MP increases, the leader leans more heavily on discipline to maintain the MP's loyalty. Similarly, as the cost to the leader of imposing discipline increases, the leader relies more on advancement to elicit the MP's support. However, because the delivery of advancement and the imposition of discipline are characterized by increasing marginal costs, the substitution effect is never complete and dissent increases.

3. Policy compromise occurs only when the electoral returns to dissent hit quite high levels, the party leader generally preferring to rely on advancement and discipline to maintain the MP's loyalty. If policy compromise is not possible (because of exogenous constraints, such as foreign policy commitments or budget limitations), the leader leans more heavily on advancement and discipline to limit the MP's dissent, but these efforts never entirely make up for the lack of policy flexibility, and hence dissent increases.

Parliamentary dissent and electoral dealignment

One implication of the first comparative statics result is that the relationship between MPs' parliamentary behaviour and advancement or discipline is contingent on their electoral circumstances. A clear statistical relationship between parliamentary behaviour and advancement and discipline is likely to be visible primarily among MPs who are at risk of losing their seats and for whom dissent may be the difference between political survival and defeat (i.e., MPs for whom the electoral returns to dissent are large). A lack of advancement or discipline should certainly push these politically insecure MPs to dissent. In contrast, MPs who hold very safe seats may exhibit loyalty quite independently of any advancement or discipline they receive because dissent offers them so little electoral advantage.

This result also provides a connection between MPs' parliamentary behaviour and a broader process of electoral dealignment. A hallmark of electoral dealignment is a decline in the extent and strength of party identification among voters. If most voters are strongly partisan, electoral behaviour is structured almost entirely by voters' affective ties to a specific party, and non-partisan cues such as dissent have little electoral impact. As party identification weakens, however, and these affective ties lose their grip over voting behaviour, the possibility – hence the incentive – exists for MPs to use dissent to generate a personal vote. In other words, electoral dealignment increases the electoral returns to dissent. This relationship between dissent and dealignment is not evident in the qualitative evidence, but the model makes a specific prediction about this relationship: as the process of dealignment unfolds, it should eventually reach a threshold and spark a surge in intra-party dissent. Note also how the dealignment interpretation helps to explain why conditions that lead to dissent in some countries and time periods (e.g., higher office costs to leaders), have little effect on party unity in other countries or eras: different levels of electoral dealignment may leave party unity intact or amplify existing incentives to dissent to the point that the party fractures.

The discounting of advancement and the impact of socialization

The second comparative statics result (the relative costs to the leader of delivering advancement and imposing discipline) also offers predictions about intra-party politics. MPs can be expected to look ahead to the inevitable decline of their parliamentary careers and discount the value of office perks and advancement accordingly. The discounting of office benefits has an impact on the game similar to that of higher advancement costs for the leader: if MPs discount advancement, every unit of advancement has a smaller marginal impact on the MP's behaviour, and the leader has to offer the MP more preferment to secure a given outcome. The game hints at the outcome of this process: as MPs' careers begin to decline (and the actuarial mathematics underpinning parliamentary careers makes this inevitable), the MPs will increasingly dissent and leaders will shift to discipline to control them. Similarly, should the cost to the leader of imposing discipline fall, leaders should rely more heavily on discipline to rein in MPs. The on-going socialization of MPs is one means by which the relative costs of advancement and discipline might shift over time. As MPs come to be socialized, they internalize the costs of violating norms of party loyalty and unity (Crowe 1986, p. 165). This lowers the cost to leaders of applying discipline because it allows them to use covert and easy-to-apply forms of social pressure (persuasion, implicit threats, and so on) rather than formal (hence highly visible and therefore potentially damaging) sanctions to control their MPs. To the extent that the discounting of advancement and socialization unfold over the same time span they should be correlated.

Thus as MPs' career prospects begin to decline, MPs are (in theory) also becoming more sensitive and responsive to social norms of loyalty, solidarity, and deference to leadership. In this fashion, socialization may prevent dissent from escalating late in the MP's career when advancement is no longer forthcoming. It is an empirical question as to whether socialization is strong enough to offset the discounting of office entirely, but in answering this question one obtains some insight into the force of progressive ambition and self-interest, on one hand, and social norms and socialization, on the other.

Conclusion

This is, of course, a *model* of intra-party politics and as such it does not contain every real-world feature of intra-party politics, e.g., leadership selection and bargaining between the parliamentary and extra-parliamentary wings of the party. Even so, the model provides a set of comparative statics which – in conjunction with the qualitative evidence presented at the beginning of the chapter – help to explain some basic mechanics of party unity and to predict the actions of MPs and party leaders. Two predictions are particularly important. The first concerns the impact of electoral dealignment on parliamentary politics. In theory, electoral dealignment increases the electoral return to dissent and in doing this, it may spark a surge in parliamentary dissent in a country. The second prediction concerns the inevitable discounting of office benefits by MPs and their increasing socialization into norms of party loyalty. By accounting for changes in the relative cost to the leadership of providing advancement and imposing discipline, the model helps to explain why leaders shift their strategy from advancement to discipline over the course of MPs' careers and why dissent need not necessarily increase over the course of MPs' careers. Of course, these two predictions hardly exhaust the list of possible causes of dissent or unity. Thus the next two chapters consider how well two other important variables, the confidence convention and a simple divergence of preferences within the party, explain dissent relative to the explanatory factors that this chapter identifies as important, e.g. electoral dealignment, advancement, discipline, and electoral security.

3 | Patterns of backbench dissent in four Westminster parliamentary systems, 1945–2005

An elite body can never satisfy all the ambitions of its members; if talents and ambitions are always more numerous than places, there are bound to be many who cannot rise quickly enough by making use of the body's privileges and who seek fast promotion by attacking them.

(de Tocqueville 1848/1965, p. 265)

Introduction

The LEADS model links dissent to a number of variables: the MP's electoral security, career advancement, and the like. These observable implications are developed within the context of an individual-level model of behaviour, but many can be tested equally well at the aggregate level. If, for example, advancement suppresses an MP's propensity to dissent, then parties in which opportunities for advancement are relatively abundant should experience less dissent than parties in which such opportunities are scarce. There is also scope at the aggregate level to test arguments about dissent that are not directly addressed by the model. The confidence convention stands out in this regard: it does not play a role in the model (by assumption, the MP's vote is not critical to the survival of the government), but it is a central feature of parliamentary government, and one that might be expected to influence the level of dissent that parties experience. Indeed, the impact of these sorts of institutional variables is often better studied at the aggregate level, where there is typically more room for institutional variation than at the individual level. For example, broad comparisons of the level of dissent within governing parties (which must maintain confidence), on one hand, and opposition parties (which are under no such obligation), on the other, can be used to assess the impact of the confidence convention on parliamentary behaviour. Of course, these sorts of aggregate-level comparisons cannot delineate precise causal linkages. Nevertheless, they provide an opportunity to trace out the contours of parliamentary dissent across time and space, even while they help to determine which variables do the best job of explaining variation in dissent.

Measuring dissent

Dissent occurs when a party member acts against his or her party (Ozbudun 1970, p. 305). As such, it encompasses a variety of activities, ranging from an MP speaking out publicly against the party, to voting against the party whip in a division, and – at the limit – defection. Many of these individual-level activities, especially parliamentary ones like voting and defection, are straightforward to measure. If, in a given division, an MP votes contrary to his or her party leadership's instructions, the MP is counted as dissenting. Tell-tale signs of the party's instructions are fairly easy to spot. By tradition, when a division is whipped, that is, when party leaders have issued instructions on how their members are to vote, the respective parties' whips are identified in the division lists as the *tellers* (the members who provide the Speaker with a count of the votes).[1] Beyond that there is the pattern of voting; very often, the parties' frontbench members vote as blocs, so backbenchers voting contrary to their parties stand out. Ambiguities can arise, of course. An MP might abstain rather than vote against the party, for example, and because abstention is not a recognized course of action in these parliaments and the division lists never reflect the activity, it can only be tracked if it is reported in the media or if the MP asks that the parliamentary record take note of his or her actions.[2] As a result it tends to be difficult (though not impossible) to disentangle purposeful abstention in a division from simple absence. Nevertheless, it is almost always possible to classify MPs who do vote in a division as dissenting or toeing the party line.

Individual acts of dissent can be aggregated to obtain measures of the level of dissent within a party, but this must be done with sensitivity because in the aggregate dissent is a multi-dimensional concept. Take, for example, the most widespread aggregate measure of dissent, the

---

[1] This tradition is weakest in Canada, where parliamentary clerks, rather than the party whips, count the votes and hand the count to the Speaker. Nevertheless, even in Canada, *Hansard* clearly records the whips informing the Speaker how their respective parties intend to vote in a given division.

[2] In the UK, MPs who wish to abstain sometimes enter both division lobbies, in effect cancelling their vote by voting on both sides of the issue.

percentage of divisions in a parliament that witness at least one MP voting contrary to the party line (Norton 1975, 1980; Cowley 2002, 2005). (I refer to these divisions as *dissenting divisions*.) The statistic is easy enough to calculate: if Conservative MPs voted against their party in 10 out of a parliament's 100 divisions, the percentage of dissenting divisions for the Conservative Party for that parliament is 10 per cent. The percentage of dissenting divisions is thus a measure of the *frequency* of dissent within a party, but it says little about the severity of that dissent. It may be the case that dissent is frequent because one or two maverick MPs vote against the party in division after division. This sort of dissent may be politically embarrassing, and it can be a significant nuisance and waste of time, especially if the rebels are constantly dividing the House when it would otherwise grant unanimous approval, but it is not automatically or immediately disastrous.[3]

Relative to this situation, there are two ways in which dissent can become a more serious threat to the party. First, dissent may be *deep* rather than superficial, with many MPs voting against the party in a given division. Second, the group of MPs who engage in dissent may be more or less *extensive*. In other words, dissent might not be the preserve of isolated mavericks, but an activity engaged in by many of the party's MPs, although perhaps in a fashion that has just a few MPs dissenting against the party at any one time. The depth of dissent is quite obviously of concern to governing parties; they need to maintain their majorities if they wish to retain control of the parliamentary agenda and remain in power. The extent of dissent, on the other hand, is of greater concern to party leaders, especially those of parties in which the caucus elects and removes the leader; as the number of disaffected backbenchers grows, so too does the risk of a leadership spill.

These considerations suggest two more measures of dissent in addition to the percentage of dissenting divisions that a party experiences during a parliamentary term. First, there is the mean number of dissenting votes cast in dissenting divisions. This figure tells one the average number of votes a party loses to dissent. If this figure is divided by the size of the party caucus so that it is standardized across parties of different sizes, one can interpret the resulting statistic as the percentage

---

[3] The inconvenience is amplified by the fact that these assemblies do not use electronic voting systems. A division at Westminster or Ottawa can take up to ten minutes, depending on how many MPs are in attendance.

of a party's voting strength that tends to be lost to dissent. This standardized statistic serves as my measure of the depth of dissent. I measure the extent of dissent, on the other hand, by the percentage of MPs in the parliamentary party who cast one or more dissenting votes during a term.

General patterns of dissent

In theory, these three measures can range from 0 to 100. Scores of zero indicate perfect (voting) unity in the party. Scores of 100, on the other hand, mean that the party is very disunited, although the nature of the party's disunity depends on the aspect of dissent that is measured. The percentage of dissenting divisions experienced by the party over the parliamentary term (i.e., the frequency of dissent) would equal 100 if every division during the term saw at least one of the party's MPs vote against it. A score of 100 on the extent of dissent indicates that every MP in the party voted against the party on at least one occasion during the parliamentary term. Similarly, the depth of dissent would be scored 100 if, when dissenting divisions occurred, all MPs voted against the party whip. Of course, collective responsibility is going to ensure that a party leader is not completely bereft of support – ministers and shadow ministers cannot engage in dissent without resigning their posts – so the 100 per cent ceilings on the extent and depth of dissent are theoretical abstractions that help one gauge the relative severity of dissent experienced by different parties.

These measures need not be highly correlated with one another. For example, an issue that deeply divides a party, but which is confined to just a few divisions, generates dissent that is deep but not frequent. Were such an issue to be dragged out over a long series of divisions with the same group of MPs dissenting in each division, the dissent would become more frequent without becoming more extensive. It is possible, then, for these three measures to tap quite distinct dimensions of dissent. Empirically, this is the case for the frequency and depth of dissent: across these four countries, the correlation between frequency and depth of a party's dissent is just $r = .13$. The extent of dissent, on the other hand, is more strongly correlated to the frequency ($r = .60$) and depth of dissent ($r = .36$), indicating that there is some overlap between the extent of dissent and the other two measures. This overlap results from two patterns in the data: in many instances, the dissent that a party

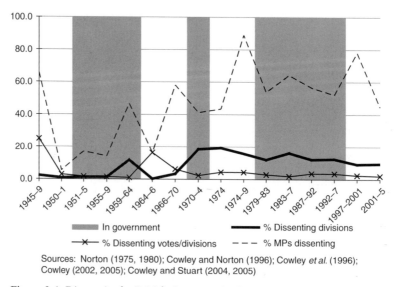

Sources: Norton (1975, 1980); Cowley and Norton (1996); Cowley *et al.* (1996);
Cowley (2002, 2005); Cowley and Stuart (2004, 2005)

Figure 3.1 Dissent in the British Conservative Party, 1945–2005

experiences is frequent and extensive, but not deep; in other cases, it is deep and extensive, but infrequent. Thus, dissent is extensive *either* because the party suffers repeated rebellions by small and disparate groups of MPs, *or* because it experiences a few isolated but massive rebellions.

Backbench dissent in the UK

Patterns of dissent in the British House of Commons are traced out in Figures 3.1 and 3.2 for the Conservative and Labour Parties, respectively. The periods in which each party formed the government are also highlighted in the figures. The surge in the frequency of dissent noted by Norton is clearly visible. Prior to 1970, the percentage of dissenting divisions experienced by both parties hovered around 5 per cent, but from about 1970 onward that figure climbed dramatically, first for the Conservatives during the Heath government's term of office (1970–4), and then quickly thereafter for Labour, during the Wilson and Callaghan governments' terms (1974–9). In both parties, the percentage of dissenting divisions reached a height of 20 per cent. In other words, during their tenures as prime minister, both Heath and Callaghan were

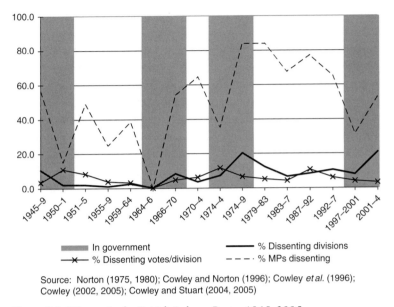

Source: Norton (1975, 1980); Cowley and Norton (1996); Cowley *et al.* (1996);
Cowley (2002, 2005); Cowley and Stuart (2004, 2005)

Figure 3.2 Dissent in the British Labour Party, 1945–2005

opposed by their own backbenchers on approximately one of every five divisions. The frequency of dissent subsided somewhat in the 1980s and 1990s, settling down to between 10 and 15 per cent of all whipped divisions. Dissent increased again during Blair's second term in office (2001–5), at least on the Labour side of the House, where the party experienced dissent in 21 per cent of whipped divisions (Cowley 2005).

Both of Britain's major parties have also suffered periodic surges in the depth and extent of dissent. The most visible example is the Conservative rebellion on Rhodesian independence in 1965, a division that saw 16.4 per cent of Conservative MPs vote against their own party. This was, however, the party's only dissenting division in the 1964–6 Parliament and it was typical of the pre-1970 pattern: one or two divisions in a session might attract widespread opposition from the parties' back benches, but the parties would otherwise exhibit perfect unity. After 1970, dissent became much more extensive, however. For the Conservatives, the growth in the extent of dissent was primarily due to its increased frequency. Small bands of Conservative MPs, the composition of which was always shifting, would frequently dissent from the party line, so that by the end of a term many Conservative MPs had engaged in dissent without the party having suffered any major breakdown in unity. Most of the time, then, the situation in the Conservative ranks reflected chronic but isolated discontent rather than internal party crisis (though the latter could and did occasionally break out). The increased extent of dissent in the Labour Party was, in contrast, due to an increase in its depth as well as its frequency. Post-1970, dissent cost the Labour Party an average of 6.9 per cent of its voting power (compared to just 3.3 per cent for the Conservatives), while not being much less frequent (10.5 per cent of dissenting divisions compared to 13.5 per cent for the Conservatives). In this respect, Labour's dissent was a more serious threat to the party, and indeed it reflected a ongoing battle throughout the 1970s and 1980s between the party's left and right factions.

Backbench dissent in Canada

The overall levels of dissent in the Canadian and British Parliaments are fairly similar. The frequency of dissent in the Canadian Liberal Party (Figure 3.3), for example, has exceeded 20 per cent of a parliament's divisions and taken in upwards of 50 per cent of the parliamentary party in several parliaments. The same is true of the Progressive Conservatives (PC) and (in the post-1993 period) the Reform Party (Figure 3.4).[4] The similarity in the overall levels of dissent aside, there are some important differences in the patterns of backbench dissent in the Canadian and British Parliaments. In particular, there is very clearly more variability in dissent in Canada than there is in Britain. Periods of frequent and extensive dissent are visible throughout the Canadian data and often occur just before or after periods of near-complete unity. Liberal dissent in the 1957–8 Parliament, for example, involved 55 per cent of the Parliament's divisions; the next term, Liberal MPs dissented on just 2.5 per cent of divisions. In the 1974–9 term, almost 60 per cent of the PC

---

[4] The last three Parliaments in Figure 3.4 reflect statistics for the Reform Party, which displaced the Conservatives on the right of the Canadian party system at the 1993 election. Given that Reform took over the Progressive Conservative's electoral position and parliamentary role (as the primary opposition party) and the fact that the two parties decided to merge in 2003, it seems appropriate to portray the data as an uninterrupted series.

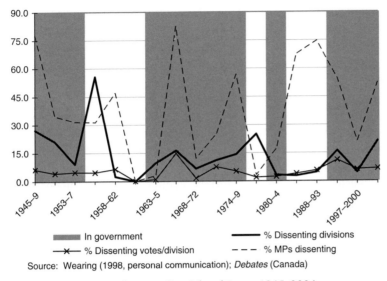

Figure 3.3 Dissent in the Canadian Liberal Party, 1945–2004

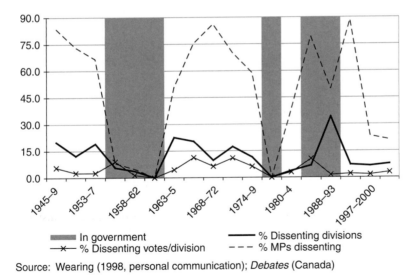

Source: Wearing (1998, personal communication); *Debates* (Canada)

Figure 3.4 Dissent in the Canadian Progressive Conservative (1945–93) and Reform Parties (1993–2004)

caucus engaged in dissent; in the subsequent term not a single Conservative dissented. The data provide no indication, then, of a sea-change in parliamentary behaviour such as occurred in Britain in the 1970s. On the contrary, wild swings between widespread dissent and perfect unity appear to be the Canadian norm.

The regular occurrence of minority government is one reason for the extreme variation in the Canadian data. Minority government makes dissent a risky proposition on the government side, and so dissent in the governing party bottoms out in these conditions (as it did for the PC minority governments of 1962–3 and 1979–80, for example). Minority governments also tend to be risk-averse and short-lived; they not only try to avoid having matters put to a division (because any vote could see the government collapse), they tend to collapse before too many divisions actually take place. This can skew the aggregate data. For example, the surge in the frequency of Liberal dissent in the 1957–8 Parliament was due to Liberal MPs dissenting on ten of just eighteen divisions in total. Minority government cannot be the sole explanation for the variation in dissent, however, as there were only five minority governments between 1945 and 2004. The wide swings in backbench dissent in Canada also reflect a tendency for dissent to be driven by a small number of mavericks. The data in Figures 3.3 and 3.4 only hint at this dynamic, but a tell-tale sign is that the frequency of dissent remains stable or increases even while the extent of dissent declines. The 1988–93 PC government is a good example of this pattern of dissent. The extent of PC dissent declined from 80 to 50 per cent, while the frequency of dissent surged upward from 6 to 35 per cent. This was primarily due to two rebel MPs, David Kilgour and Alex Kindy, constantly voting against their own party. Sometimes the two rebels would be joined by a few other Conservative MPs (and there were one or two issues that attracted broader internal dissension), but often Kindy and Kilgour were the only dissidents. In this fashion, the presence of just a few mavericks in a parliament contributes to wide swings in the frequency of dissent. That pattern changed, however, during Jean Chrétien's time as prime minister (1993–2003), when it became more common to see Canadian MPs voting against their parties in numbers.[5]

---

[5] The return to minority government in Canada since 2004 has once again reined in dissent in Canada – at least as far as voting is concerned. Eight Canadian MPs have left their parties to sit as independents or members of other parties since the 2004 election, however.

Backbench dissent in Australia

The Australian dissent data include figures for both the House of Representatives and the Senate.[6] There is a variety of reasons to include the Senate in the analysis. First, unlike the British House of Lords and the Canadian Senate, the Australian Senate is elected and powerful. In theory, Australian governments are responsible only to the House, but in practice, with the Senate's proportional electoral system typically denying the government of the day a corresponding Senate majority, Australian governments have to bargain with the Senate over legislation. In this environment, the loss of just a few votes to dissent in the Senate can represent a significant legislative roadblock to an Australian government. Second, with Australian party leaders elected by their parliamentary parties, senators are potentially pivotal players in the parties' internal politics. Rebellion, regardless of whether it originates in the House or the Senate, can undo Australian party leaders.

On the whole, the Australian Senate has also been the main source of Australian parties' disunity. The contrast is most striking for the Australian Labor Party (ALP). Whereas the ALP experienced some fairly serious (albeit isolated) rebellions in the Senate in the 1980–2 and 1985–7 terms (see Figure 3.7), it was almost perfectly united in the House of Representatives. In fact, I do not chart the ALP's dissent in the House of Representatives precisely because there is nothing to show: in the 3,020 divisions that I sampled, the ALP saw just a single vote cast against the party. The same contrast comes through in the Coalition data. While there were times, as in the last term of the Fraser government (1980–2), during which dissent in the Coalition involved 5 per cent of divisions in the House (see Figure 3.5), it has on occasion reached upward of 20 per cent of divisions in the Senate (see Figure 3.6). The Coalition's Senate dissent has also tended to be deeper, costing the Coalition between 10 and 20 per cent of its voting power in the Senate as compared to just 7.5 per cent (at most) in the House. The difference in the severity of dissent between the House and Senate partly reflects the smaller size of the Australian Senate relative to the House (and, indeed, to the British and Canadian Commons, too). With governing parties in Australia controlling an average of eighty House seats

[6] As the bulk of the Australian data are taken from Lucy (1985), the Australian time series starts only in the 1970s. I have continued the time series by sampling from parliamentary records at the point in time when Lucy ends his analysis (1982).

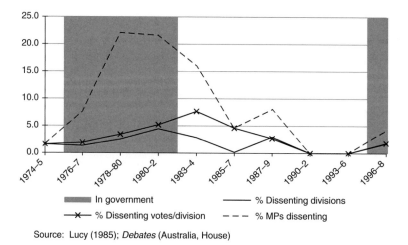

Source: Lucy (1985); *Debates* (Australia, House)

Figure 3.5 Dissent in the Australian Coalition (House), 1974–96

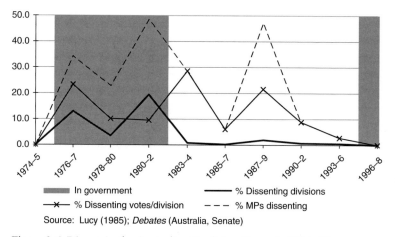

Source: Lucy (1985); *Debates* (Australia, Senate)

Figure 3.6 Dissent in the Australian Coalition (Senate), 1974–98

but just thirty Senate seats, a loss of just three to five senators to dissent results in a precipitous loss of voting power and practically ensures the party's defeat in Senate divisions. None of this, however, should obscure the larger message of the data, namely that dissent in Australia, even in the more fractious Coalition, is a much rarer phenomenon than it is in either Britain or Canada.

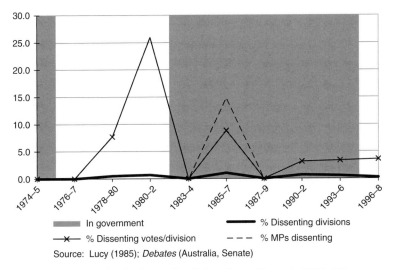

Source: Lucy (1985); *Debates* (Australia, Senate)

Figure 3.7 Dissent in the Australian Labor Party (Senate), 1974–98

Backbench dissent in New Zealand

A similar message can be delivered about dissent in New Zealand: it is just not that common.[7] The percentage of dissenting divisions has only rarely approached 5 per cent (see Figures 3.8 and 3.9), and just as in Australia, it is the party on the political right, the National Party in New Zealand's case, that is the more fractious. The key difference between Australia and New Zealand is that dissent in New Zealand became noticeably deeper and more extensive from the mid-1980s onward. The figures are low compared to the British and Canadian data, with the extent of dissent never exceeding 50 per cent, but other indicators of dissent, such as the number of MPs defecting from their parties, back up the impression of a recent surge of parliamentary dissent in New Zealand. The upward trend in defections began in 1988, when a Labour MP, Jim Anderton, left the party to sit as the lone member of the New Labour Party. The following term, the National government saw four of its members defect: Gilbert Myles, Hamish MacIntyre,

---

[7] Note that the New Zealand data only go up to 1996 because the House of Representatives changed its voting rules early in 1996 to allow 'party votes' to be cast. This was one of the procedural changes adopted in advance of the change to a mixed-member electoral system.

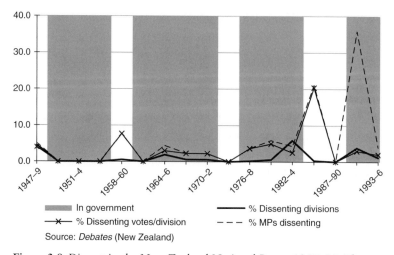

Figure 3.8 Dissent in the New Zealand National Party, 1947–96. The source for New Zealand data prior to 1987 was Hobby (1987).

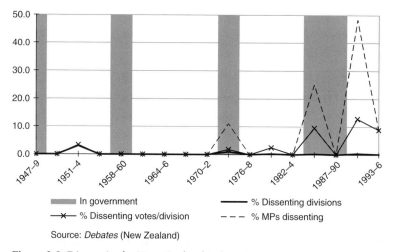

Figure 3.9 Dissent in the New Zealand Labour Party, 1947–96

Cam Campion, and Winston Peters. Peters's defection was especially important; the ex-cabinet minister had a high profile that helped to quickly establish his new party, New Zealand First, as a viable alternative to National and Labour. The adoption of proportional representation in 1993 merely accelerated the trend: over the next three years (i.e., before an election was contested under PR) nine National MPs and four Labour MPs left their parties. These defections robbed Bolger's National government of its slim majority, forcing it at various points in the 1993–6 term to govern as a minority or as part of a coalition. Political tensions that would have been the grist of intra-party politics under the old rules of the game were, in this fashion, transformed into the material for inter-party bargaining. One can speculate, then, that backbench dissent remained at a relatively low level in New Zealand not because the National and Labour parties were especially united, but rather because the social and electoral forces behind electoral dealignment were so powerful that they blew apart the two established parties.

Summary

These cases reveal several basic patterns of dissent. First, there are instances of perfect unity. The ALP (in the House) and the New Zealand Labour Party exemplify this pattern, but it appears periodically in Canada, especially during periods of minority government, and in Britain prior to 1970. A second pattern sees this unity punctuated by isolated but quite serious revolts. Britain before the 1970s and New Zealand in the late 1980s and 1990s show evidence of this pattern. A third pattern, most common in Canada, is for dissent to be frequent but not especially severe. This is generally the product of a few mavericks constantly voting against their own parties. Only rarely is dissent simultaneously frequent, deep, and extensive and when it is, it signals a party in a great deal of distress: the British Labour Party in the early 1980s, with the party's right and left factions locked in a decade-long battle over the party's identity, is the best example. Beyond these patterns, there are some obvious cross-national and temporal contrasts. First, there is simply more dissent in the British and Canadian Parliaments than in the Australian and New Zealand Parliaments. Second, dissent has increased over time in Britain and New Zealand, whereas, if anything, it has declined in Australia.

Explaining variation in party-level dissent

I consider five factors that might explain these patterns. The first, the force of the confidence convention, is outside the scope of the LEADS model.

The remaining factors – the party's popularity, the level of party identification in the electorate, the availability of advancement in the party, and the balance of parliamentary experience among a party's MPs – are more directly connected to the LEADS model, either intensifying MPs' incentives to dissent or altering the relative costs of advancement or discipline.

The confidence convention

The golden rule of parliamentary politics is that the cabinet must maintain the confidence of the House. If it cannot do this, it must either give way to a new cabinet or dissolve Parliament and call an election. Given this rule, backbenchers, especially on the government side of the House, should hesitate to vote against their party. It is not surprising then that some authors see the confidence convention as the necessary and sufficient condition for party cohesion (Diermeier and Feddersen 1998) and the breakdown of that convention as the chief cause of backbench dissent (Schwarz 1980). In its barest form (and this is essentially what Diermeier and Feddersen's position boils down to), the argument is that the confidence convention suppresses dissent because government backbenchers do not want to bring down their government and deprive themselves of the privileges of power. Schwarz (1980) adopts a similar stance, arguing that dissent in the British Commons increased in the early 1970s because of a weakened confidence convention. The demise of the 'parliamentary rule' that the government must resign upon a parliamentary defeat invited dissent, backbench logic being that if the government did not collapse upon defeat, then voting against the party was less risky.[8] Indeed, two pieces of evidence discussed briefly above support these arguments: the lack of dissent among Canadian minority governments (which are always on the brink of collapse) and the greater frequency and depth of dissent in the Australian Senate than in the House (where governments need to maintain confidence).[9]

---

[8] Norton (1980, 1985) shares Schwarz's position, but also argues that it was Edward Heath's abrasive leadership style that initially sparked the dissent. Dissent was then ratcheted upward by the government's subsequent survival despite defeats in the House.

[9] In 1975 the Senate refused supply to the Whitlam government, and the governor-general ruled that the Whitlam government had lost Parliament's confidence and ordered a double dissolution. The governor-general's actions were highly controversial, however, and opinion is that they are highly unlikely to be repeated (Jaensch 1992).

The confidence convention is an imposing parliamentary rule, but it is a much less rigid constraint on the behaviour of party leaders and ordinary backbenchers than many people believe. At the margin, such as when the government has an extremely narrow majority and when a division is implicitly or explicitly on a matter of confidence, the confidence convention is certainly all that is required to induce perfect or near-perfect cohesion among members of the governing party.[10] Parliamentary politics is, however, only rarely played out under these conditions, conditions which, as Schwarz's argument implies, also change over time (and between countries). The fact is that few divisions are implicitly or explicitly on matters of confidence, and so a government can be defeated in the division lobbies without losing the confidence of the House.[11] This does not mean that government defeats are costless – they can derail a government's legislative agenda and generate an image of weakness in voters' eyes – but they are not automatically catastrophic.[12] In addition, the confidence convention would seem to be

[10] There are examples of MPs dissenting on votes of confidence. Rupert Allason, a British Conservative MP, abstained from voting for Major's confidence motion on the Maastricht Treaty; in the 1993–7 Canadian Parliament, John Nunziata, a Liberal MP, voted against the Chrétien cabinet's budget as a whole; in 2007, William Casey, a Canadian Conservative MP, also voted against his own (minority) government's budget. (Votes on main supply motions are automatically considered to be matters of confidence.)

[11] Norton records that British governments were defeated sixty-five times between 1970 and 1979 without resigning (1980). In Canada, Franks (1987, p. 139) notes that the Trudeau government was defeated eight times between 1972 and 1974 without resigning. The Pearson government also lost a third-reading vote on its budget in 1968. Pearson, however, asked the House to acknowledge explicitly that this defeat did not constitute a loss of confidence. The House acquiesced (to a minority government), and Pearson's cabinet continued in office (Ward 1987, p. 145).

[12] Given these costs, one might ask why prime ministers (PMs) do not declare every vote a matter of confidence. This would ensure perfect, or near-perfect, cohesion. This is the thrust of Huber's (1996b) model of the vote of confidence. Huber's model imposes a cost on the PM for calling a vote a matter of confidence – and so the PM invokes the confidence convention only when the legislative measure merits this cost. This is all quite sensible, but what the reader has to recognize is that the costs faced by the PM are very high indeed. They are not simply electoral in nature (the parliamentary tactic revealing to voters that the PM is barely in control of his or her party) and shared, therefore, by all party members. In some parties, leaders can be elected and removed peremptorily by the parliamentary party. Under these conditions a PM who too readily invokes confidence is almost certain to be replaced by the very backbenchers whom he or she seeks to control. Thus the cost of making a vote a matter of confidence may well be the loss of the

of little use in explaining the behaviour of opposition MPs (Franklin *et al.* 1986, p. 146). It is true that the convention provides an incentive for opposition MPs to stick together in the hope of bringing down the government, but they suffer no serious consequence should they fail to do so.

The upshot of all this is that parliamentary behaviour is not a deterministic function of the confidence convention. That said, the confidence convention should have an impact on dissent. In particular, dissent should increase – on both government and opposition benches – as the probability of a loss of confidence declines. In practical terms, this probability declines as (a) the size of the government's majority increases, and (b) as the opposition becomes more fragmented (i.e., as the number of opposition parties increases). On the government side, a large majority allows backbenchers to dissent more freely because they know that a few dissenting votes will not bring their government down. If, in addition, the opposition is fragmented, government members can rely on co-ordination failures among opposition parties to preserve the government in office. Indeed, even minority governments can survive dissent providing the opposition is divided.[13] Overall, the confidence convention should have a much weaker impact on the behaviour of opposition MPs (their parties are under no obligation to maintain the confidence of the House). Nevertheless, opposition backbenchers have stronger incentives to stick together when their actions have at least some possibility of inflicting serious damage on the government. This is most likely when the opposition is both relatively united and controls a significant share of parliamentary seats. This suggests the following hypotheses about the confidence convention and party-level dissent:

Hypothesis 1. Dissent should be higher in opposition parties than in governing parties.

Hypothesis 2. For governing parties, dissent should increase alongside the party's seat share, whereas for opposition parties, dissent should decrease alongside the party's seat share.

Hypothesis 3. For both government and opposition parties, dissent should increase as the opposition becomes more fragmented.

premiership. It is little wonder then that PMs are averse to employing the tactic under all but the most desperate circumstances.

[13] Logically, some degree of opposition fractionalization is a necessary precondition of minority government. If the opposition were united in a single party, it would, by definition, control a majority of seats.

Party popularity

Beyond the confidence convention lie a number of other variables that the LEADS model of intra-party politics links to dissent. The model casts intra-party politics in terms of a trade-off between the MP's desire for electoral security and the pursuit of career advancement. It is not possible to control for the electoral environment of individual MPs within the confines of an aggregate-level model, but one can use measures of party popularity to get an idea of how the party as a whole is faring politically. Low or declining levels of party popularity over the parliamentary term indicate that the electoral environment in which the party's MPs must seek re-election is an uncongenial one. Toeing the party line in these circumstances is potentially costly, heightening the MP's incentive to distance herself from the party and making dissent more likely. At the party level, then, low or declining levels of party popularity should coincide with surges in dissent.

Hypothesis 4. Dissent increases as party popularity declines.

Electoral dealignment and party identification

The party's unpopularity may well create incentives for MPs to dissent, but as the LEADS model makes clear, these incentives are contingent on the effectiveness of dissent. The level of party identification in the electorate has a direct bearing on the effectiveness of dissent. If party identification is strong and extensive, most voters vote on the basis of affective ties to a specific party rather than on the basis of the parties' policy positions or the individual candidates' characteristics. Under these conditions, the party label is a valuable electoral asset that the MP has little incentive to devalue by dissenting. However, even if the MP were to dissent, the fact that most voters vote on the basis of affective ties to a party would limit the impact of the MP's dissent. Generally speaking, then, strong and extensive levels of party identification among voters undercut MPs' incentives to dissent *and* their ability to translate their dissent into a tangible electoral benefit.[14]

---

[14] Note that the partisan balance of the electorate is irrelevant to the argument. If party identification is strong and extensive, some segment of the electorate votes for the MP entirely on the basis of the MP's party affiliation, whereas another segment of the electorate votes against the MP for precisely the same reason. The MP can do nothing to sway either camp (save switching parties), and so the relative size of these two camps is moot.

Conversely, as dealignment sets in and the proportion of the electorate who vote exclusively or predominantly on the basis of partisan affiliations shrinks, the effectiveness of dissent grows. Part of the process of dealignment is the replacement of partisan identifiers by non-partisan voters who lack strong affective ties to established political parties. The shift in the relative balance between identifiers and non-partisans is not necessarily consequential. If non-partisans are politically inactive or politically unsophisticated, casting their votes randomly rather than systematically on the basis of available political information, then electoral outcomes will still be determined by the partisan balance of identifiers. Evidence suggests, however, that non-partisans are neither politically inactive nor unsophisticated (Dalton 2000). On the contrary, dealignment has generated within the electorates of advanced industrial democracies a growing pool of non-partisan but still politically active and sophisticated voters who are willing and cognitively able to vote on the basis of non-partisan cues. In this fashion, dealignment has simultaneously diminished the electoral security that the party label affords the MP and increased the incentive for the MP to act independently of the party (Thies 2000). Dealignment has therefore markedly changed the cost-benefit ratio of dissent, with dissent offering a potentially better electoral return than it ever did. At the macro-level, this argument suggests that a negative relationship should exist between the extent and strength of party identification among voters and the level of dissent in the party.

Hypothesis 5.   Dissent increases as party identification among voters becomes weaker and/or less extensive.

The availability of advancement

Party leaders use institutional and sociological tools to maintain unity in the face of the incentives generated by political unpopularity and dealignment. The double monopoly of power at the heart of Westminster parliamentary government points to the party leadership's monopoly of advancement as the most relevant of these institutional tools. This double monopoly of power fuses professional advancement and policy influence into a single indivisible good, a cabinet position, and places the pathways to these positions under the control of a single party's leadership. Even the opposition parties conform to this template. While shadow ministers do not enjoy the perks or power of cabinet ministers, they get a disproportionate share of the opposition's meagre resources, bask in the media spotlight, and have greater influence over their party's policy proposals and are in a strong position to get a cabinet position should their party win the next election. The fusion of office perks and policy influence makes these frontbench positions attractive to both office- and policy-seeking MPs and generates a high demand for advancement.

In theory, the level of dissent in a party should depend on the party leadership's ability to meet this demand. The individual-level logic underpinning this argument follows directly from the LEADS model, that is, as the cost to the leader of delivering advancement increases, less advancement is delivered to MPs, and MPs then dissent because they are not receiving enough advancement to offset the electoral damage of unpopular party policies. Moreover, as the probability of obtaining advancement to the front bench declines, MPs begin to discount the value of advancement accordingly, further exacerbating the problem. Hence when opportunities for advancement in the party are limited (i.e., when there is little chance of promotion), one can expect that there will be a number of MPs who find little reward in toeing the party line and who will, especially in times of political difficulty, have every incentive to distance themselves from the party. A simple estimator of an MP's probability of obtaining higher office (and the best aggregate-level proxy of the expected utility of a frontbench office) is the proportion of the parliamentary party that hold frontbench posts in the ministry or shadow ministry.[15] This is a rough measure of an MP's probability of promotion, but even so it provides a fairly good comparative measure of the abundance or scarcity of career opportunities across parliamentary parties. As this percentage declines, that is, as opportunities for advancement become relatively scarce, dissent should increase.

Hypothesis 6.   Dissent increases as the percentage of a party's MPs holding frontbench positions declines.

The balance of parliamentary experience

In a descriptive turn of phrase, Crowe (1986, p 162) describes parliamentary parties as webs of informal authority. Norms of loyalty,

---

[15] The usage of 'ministry' rather than 'cabinet' is intentional here. Included in the ministry are cabinet ministers, junior ministers, parliamentary secretaries, whips, and House leaders (who need not be ministers).

solidarity, and deference to leadership are the key components of these webs of informal authority, and in the LEADS model these social norms serve to reinforce the party's more direct appeals to a younger MP's progressive ambition or to substitute for an older MP's loss of upward mobility. Crowe's description also engenders a picture of MPs becoming increasingly enmeshed in this web of informal authority over time, with these social norms exerting ever greater force over the MP the longer he or she remains part of the parliamentary party.

If socialization is indeed vital to individual loyalty, it follows that neophyte MPs, who by definition are less likely to have been socialized into acceptable patterns of parliamentary behaviour, are more likely to dissent than their more experienced colleagues. Efforts at socialization are also likely to be impaired when turnover in the party's parliamentary membership is very high. Effective socialization requires, after all, that group norms of loyalty, deference to leadership, solidarity, and teamwork be transmitted from generation to generation (Asher 1973, p. 499; Crowe 1986, p. 177). High and chronic levels of turnover disrupt this transmission process by draining parties of the experienced members required to mentor newcomers in the party's values. Short tenures of office also make it much harder for leaders to develop close personal ties with their backbenchers, ties that can be relied upon to deliver loyalty in politically stressful times. Absent mentoring and close personal relationships with party leaders, newcomers are unlikely to become fully integrated into the party's web of informal authority and will, as a consequence, be far more likely to dissent. The critical party-level variable to test, then, is the percentage of new MPs entering the party's caucus in any term: as this percentage rises, so too should dissent in the party.

Hypothesis 7.   As the percentage of new MPs entering the party at each parliamentary term increases so too should dissent.

Data and methods

I test these hypotheses with three multivariate models of dissent, one for each dimension of dissent. The main independent variables are as follows:

1. *Government status.* This is simply a dummy variable that marks the party's governing (1) or opposition status (0).

2. *Seat share (percentage seats).* This is measured as the percentage of parliamentary seats held by the party at the beginning of the term. The models also include an interaction between this seat share variable and the party's government–opposition status. This specification allows the seat share coefficient to differ depending on whether the party is in government or opposition.

3. *Effective number of opposition parties (ENOP).* This variable is measured by restricting Laakso and Taagepera's (1979) index for the effective number of legislative parties to opposition parties. Thus, $ENOP = 1/\sum_{i=1}^{n} s_i^2$ where s_i is the percentage of seats held by the ith opposition (i.e., non-government) party at the start of the parliamentary term. To allow for the possibility that government and opposition parties respond differently to the effective number of opposition parties in parliament, some specifications also include an interaction between *Government status* and *ENOP.*

4. *Percentage of very strong party identifiers in the electorate (percentage strong ID).* This measure is derived from surveys conducted just prior to the start of the parliamentary term. So, for example, the figures for the 1993–6 Australian Parliament were drawn from the 1993 *Australian Election Study.* The measure counts only those voters who indicated that they identified 'very strongly' with a party.[16]

5. *Party popularity.* Popularity is defined as the party's share of declared vote intentions in public opinion surveys. Two measures of party popularity are employed. The first is the range of the party's popularity over the parliamentary term multiplied by –1 if net party popularity fell over the term or +1 if it climbed over the term. This variable (*Popularity trend*) not only indicates the general trend in the party's popularity, it also provides a sense of its volatility. One imagines that politicians prefer a predictable environment to a volatile one. Large shifts in voting intentions, even if they result in only a small net change in popularity over the course of the term, are likely to make MPs uncertain about their chances for re-election, therefore leery of relying too heavily on the party label for re-election and so

---

[16] These election studies tend to adopt a similar series of questions to tap respondents' partisanship, first asking them if they (very strongly, strongly, weakly, etc.) support a party or not, and if not, whether they lean toward one particular party.

more likely to dissent in the hope of building up a more predictable personal vote.

The second popularity measure is simply the party's level of popularity at the start of the parliamentary term (*Popularity at start*). This variable provides a benchmark of the party's starting position that helps to place the trend measure of popularity in context. For example, for a party that starts at 60 per cent in the polls, a 5 per cent drop over the course of the parliamentary term is no barrier to re-election. If, however, the party starts the term with a popularity rating of just 35 per cent, a 5 per cent decline is a major crisis.

6. *Percentage of the parliamentary party holding frontbench positions (percentage frontbench MPs)*. Included in these figures are ministers, junior ministers, and parliamentary secretaries (or the opposition counterparts to these positions).[17]

7. *Percentage of new MPs entering the parliamentary party per term (percentage new MPs)*. This is simply the percentage of MPs in the parliamentary party with no previous parliamentary experience. In the Canadian and Australian cases, this means no federal parliamentary experience, and in the Australian case this also means no experience in either the House or the Senate.

All of these variables are measured by party from 1945 onward, save in Australia, where they date from 1974 onward. The data end in 2005 in Britain, 2004 in Canada, 1998 in Australia, and 1996 in New Zealand. The sampling frame includes sixteen British, ten Australian, seventeen New Zealand, and eighteen Canadian Parliaments. Each Australian Parliament provides an observation for the House and Senate, however, and so the Australian case provides an extra ten observations. With all

---

[17] In the Canadian, Australian, and New Zealand Parliaments, one finds parliamentary secretaries. These posts are salaried (at least on the government side), but are not always considered part of the ministry (i.e., rigidly subject to collective responsibility), depending on the country and the era (on Canada, for example, see Ward 1987, pp. 196–7). These posts are, however, typically an MP's first step up the parliamentary career ladder, much as a parliamentary private secretaryship (PPS) is in the UK. To maintain comparative validity, I include PPSs in my count of British ministries, despite the fact that these posts are neither salaried nor legally part of the ministry (Silk and Waters 1987, p. 42). I do not include the Law Officers in the British numbers because these offices tend to be handed to legal specialists out of necessity. This is not especially problematic, however, as the fixed number of Law Officers means that excluding them simply subtracts a constant from the size of the British front benches.

parliaments providing observations for a governing and an opposition party, there are 142 cases in total.[18] I used multiple imputation techniques to ameliorate missing data problems and to ensure that all 142 cases entered the analysis. The imputation primarily was targeted at popularity and party identification figures which are quite spotty for the earlier time periods. Overall, however, missing data were not a serious problem, and analyses limited to the seventy-nine fully observed cases deliver the same substantive message as those shown below.

The data comprise a time-series cross-section with panels defined by the parties and the time periods defined by parliamentary terms. The unit of analysis is therefore the Labour or Conservative, etc. Party in the 1945–9 Parliament, the 1950–1 Parliament, and so on. This data structure produces a number of complications, some of which are well known from the literature (e.g., Stimson 1985; Beck and Katz 1995) and others which are less obvious. One of the less obvious problems is that parliamentary terms in these countries are not regular and equal time intervals. This means that some parliaments have more time to have divisions (and, therefore, more dissenting divisions or more dissenting MPs) than other parliaments.[19] To help solve this problem I control for the number of months in the parliamentary term.

A second econometric issue is the extent to which observations are independent of one another. One might argue, for example, that exogenous shocks to a party system affect all parties in the country and the

---

[18] In Canada, the identity of the opposition party changes in 1993 from the Progressive Conservative Party (which was almost completely annihilated at the 1993 elections) to the Reform Party.

[19] The irregularity of parliamentary terms may generate non-constant diagonal terms on the unit variance–covariance matrices. In a purely cross-sectional structure one would recognize this problem as heteroskedasticity, but in time serial data like these, it takes the form of autoregressive conditional heteroskedasticity (ARCH). A common way to deal with regular heteroskedasticity is by weighted least squares and one can think in analogous terms here. One dependent variable is the percentage of dissenting divisions observed per parliament. Since this variable is constructed by dividing the number of dissenting divisions by the total number of divisions, it already partially controls for the greater number of divisions that can occur in longer Parliaments (personal communication, Peter Kennedy, July 1997). This solution does not apply to the depth or extent of dissent, however, because one is not dividing these dependent variables by the number of divisions in the parliament or some other proxy for parliamentary duration. A broader solution is to model the variance of dissent in the mean of the equation by explicitly including the length of the parliament in the model.

model's error structure should account for this dependence (i.e., that the observations should be clustered by country). Beyond this, there are the standard issues of autocorrelation and heteroskedasticity common to all time-series cross-section models. A number of methods exist to deal with these problems (e.g., panel-corrected standard errors (Beck and Katz 1995)), but I opt for simplicity here and estimate the models via OLS with robust standard errors. I do not cluster the observations by party or country, because doing so tends to reduce the models' efficiency without materially affecting the results. In view of the relatively small number of observations per panel (an average of fourteen per party), I also avoid more sophisticated estimation techniques that rely on asymptotics (i.e., large-N properties) to correct the variance–covariance matrix; these techniques are often biased and inconsistent in small samples.[20]

Results

The statistical results are presented in Tables 3.1–3.3. The hypotheses are all directional in nature (the expectations for each coefficient are noted in the second column of each table) and in view of that I use one-tailed significance levels. Although the models are all straightforward linear regressions, some care must be exercised in interpreting the results. There are two areas where one can be led astray. First, the coefficients of the interaction terms cannot be interpreted as in regular additive models since the marginal effects and standard errors of these terms are conditional on the value of the modifying variable (Friedrich 1982; Golder 2003). Second, some attention must be paid to whether the coefficients reflect variation over time or across party systems. This can be determined by running two versions of each specification, one with a set of dummy variables for each political party (i.e., a fixed-effects model) and one without (i.e., OLS on the entire sample). The fixed-effects regression line is driven by the changes that a particular party experiences over time, whereas the OLS regression line also takes account of variation across parties and countries. Differences between the fixed-effects and OLS regression lines can have a bearing on

---

[20] Moreover, estimating the models with panel-corrected or Newey-West standard errors or via fixed- or random-effects models with first-order autocorrelation lag structures does not substantially alter the results.

Table 3.1. *The frequency of backbench dissent (percentage of divisions witnessing dissent), 1945–2005*

	Expectation	Model 1 (OLS)	Model 2 (fixed effects)	Model 3 (OLS)	Model 4 (fixed effects)
Months		.05	−.06	.05	−.05
		(.08)	(.09)	(.08)	(.08)
Government status	−	2.94	−7.68	1.54	2.76
		(7.21)	(8.93)	(8.11)	(10.20)
Percentage seats	−	.31**	.07	.30	.14
		(.14)	(.16)	(.14)	(.17)
ENOP	+	6.26***	.91	5.91**	3.66
		(1.92)	(2.91)	(3.25)	(4.19)
Government status × percentage seats	+	−.11	.12	−.09	−.01
		(.14)	(.17)	(.13)	(.16)
Government status × ENOP	−	−	−	.61	−4.53
				(3.50)	(4.92)
Popularity at start	−	−.49***	−.23	−.50***	−.14
		(.15)	(.18)	(.15)	(.18)
Popularity trend	−	−.14***	−.10**	−.14***	−.09**
		(.05)	(.05)	(.05)	(.05)
Percentage strong ID	−	−.06	−.24**	−.06	−.26**
		(.09)	(.13)	(.09)	(.13)
Percentage frontbench MPs	−	−.16**	−.17*	−.16**	−.18*
		(.09)	(.12)	(.09)	(.12)
Percentage new MPs	+	−.05	−.11	−.05	−.13
		(.05)	(.05)	(.05)	(.05)
Intercept		11.21	−	12.70	−
		(10.29)		(10.85)	
Party dummies		−	Included	−	Included
R^2		.41	.69	.41	.69
N		142	142	142	142

Cell entries are OLS regression coefficients with robust standard errors in parentheses.

* 1-tail $p < .10$
** 1-tail $p < .05$
*** 1-tail $p < .01$

Table 3.2. *The depth of backbench dissent (mean percent voting power lost to dissent), 1945–2005*

	Expectation	Model 5 (OLS)	Model 6 (fixed effects)	Model 7 (OLS)	Model 8 (fixed effects)
Months		.01 (.04)	–.03 (.04)	.01 (.03)	–.03 (.04)
Government status	–	–1.19 (5.10)	–11.02* (6.65)	2.35 (7.59)	–15.12** (7.57)
Percentage seats	–	–.04 (.12)	–.17 (.14)	–.01 (.13)	–.19* (.14)
ENOP	+	1.23 (1.00)	–1.26 (1.41)	2.34 (2.79)	–2.34 (2.12)
Government status × percentage seats	+	–.02 (.11)	.20 (.14)	–.05 (.13)	.25** (.13)
Government status × ENOP	–	–	–	–1.54 (2.72)	1.78 (2.69)
Popularity at start	–	–.01 (.10)	.00 (.15)	.02 (.12)	–.03 (.17)
Popularity change	–	–.01 (.03)	–.01 (.04)	–.01 (.03)	–.02 (.04)
Percentage strong ID	–	.02 (.06)	–.00 (.07)	.02 (.06)	.01 (.08)
Percentage MPs on front bench	–	–.02 (.05)	.01 (.07)	–.02 (.05)	.01 (.07)
Percentage new MPs	+	–.01 (.04)	–.01 (.04)	–.02 (.04)	–.01 (.04)
Intercept		6.31 (6.70)	–	2.59 (10.21)	–
Party dummies		–	Included	–	Included
R^2		.09	.57	.09	.57
N		142	142	142	142

Cell entries are OLS regression coefficients with robust standard errors in parentheses.
* 1-tail $p < .1$
** 1-tail $p < .05$
*** 1-tail $p < .01$

Table 3.3. *The extent of backbench dissent (percentage of parliamentary party engaged in dissent), 1945–2005*

	Expectation	Model 9 (OLS)	Model 10 (fixed effects)	Model 11 (OLS)	Model 12 (fixed effects)
Months		1.04^{***}	$.60^{***}$	1.02^{***}	$.59^{***}$
		(.13)	(.14)	(.14)	(.14)
Government status	−	−12.03	-43.29^{**}	−29.49	-54.25^{*}
		(25.112)	(25.40)	(31.64)	(34.93)
Percentage seats	−	−.08	$-.73^{**}$	−.22	$-.79^{**}$
		(.42)	(.42)	(.44)	(.43)
ENOP	+	5.97^{*}	−4.46	.46	−7.39
		(4.29)	(7.16)	(9.30)	(10.97)
Government status × percentage seats	+	.18	$.89^{**}$	.36	1.00^{**}
		(.52)	(.52)	(.55)	(.58)
Government status × ENOP	−	−	−	7.61	4.73
				(9.93)	(10.11)
Popularity at start	−	-1.48^{***}	$-.68^{*}$	-1.60^{***}	$-.77^{**}$
		(.36)	(.41)	(.40)	(.45)
Popularity trend	−	$-.37^{***}$	$-.26^{**}$	$-.38^{***}$	$-.27^{**}$
		(.16)	(.14)	(.16)	(.15)
Percentage strong ID	−	−.01	$-.50^{***}$	−.01	−.49**
		(.21)	(.23)	(.21)	(.23)
Percentage frontbench MPs	−	$-.54^{***}$	−.32	$-.56^{***}$	−.31
		(.20)	(.26)	(.20)	(.27)
Percentage new MPs	+	$.22^{**}$	.03	$.23^{**}$	.04
		(.11)	(.13)	(.11)	(.13)
Intercept		62.37^{***}	−	80.61^{**}	−
		(24.37)		(33.88)	
Party dummies		−	Included	−	Included
R^2		.58	.83	.59	.83
N		142	142	142	142

Cell entries are OLS regression coefficients with robust standard errors in parentheses.

* 1-tail $p < .1$

** 1-tail $p < .05$

*** 1-tail $p < .01$

interpretation. For example, if the OLS model indicated that dissent increased alongside the effective number of opposition parties (*ENOP*) whereas the fixed-effects model indicated no such effect, one would not automatically interpret the result as supporting the confidence convention thesis. Such a result tells us instead that more fragmented party systems (i.e., where the *ENOP* is high) experience more dissent than consolidated party systems (i.e., where the *ENOP* is low), suggesting a further link between dissent and the dealignment of the party system.[21]

The frequency of dissent

Table 3.1 provides the results for the frequency of dissent. Three results stand out. First, declining trends in popularity are associated with an increased frequency of dissent, with a 10 per cent drop in popularity generating a further 0.9–1.4 per cent of dissenting divisions on average. (Drops of 15–25 per cent in party popularity are regularly observed in the data.) Second, increasing the percentage of MPs in the party who hold frontbench positions appears to decrease dissent; increase the percentage of MPs on the frontbench by 10 per cent and the frequency of dissent declines by about 1.6–1.8 per cent. Both of these results hold within and across political parties. A third clear result, albeit a negative one, is that there is no link between the frequency of dissent and the percentage of new MPs in the party.[22]

---

[21] Time-series cross-section analysts are conditioned to employ unit dummy variables to control for different levels of the dependent variable across units (thereby eliminating a form of heteroskedasticity (Stimson 1985)) and to prevent the analyst from accepting ecological fallacies (Green *et al.* 2001). The addition of unit-specific dummy variables to the model is not costless, however: they result in inefficiency (because they use up degrees of freedom and drain variance from the substantively relevant variables in the model) and obscure some potentially useful information conveyed by the overall regression line (Beck and Katz 2001). Indeed, one can read my point here as being that there is no ecological fallacy – rather both regression lines tell us something relevant about backbench dissent.

[22] This can perhaps be taken as evidence that socialization is indeed a secondary rather than principal bulwark of party unity, but one might also argue that my measure of advancement opportunities, the relative size of the party's front bench, is confounded with the socialization process. In conversations with the New Zealand Labour and National Party whips, I asked how the dynamics of socialization and mentoring had been affected by recent electoral volatility. The electoral environment had led to a high degree of turnover in each party, putting them in a position where they came to government with only a few MPs with

There is evidence of dealignment driving up dissent. The fixed-effects specifications (Models 2 and 4) indicate, for example, that a 1 per cent decline of very strong identifiers in the electorate is associated with a .25 per cent increase in dissenting divisions. Note that this effect is driven by changes in the percentage of very strong identifiers over time within each party system rather than differences in levels of party identification across party systems (the coefficients are statistically insignificant in the OLS specifications). The across-system effects of dealignment are, in fact, picked up by the parties' starting levels of popularity. A party's starting popularity, for example, has a strong negative effect on dissent in Models 1 and 3 (the OLS models), but no statistical effect in the fixed-effects models. The OLS result shows, then, that parties with lower average starting popularity ratings tend to have higher levels of dissent than parties with higher average starting popularity ratings. Where does one find parties with high average popularity ratings? In party systems dominated by two major parties (e.g., Australia). Conversely, parties with low average popularity ratings are found in fragmented party systems (e.g., Canada), the greater number of parties tending to limit the amount of electoral support that any one party captures. Fragmentation of the party system (along with a decline in party identification) is symptomatic of dealignment, and in that respect the link between starting popularity and dissent shown in Models 1 and 3 reflects a connection between dealignment and dissent.

Determining the extent to which the confidence convention shapes parliamentary behaviour is not straightforward. Be aware that the OLS models pick up cross-system differences that say more about the impact

prior ministerial experience. The whips noted the consequences: virtually all experienced MPs ended up in the cabinet, swamped with work and surrounded by civil servants, leaving few veteran MP on the back bench to mentor new MPs on the informal folkways of party and parliament. Both whips felt that this environment had contributed to dissent. The whips' interpretation of the intra-party environment suggests that it is not turnover as such that causes dissent as much as an imbalance between veteran and neophyte backbenchers – and cabinets and shadow cabinets, by necessity, remove veteran MPs from the back bench. While plausible, this argument cannot be sustained. First, it suggests that the size of the ministry should be positively related to the party's level of dissent; this runs against the facts. Second, the ratio of new to veteran backbenchers (with the percentage of veterans measured as 100% – % new MPs – % MPs on the front bench) is entirely unrelated to the frequency, depth, or extent of a party's dissent. The results, then, are not simply the result of the ministry soaking up parties' supplies of mentors.

of dealignment than the confidence convention. Models 1 and 3, for example, indicate that a higher effective number of opposition parties (*ENOP*) is associated with a higher frequency of dissent, but this is just a practical illustration of the hypothetical example noted above, namely that dissent is more frequent in systems that have a greater effective number of parties, i.e., in more fragmented party systems. The results of the fixed-effects specifications are therefore more relevant to the confidence hypothesis, but even when the marginal effects and standard errors of the interaction terms are calculated, they reveal no support for the confidence convention argument. Model 2, for example, shows that the marginal effect of seat share on dissent for governing parties is *b* % *Seats* + *(b% Seats × Gov. status)* = .07 + .12 × (*Government status*) = .19. This is in line with Hypothesis 2, which predicts seat shares to be positively related to dissent in governing parties, but the effect is not statistically significant.[23] There is, moreover, no evidence that government status in and of itself suppresses dissent as per Hypothesis 1 (the government status dummies are always statistically insignificant).

The depth of dissent

The confidence convention hypothesis cannot be written off entirely on the basis of these results, but if the convention does structure parliamentary behaviour, its influence should show up on the depth of dissent. The frequency of dissent, after all, can be inflated by a single maverick, and typically a single MP does not hold the balance of power. The depth of dissent, on the other hand, is a more critical variable for government survival. With the average seat share for governing parties in this data set at 55.2 per cent, governing parties can afford frequent rebellion provided that its depth never exceeds 5.2 per cent (i.e., that it does not lose more than 5.2 per cent of its voting power to dissent); any more than that threatens the government's survival.

The results in Table 3.2 certainly suggest that the depth of dissent is more strongly structured by the confidence convention than the

---

[23] The standard error for this prediction is computed as:

$$SE = [\text{var}(b_{\%Seats}) + \text{var}(b_{\%Seats \times Gov\ Status})$$
$$\pm\ 2\text{cov}(b_{\%Seats}, b_{\%Seats \times Gov\ Status})]^{1/2},$$

which turns out to be .15. The marginal effects are, therefore, not significant (t = $b_{\%\ Seats \times Gov.\ status}$/SE = .19/.15 = 1.27), and Hypothesis 2 can be rejected.

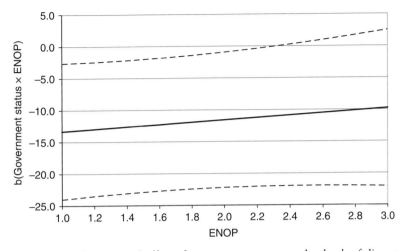

Figure 3.10 The marginal effect of government status on the depth of dissent modified by the effective number of opposition parties

frequency of dissent. The only variables affecting the depth of dissent are those connected to the confidence convention: government status, party seat shares, and the effective number of opposition parties. There is evidence, for example, that government status not only suppresses the depth of dissent directly (the government status dummies in Models 6 and 8 are negative), but that an increasing seat share has a negative impact on opposition dissent ($b = -.17$ in Model 6) and a slightly positive (albeit statistically insignificant) effect on government dissent ($b = -.17 + .20 = .03$). In other words, whereas the depth of government dissent is unresponsive to the party's seat share, the depth of opposition dissent declines as the party's seat share increases, a result that is at least partly supportive of Hypothesis 2.

There is another way to look at the interactions that bears on the confidence convention argument. Instead of viewing the party's government status as modifying the impact of the party's seat share on dissent (as per Hypothesis 2), one can also see the governing party's seat share or the *ENOP* as modifying the impact of the party's government status on dissent (a variation on Hypothesis 1). In other words, being in government may suppress dissent, but this effect might diminish as the party's seat share or the *ENOP* increases. To assess this possibility the marginal effect of government status on dissent must be examined while the party's seat share or the *ENOP* varies. This is done in Figure 3.10, which in addition to tracing out the estimated marginal effects of government status from Model 8, provides the 90 per cent confidence intervals for this estimate (the dashed lines). Figure 3.10 is read as follows. When there is just a single opposition party (i.e., $ENOP = 1$), the marginal effect of government status on dissent is estimated to be -13.34 ($= -15.12 + 1.78 \times ENOP$) (i.e., on average, government parties lose 13.34 per cent less of their voting power to dissent than opposition parties). As the $ENOP$ rises to 2 (i.e., a government facing two evenly balanced opposition parties), the average difference between the depth of the government and opposition dissent shrinks from 13.34 to 11.56 per cent ($= -15.12 + (1.78 \times ENOP)$). These effects are statistically significant only when the upper and lower confidence bounds are both above or below the zero y-axis. Clearly, the substantive effect of an increasingly fragmented opposition is small – increasing $ENOP$ from 1 (a single opposition party) to 1.5 increases the depth of government dissent by approximately 1 per cent – nevertheless, the effect is statistically significant up until about 2.3 effective opposition parties. In short, governments tend to lose more of their voting power to dissent when they face a more divided, hence weaker, opposition.

The extent of dissent

Empirically, the extent of dissent overlaps both the frequency and depth of dissent: parties tend to experience either frequent and extensive dissent or deep and extensive dissent. Quite sensibly, then, the extent of dissent is affected by a combination of the factors that structure the frequency and depth of dissent. The impact of the confidence convention, for example, is quite visible in Table 3.3. The government status dummy variables in Models 10 and 12 are negative, indicating that governing parties tend to experience less extensive dissent than opposition parties (as per Hypothesis 1). Models 10 and 12 also show the seat share coefficient reversing for governing and opposition parties (as per Hypothesis 2). The effect is less stark once the confidence bounds on the interactions are calculated, but it is clear that in opposition dissent becomes less extensive as the party's seat share rises. Finally, if one views the party's seat share as modifying government status, there is evidence that the suppressive effect of government status diminishes as the government's seat share increases. The effect is illustrated in Figure 3.11 (using the coefficient estimates from Model 10).

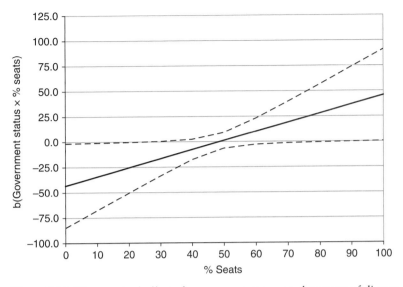

Figure 3.11 The marginal effect of government status on the extent of dissent modified by party seat share

Governments with majorities in the neighbourhood of 70–80 per cent exist in the data set and for these governments dissent is no longer less extensive than for opposition parties, but rather 20–25 per cent more extensive.

The level of party identification in the electorate and abundance of opportunities for advancement in the party also matter, with a 1 per cent decline in the percentage of very strong identifiers in the electorate increasing the extent of dissent by approximately 0.5 per cent. The percentage of MPs on the front bench has a similar marginal effect. Strong popularity effects are also visible, an indication that the party's electoral fortunes influence the extent of dissent. For every 1 per cent drop in the party's starting level of popularity, the extent of dissent climbs by between 0.68 and 1.60 per cent, depending on the model. Downward trends in popularity also extend dissent through the party. A 10 per cent decline in the party's popularity during the term, for example, increases the extent of dissent by between 2.6 to 3.8 per cent (even if much of this decline is recovered before the election). One might argue (along the lines expressed by some of the MPs quoted in Chapter 2) that this interpretation of the results mixes up cause and effect and that it is the party's disunity that leads to its unpopularity.

Further statistical tests make clear, however, that the causal arrow points from unpopularity to dissent rather than from dissent to unpopularity.

There is one way in which the extent of dissent is unique: it is the only dimension of dissent that is affected by the percentage of new MPs in the parliamentary party. The effect is positive, with every 1 per cent of new MPs increasing the extent of dissent by somewhere between 0.22–0.23 per cent. This effect shows up only in the OLS models (Models 9 and 11), however, suggesting that the result is driven by across-system rather than over-time differences. This raises the question of whether the extent of dissent is driven by the lack of socialization of a large number of neophyte MPs (in line with Hypothesis 6) or whether it reflects the fact that dissent is higher in party systems marked by electoral volatility and, in consequence, high levels of parliamentary turnover. The second interpretation casts the percentage of new MPs as a measure of electoral security and dealignment rather than socialization, a possibility that is hard to dismiss here. True, the model already controls for the party's electoral standing and the degree of dealignment (via the party popularity measures and the percentage of very strong identifiers), so the effect of an influx of new MPs on dissent is somewhat independent of these factors. Equally, the null coefficients in the fixed-effects models (Models 10 and 12) warn us that the interpretation here is *not* that dissent becomes more extensive as the percentage of new MPs in the party increases. It is rather that parties with a high percentage of new MPs have, on average, more extensive dissent than parties with a low percentage of new MPs. The causal argument between a lack of socialization and dissent is harder to maintain given the latter interpretation, and the issue can only be resolved by an individual-level analysis that examines whether new MPs are, in fact, more likely to dissent than veteran MPs.

Discussion

These results generate two comments and two questions. The first comment concerns the extent to which the confidence convention displaces the LEADS model as an explanation for patterns of party unity and backbench dissent. There is no doubt that the confidence convention influences the pattern of backbench dissent: dissent in government parties is neither as deep nor as extensive as dissent in opposition parties

(Models 6, 8, 10, 12) – though these differences diminish as the opposition becomes more fragmented (Model 8 and Figure 3.10) and as government's seat share increases (Model 10 and Figure 3.11), in short, as the confidence convention becomes an increasingly remote threat to the government's survival. The same dynamic appears among opposition parties, though working in the opposite direction, with dissent becoming less severe as the opposition's seat share increases (Models 8, 10, 12). That said, the frequency (certainly) and extent of dissent are as strongly affected by the variables associated with the LEADS model as they are by the confidence convention. This is worth emphasizing: even after accounting for the pressures of the confidence convention on parliamentary behaviour, the abundance of career advancement opportunities, the party's popularity (hence MPs' electoral prospects), and the level of party identification in the electorate (hence the incentive to dissent) still influence the pattern of backbench dissent.

The second comment concerns the importance of dealignment in accounting for cross-national differences in levels of dissent. One of the striking contrasts in the aggregate dissent data is how frequent and extensive dissent is in the UK and Canada as compared to Australia and New Zealand. Only dealignment in the party system can account for these cross-national differences. The confidence convention cannot explain these differences; all of these systems operate under the convention. They cannot be due to the ebb and flow of popularity during the term or the size of the ministry; these variables affect all parties fairly equally and operate to explain temporal rather than spatial variation in dissent. Dealignment, however, is the sort of large-scale environmental change that can account for these sorts of cross-national differences, and it seems an especially compelling explanation in the British case. Between 1964 and 2004, the percentage of British voters identifying themselves as very strong party identifiers declined from 44 to 14 per cent. The parliamentary impact of this 30 per cent slide in the strength of party identification in the UK was (according to these models) a 7.5 per cent increase in the frequency of dissent and a 15 per cent increase in its extent. What's more, half of this decline in the strength of party identification occurred between 1970 and 1974, right alongside the surge in parliamentary dissent. By way of contrast, Australia's highly cohesive parties have continued to inhabit a remarkably stable political environment in which party identification levels have remained robust (McAllister 1992, 2006) and other symptoms of dealignment, such as fragmentation, minimal. The effective number of opposition parties in the Australian House, for example, increased from 1.00 in 1974 to just 1.06 in 1998. During the same time period, the *ENOP* in Britain increased from 1.09 in 1970, to 1.26 by 1974, to 1.98 in 2001, an increase that might account for as much as a 6 per cent surge in the frequency of dissent. In short, the impact of dealignment can easily account for the broad cross-national differences in the data.

Two questions follow these two comments and both are aimed at the LEADS model. First, are these aggregate-level results also found at the individual level? For example, while the aggregate results indicate that a contraction of the front bench is associated with an increase in the frequency of dissent, is it the case that individual MPs denied a position on this smaller front bench engage in dissent? Dealignment and dissent appear to travel together, but is it really the case that the weakening of party identification has made dissent a more electorally profitable strategy for the individual MP? These sorts of individual-level observations are critical because they establish a causal link between the basic mechanisms of the LEADS model and the MP's dissent in a way that aggregate analyses cannot.

Second, is it possible that the above results are due to other factors or another model of parliamentary behaviour? In particular, could a spatial model of the sort Krehbiel proposes account for these patterns of dissent? This is not implausible. In fact, Krehbiel himself argues that the surge of backbench dissent witnessed at Westminster in the 1970s could be due simply to a change in the distribution of preferences in the two main parties (Krehbiel 1993, pp. 259–60). Certainly, one can imagine the social changes underpinning dealignment (e.g., the general embourgeoisement of society) bringing into both parties an ideologically homogeneous cohort of university-educated, middle-class professionals. The influx of these members would make the parties more internally heterogeneous while also making them more similar to one another, a situation that generates dissent in Krehbiel's model. Dealignment is still the root cause of dissent in this story, and not because it heightens MPs' incentives to dissent, but rather because the social changes that accompany dealignment alter the distribution of preferences within and between parties. Determining whether this is, in fact, the case is the topic of the next chapter.

4 | Policy preferences and backbench dissent in Great Britain and Canada

In the British case, this means inspecting more carefully the hypothesis that even in peak periods of the Westminster model legislative parties only appeared to be strong because their members had homogeneous preferences.

(Krehbiel 1993, p. 260)

Introduction

Do parties force or entice their members to vote together *in spite of their disagreements* about policy, or do party members vote together *because they already agree* over policy? The high levels of cohesion displayed by parliamentary parties tend to discourage students of parliamentary politics from asking this question. There is, perhaps, an underlying assumption that if parliamentary parties are highly cohesive, it must be because they can and do enforce discipline. For Krehbiel (1993, 1999), however, the answer to this question is not clear a priori, and the inferential link between policy preferences and discipline, on the one hand, and individual loyalty and party unity, on the other, not necessarily correct; MPs' voting behaviour could just as well be determined by their 'preferenceship', that is, by their ideological proximity to various voting coalitions in the chamber, as by their party affiliation.

There is a temptation to dismiss preferenceship out of hand as an abstraction that is too far removed from the realities of parliamentary politics to yield valuable insights; this temptation should be resisted. Preferenceship, after all, is less a comprehensive model of legislative politics than a starting-point for further investigation. If, for example, party unity is in fact produced largely by members' shared policy preferences, then models that explain unity as a function of the disciplinary mechanisms available to parties once the MP is in parliament (e.g., the distribution of patronage, threats of expulsion, etc.) are not useful. Time would be better spent thinking about how individual loyalty and party

75

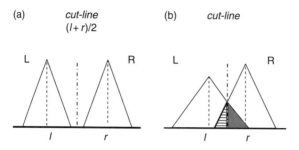

Figure 4.1 Hypothetical distributions of ideal points in two parliamentary parties

unity are affected by screening mechanisms (e.g., candidate selection rules) that allow party leaders to weed out candidates with uncongenial preferences. The issue, moreover, is not whether dissent is rooted in a divergence in policy preferences between party leaders and members, but whether leaders can maintain unity in the face of policy disagreements. In this respect, a good deal rides on determining the extent to which party unity is a function of shared policy preferences. The chapter, then, should not be read as an effort to falsify a straw-man model of parliamentary politics, but rather an attempt to discern how and how much individual loyalty and party unity depend on the distribution of policy preferences within and between parties.

Preferenceship and party unity

Figures 4.1a and 4.1b help to illustrate Krehbiel's argument. The triangles L and R represent the distribution of policy preferences within two political parties. The two parties have median policies of *l* and *r* respectively, but in both parties there are MPs who are to the left or right of their respective parties' policies. Now suppose that MPs vote for the policy option (i.e., *l* or *r*) closest to their ideal point. If the distribution of preferences is as it is in Figure 4.1a, the parties will remain perfectly united because the ideal point of every member of L is closer to *l* than *r*. All members of R vote for *r* for exactly the same reason. If, however, the ideal points of some members of L and R are closer to the opposing party's position (those with preferences in the shaded area in Figure 4.1b), each party faces the prospect that these outlying MPs may break ranks and vote against the party. Party leaders might, of course, use discipline to force these outlying MPs to vote the party line – but this opens the door to an observability problem: unless parliamentarians' preferences are measured directly, the analyst does not know whether the parties remained united because of a congenial configuration of preferences (as in Figure 4.1a) or because party leaders successfully imposed discipline on outlying MPs (as in Figure 4.1b).

Measuring policy preferences

In theory, only two variables are required to test this model, a summary indicator of MPs' voting records (the dependent variable) and a measure of their policy preferences (the independent variable).[1] MPs' voting records are (as explained in Chapter 3) straightforward to compile, but estimating their policy preferences is a challenge. MPs' votes, after all, can be observed; their preferences only inferred. A common technique is to use scaling or unfolding techniques to estimate MPs' policy preferences from their past votes (e.g., Poole and Rosenthal 1997; Londregan 1999; Snyder and Groseclose 2000), but there are several problems with this approach.[2] First, these scaling methods require some variance in

---

[1] If MPs' preferences are electorally induced, it should not be necessary to take separate account of MPs' electoral environments or circumstances (Krehbiel 1999, p. 158). Presumably, preferences held at any particular time have been induced by, and hence reflect, the states of these other variables up to that time.

[2] In rough terms, these scaling techniques work by placing MPs with completely opposite voting records (i.e., one MP always votes 'yes' while the other always votes 'no') at opposite ends of the policy space (which may, of course, be multidimensional). MPs with mixed voting records occupy the middle region of the policy space (i.e., an MP who votes 'yes' half the time and 'no' half the time will be at the centre of the policy space). If, however, the parties are perfectly united on floor votes, the middle of the policy space will be empty, and the scaling techniques will identify the parties as single points at opposite ends of the policy space. In other words, if the parties were perfectly united, there is no way that these scaling techniques could show the parties as occupying overlapping ideological territories; a priori, discipline is ruled out as an explanation for the parties' cohesion.

   One potential solution to the lack of variance in MPs' voting records is to estimate ideological preferences from free votes. By definition, free votes are free of party leaders' dictates, so one tends to observe more MPs voting against their parties in these situations. This might enable one to estimate MPs' preferences from their free voting records and then use those estimates to assess the degree to which MPs' voting behaviour in whipped divisions is consistent with preferenceship. There are, however, three flaws in this method:

   1. Leaders, even if they declare a vote to be free, are not shy about making public their preferred position or otherwise trying to influence MPs' voting intentions

members' voting records before they can produce valid estimates of legislators' policy preferences. This is not a problem when these techniques are applied to voting data from legislatures such as the US Congress, where party cohesion is low relative to most parliamentary systems. However, in many parliamentary systems, this sort of variance cannot be taken for granted. Second, voting patterns may not be a good proxy for members' policy preferences. If, for example, parties can and do influence members' votes, then votes reveal preferences that are endogenous to party discipline. Alternatively, party leaders may only allow votes on which the parties occupy clearly divergent policy positions (as in Figure 4.1a). In either case, observed votes suffer from selection bias. Strategic voting creates additional problems. During Blair's time in office, for example, the Conservatives would sometimes take advantage of splits in the Labour Party by joining with left-wing Labour MPs to vote against the government. When scaling techniques are applied to these sorts of votes, they mistakenly place Labour MPs like Dennis Skinner and Jeremy Corbyn, champions of the party's hard-left wing, on the ideological right alongside the Conservative MPs with whom they sometimes vote (Spirling and McLean 2007, p. 86). All this prompts doubts that legislators' preferences can be recovered from their votes (Vandoren 1990; Jackson and Kingdon 1992; Hixon and Wicks 2000).

To avoid these problems I estimate MPs' policy preferences from their responses to the 1993 *Canadian Candidate Study* (Erickson 1993) and the 1992 *British Candidate Study* (Norris and Lovenduski 1992). Both surveys polled the attitudes of all major party candidates (of which MPs are a strict subset) in the elections to the two Parliaments examined here.[3] The great advantage of this method is that MPs' responses to surveys conducted just before the beginning of a parliament are clearly exogenous to their subsequent behaviour and to parliamentary and

(see, for example, Major 1999, p. 213). In this case, free votes are not completely free of party influences.

2. Party leaders intent on preserving a façade of unity might submit to a whipped division only those matters which they are sure will not split their parties (as in Figure 4.1a). (For an example, see Berkeley 1972, p. 125.) In this instance, free votes would suffer from a form of selection bias.

3. Free votes typically involve moral issues (e.g., abortion and capital punishment). It is not clear how well MPs' preferences on these matters help one predict their preferences on broader economic and social issues.

[3] The response rates for these surveys were 53.1 per cent for the Canadian survey and 69.0 per cent for the British survey. See Erickson (1997, p. 666) and Norris and Lovenduski (1994).

party institutions (including party discipline, agenda setting, log-rolls, and the like). Appendix 2 provides a detailed description of how I used the survey data to develop measures of MPs' policy preferences, but briefly the procedure entailed the following steps:

1. I factor-analysed the responses to policy questions of all major party candidates. Each national survey produced a clear left–right dimension, but secondary ideological dimensions were also visible. In addition to the left–right dimensions, I used two of these secondary dimensions, a constitutional dimension that taps British MPs' attitudes toward the devolution of power from Westminster and a social conservatism dimension that taps Canadian MPs' attitudes toward non-traditional lifestyles.[4]
2. I then used the factor solutions to construct additive ideological scales. That is, I took items that loaded heavily on a factor, scaled each item so that it ranged between 0 and 1 from left to right and then added the items together.
3. Multiple imputation (Rubin 1987; Schafer 1997) was used to impute the scores of MPs who failed to respond or responded only partially to the candidate surveys. Imputed scores were not constrained to fall on the scale intervals, and so after imputation, the scales were, for all intents and purposes, continuous.
4. Finally, the scales were normalized on the unit interval so that all MPs occupy ideological positions between 0 and 1. This step simply eases interpretation.

Once MPs' preferences were estimated, I calculated the party medians and the cut-lines between the parties. I assume that a party's policy position (the empirical counterparts to l and r in Figure 4.1) is defined by its front bench (i.e., its parliamentary leadership). I further assume that within the front bench, the collective policy choice is determined by the median cabinet or shadow cabinet member. Hence, a party's policy positions (on the left–right, devolution, or social conservatism scales) are equal to the policy positions of the median cabinet or shadow cabinet

---

[4] In this context, 'devolution' refers simply to the handing over of some measure of authority by one body to another and not specifically to the recent constitutional changes in Scotland and Wales. 'Devolution scale' is simply more concise than 'decentralization of national sovereignty scale'. The devolution scale and the British left–right scale are correlated at $r = -.70$. The Canadian economic left–right and social conservatism scales are correlated at $r = .43$.

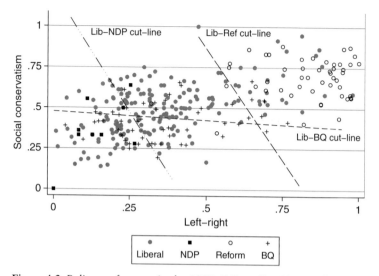

Figure 4.2 Policy preferences in the 1993–7 Canadian House of Commons

minister.[5] Once party medians are defined, the cut-lines are easy to compute. The only difficulty occurs when there is more than one opposition party. In these cases I define each opposition party's cut-line with respect to the governing party alone (not to another opposition party).[6]

An initial look at preferences and dissent

Scatter plots of the distribution of policy preferences in each Parliament are good starting points. Figure 4.2 shows the situation in the 1993–7 Canadian Parliament. The cut-lines superimposed on the scatter-plot trace the half-way point between the governing Liberal Party's median position and the median positions of the three main opposition parties. Only the economically right-wing and socially conservative Reform

---

[5] This operational decision has little if any impact on the chapter's results because there is not much difference between the ideological medians of the parties' front and back benches.

[6] Cut-lines dividing the opposition parties from one another are omitted because opposition parties tend to focus on amending or overturning the governing party's legislative agenda rather than proposing amendments to each other's amendments.

Party can claim to occupy a distinct ideological position in the upper-right quadrant of Figure 4.2. The Liberal Party, in contrast, sprawls over the policy space, flanked on the right by Reform and on the economic and social left by the Bloc Quebecois (BQ) and the small New Democratic Party (NDP). This ideological sprawl should not be taken as an indicator of measurement error; quite the opposite. The parties' ideological locations are sensible (see, e.g., Laver and Hunt 1992; Huber and Inglehart 1995; Gabel and Huber 2000), and the result is in keeping with qualitative descriptions of Canadian parties (the Liberals especially) as electoral vehicles largely devoid of ideological content (Carty 2002).

The issue here is whether dissent is concentrated among MPs who have policy positions closer to a party other than their own. The cut-lines superimposed on Figure 4.2 help to determine this. For example, Reform MPs below and to the left of the Liberal–Reform cut-line are ideologically closer to the Liberal Party's position. On average, these more economically and socially liberal Reform MPs should be inclined to vote with the Liberal Party. Reform dissent should therefore be concentrated below and to the left of the Liberal–Reform cut-line. For similar reasons, Reform MPs above and to the right of the Liberal–Reform cut-line should vote with their party. Graphs of the ideological location of dissent in each party (Figures 4.3, 4.4, and 4.5) thus provide direct tests of the preferenceship model.[7]

Figure 4.3 indicates that Reform dissent does not follow the expected pattern; most Reform dissidents are, in fact, on the Reform side of the cut-line. In other words, Reform MPs are dissenting despite being ideologically closer to their own party than any other. Exactly the opposite behaviour is found among BQ MPs. Many BQ MPs fall beyond the Liberal–BQ cut-line (indicating that they are closer to the Liberal median position than the BQ), but they rarely dissent (see Figure 4.4). Thus even though a preference-driven model would predict these MPs to act against their party, for some reason most BQ MPs do not. Finally, among Liberal MPs (Figure 4.5) one observes many MPs who occupy almost identical ideological positions but behave in very different ways, some dissenting a lot, others remaining very loyal. If only policy preferences guide behaviour, and policy preferences are identical, then behaviour too should be identical – but it is not.

---

[7] Because of its small size (just nine MPs), the NDP is dropped from the analysis.

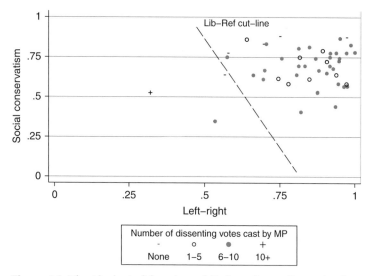

Figure 4.3 The ideological location of Reform Party dissent in the 1993–7
Canadian House of Commons

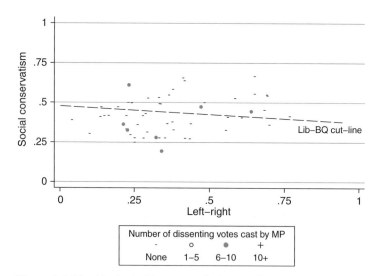

Figure 4.4 The ideological location of Bloc Quebecois dissent in the 1993–7
Canadian House of Commons

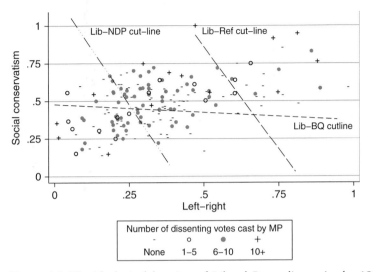

Figure 4.5 The ideological location of Liberal Party dissent in the 1993–7 Canadian House of Commons

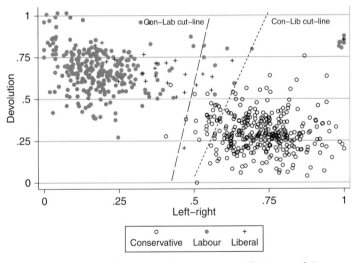

Figure 4.6 Policy preferences in the 1992–7 British House of Commons

Figure 4.6 is a counterpart to Figure 4.2 for the 1992–7 British Parliament, when the Conservatives were in power under John Major and Labour in opposition. Just as one expects, Conservative MPs are on the political right and Labour MPs on the left, Liberal Democrat MPs tending to occupy a middle position just off to the left of centre. High scores on the devolution scale imply favourable attitudes toward devolving power from Westminster to the European Union and to regional assemblies in Scotland and Wales. This ideological space is populated primarily by Labour and Liberal Democrat MPs, with the bulk of Conservative MPs occupying the opposite pole on the devolution scale. Thus a rough divide can be drawn between left and centre-left, pro-European, pro-devolution Labour and Liberal Democrat Parties and a right-wing, anti-European, anti-devolution Conservative Party.

This division is not a clean one, however. Many MPs, Conservatives especially, fall on the wrong sides of the cut-lines and find themselves ideologically closer to the policy position of one of the opposition parties. If it is all preferenceship at work, these are the MPs who should dissent. Other MPs, who are ideologically closer to their own parties, should for similar reasons exhibit loyalty. Again, graphs of the ideological location of dissent in each party provide a test of this hypothesis. Whereas preferenceship predicts that dissent will be concentrated among centrist, pro-devolution Conservatives above and to the left of the cut-lines and among right-wing, anti-devolution Labour MPs below and to the right of the cut-lines, Figures 4.7 and 4.8 show that quite the opposite is the case.[8] Dissent is instead concentrated among the most right-wing, anti-devolution Conservative MPs and the most left-wing, pro-devolution Labour MPs, in short, among extremists in both parties.

These are not one-off results. Figures 4.9–4.11 repeat the exercise for the 1997–2001 British Parliament. The ideological positions of the major parties are much the same as they were in the previous Parliament, though one can see from Figure 4.9 that the net effect of Labour's victory at the 1997 election was to add a significant number of fairly centrist, pro-devolution MPs to Labour's ranks and to reduce the Conservatives to a somewhat more right-wing, anti-devolution rump. The tendency for dissent to occur at the Conservative and Labour Party's extremes is less marked in Figures 4.10 and 4.11 than it is in Figures 4.8 and 4.9, but there is certainly no indication in either case of dissent being concentrated at or near the parties' cut-points.

---

[8] Cowley and Norton do not provide Liberal Democrat dissent figures, so a corresponding Liberal Democrat graph could not be constructed. See: Cowley and Norton (1996) and Cowley *et al.* (1996).

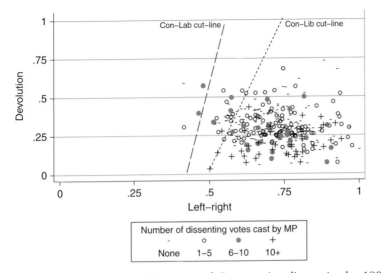

Figure 4.7 The ideological location of Conservative dissent in the 1992–7 British House of Commons

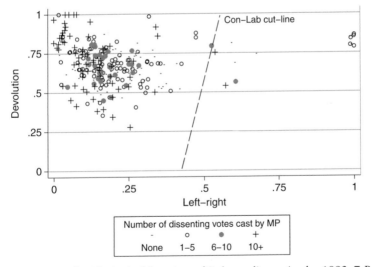

Figure 4.8 The ideological location of Labour dissent in the 1992–7 British House of Commons

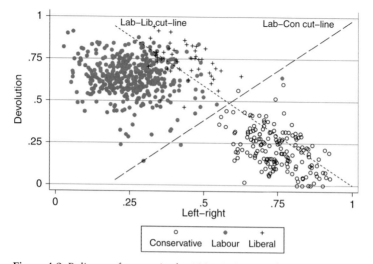

Figure 4.9 Policy preferences in the 1997–2001 British House of Commons

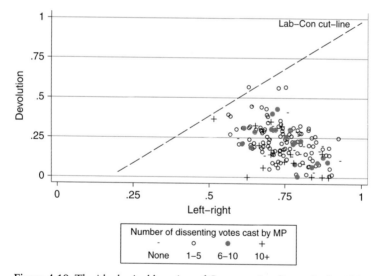

Figure 4.10 The ideological location of Conservative dissent in the 1997–2001 British House of Commons

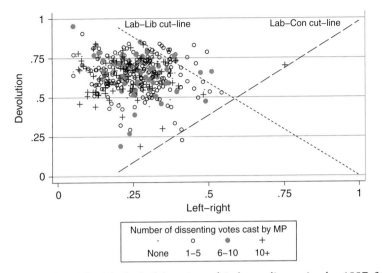

Figure 4.11 The ideological location of Labour dissent in the 1997–2001 British House of Commons

Frontbench abstentions and ends-against-the-middle voting

The overall impression that one gets from these scatter plots is that the relationship between MPs' policy preferences and parliamentary voting behaviour is not as clear-cut as one might expect given a simple preference-driven model of behaviour. The British case, with dissent concentrated at the ideological extremes of the Labour and Conservative Parties rather than beyond the cut-lines, is especially puzzling. This odd voting pattern may reflect an 'ends-against-the-middle' dynamic, with the Conservative and Labour front benches opposed (at different times and for different reasons) by ideological extremists from both parties.[9] On the Labour side, one could well argue that backbench dissent reflected Labour leftists' resistance to New Labour's drive toward the political centre. That is to say, on some issues the political status quo may have been at or just to the left of the Labour median, and Labour leftists may simply have voted against efforts of both right-leaning Labour MPs and the Conservative Party to move the status quo on these issues rightward. This is actually quite plausible. Frequently in the British Parliament the

---

[9] Ends-against-the middle voting can occur whenever politics involves multiple-issue dimensions (Poole and Rosenthal 1997, p. 228).

opposition front bench will abstain from voting in a division and allow the government to have its way unopposed. It may be the case that left-leaning Labour MPs are defying their front bench by participating in these divisions (they may well be the ones forcing them), but still voting against the Conservatives.[10] Similarly, on the Conservative side during the 1992–7 term, anti-devolution Conservatives may have rebelled against the efforts of their own front bench to accelerate the devolution of power from Westminster to the European Union.

Voting on the Maastricht Treaty, the largest and most contentious piece of EU legislation considered by the 1992–7 Parliament, provides a good example of this dynamic. The treaty moved Britain closer to Europe, but John Major had also secured an opt-out of the accompanying social chapter to prevent the British labour market and social policies moving leftward. Isolating the treaty from the social protocol appears to have created four distinct blocs in the Commons, to wit:

1. Conservative loyalists who supported the treaty's passage (given the omission of the social chapter);
2. Eurosceptics (mostly Conservatives) who voted against the Maastricht Treaty because of their opposition to the devolution of power from Westminster;
3. Labour frontbenchers who tended to abstain, because even if they did not get the leftward policy movement that the social chapter offered they did not wish to oppose any legislation that secured a closer relationship with the EU;[11]
4. Labour leftists acting against their leaders' instructions to abstain and opposing ratification because of the omission of the social chapter.

If this interpretation is correct, then Conservative dissent in the 1992–7 Parliament was driven primarily by anti-devolution sentiment, whereas Labour dissent was driven by economic leftism. What's more, the argument also implies that left-wing Labour MPs and anti-devolution

---

[10] It should be noted that Norton (1975, 1980) still counts votes cast in this fashion as instances of dissent. This is quite sensible: even though these votes are not cast against party policy, they are cast against the instructions of the party whip and the latter, not the former, is the standard by which a dissenting vote is defined.

[11] It would be difficult to footnote each and every division where this occurred, but two prominent examples are the second (*Parliamentary Debates (Hansard)*, 21 May 1992, pp. 597–600) and third (*Parliamentary Debates (Hansard)*, 20 May 1993, pp. 469–71) readings of the Maastricht Treaty.

Conservative MPs were resisting legislative initiatives designed to move the status quo from outside the party medians to the policy interval between the party medians. This is the only configuration that could explain why ideological extremists (i.e., MPs on the far sides of the parties' medians) rather than moderates (i.e., MPs between the party medians) were dissenting. To see this, consider the counterfactual situation with the status quo in the policy space between the party medians as in Figure 4.1. Such a configuration results in the two parties voting against one another, with backbench dissent concentrated among MPs who fall beyond the cut-line nearer the opposing party's position. Only if the status quo were outside the party medians would one observe the party front benches in agreement as to the desirability of moving policy toward the political centre, and only MPs on the far side of the relevant party median would be made worse off by such policy moves.

I test this possibility by regressing the number of dissenting votes that Labour and Conservative MPs cast on their policy preferences on devolution *and* left–right issues.[12] The expectation is that Labour dissidents should be located to the left of the Labour Party median on the left–right dimension, whereas Conservative dissidents should be found below the Conservative median on the devolution dimension. To operationalize this idea, MPs' positions on these ideological dimensions are normalized about the party medians so that positive scores indicate that the MP is to the left of the Labour median on the left–right dimension or below the Conservative median on the devolution dimension. A party dummy and interactions allow the ideological coefficients to vary by party. The rival model here is a simple one in which MPs' voting behaviour is determined by their positions relative to the cut-line. MPs who fall beyond the cut-line (i.e., who are closer to an opposing party's position) are predicted to dissent, and the farther beyond the cut-line the MP is located, the more dissenting votes the MP is predicted to cast.[13]

---

[12] The sample of EU-related divisions included sixty-four divisions on the European Communities (Amendment) Bill, two on the Treaty of Maastricht (Social Protocol), two on the European Communities (Finance) Bill, one on European Communities, one on the European Union, and one on Europe and a referendum. See Norton and Cowley (1999).

[13] In this model the MP's ideological position is computed as the Euclidian distance to the Labour–Conservative cut-line. This position is then normalized relative to the cut-line so that MPs beyond the cut-line have positive ideological scores while MPs on their own party's side of the cut-line have negative scores.

Table 4.1. *Regression model of dissenting votes cast by British Labour and Conservative MPs in the 1992–7 House of Commons*

Covariates	Ends-against-the-middle model			Cut-line model		
	B	95% confidence interval[†]		B	95% confidence interval	
		Lower	Upper		Lower	Upper
Labour MP	5.60	−5.26	16.46	–		
Left–right position	3.05	−11.78	17.88	–		
Devolution position	31.65***	17.67	45.63	–		
Labour MP × left–right position	16.98**	0.88	33.08	–		
Labour MP × devolution position	−37.46	−90.34	15.42	–		
Ideological distance to cut-line	–			−2.32	−7.11	2.47
Constant	−8.00**	−14.33	−1.67	5.84***	3.34	8.34
R^2		.10			.00	
N		617			617	

*$p < .10$
**$p < .05$
† Multiple imputation estimates follow a t-distribution with the degrees of freedom based on the proportion of missing data. The confidence intervals reflect these facts and are based on Huber-White standard errors. Estimates and confidence intervals generated using Tomz *et al.* 2001.

The results of these two models are shown in Table 4.1 and are fairly straightforward. The ends-against-the-middle model shows that Conservative MPs' dissent is related to their position on the devolution scale; the farther the Conservative MP is beyond the Conservative Party's median position on the devolution scale, the more dissenting votes he or she casts. In contrast, Labour MPs' dissent is unrelated to their position on the devolution of power from Westminster. (The marginal effect for Labour MPs is $31.65 - 37.46 = -5.81$, which is statistically insignificant.) The opposite is true with respect to the left–right dimension. For Conservative MPs the left–right coefficient is statistically insignificant, indicating that their voting behaviour is uncorrelated to their position on the left–right scale. For Labour MPs, on the other hand, left–right preferences have a strong impact on their voting behaviour, with dissent increasing the more the Labour MP is to the left of the Labour Party median.[14] The results of the simple cut-line model are even more straightforward: British MPs' voting behaviour is entirely unconnected to their ideological proximity to the Labour–Conservative cut-line.

What conclusions can be drawn from these results? First, they suggest that MPs' policy preferences have an impact on how they vote in parliamentary divisions. It would be strange if this was not the case, and certainly this positive result provides some confidence that the policy preferences estimated from MPs' survey responses are valid measures. That said, the results speak to the fact that much depends on correctly discerning the position of the status quo. Only when the possibility that the legislative status quo lies outside party medians is admitted to the model do policy preferences begin to explain the variation in British MPs' voting records. Moreover, even when this possibility is admitted, the fact remains that MPs' policy preferences do not entirely explain their voting behaviour. (The ends-against-the middle model's R-squared statistic is just .10.) There is either a great deal of random noise in the data, or something beyond MPs' policy preferences explains parliamentary behaviour. Finally, the failure of the simple cut-line model to predict backbench dissent suggests that the MPs' proximity to other voting coalitions in the House is irrelevant.

An individual-level analysis: voting on Bill C-41 in the Canadian House of Commons

One of the problems with evaluating preferenceship with aggregate-level voting data is that in any large group of divisions it is not clear precisely where the status quo points and the alternatives are located. As a consequence, it is entirely possible (and probably very likely) that dissent is a function of both extremists resisting their party's moves to the political centre and moderates resisting the party's moves – in different divisions – to the political extremes. If this is the case, the aggregate-level relationship between dissent and ideological preferences

---

[14] The marginal effect of left–right preferences for Labour MPs is 3.05 + 16.98 = 20.03, $t = 3.06$.

may appear random. The remedy is to delve beneath the aggregate data and look at how more focused ideological scales predict dissent in a few specific divisions. The challenge is to find divisions (with dissent) on matters that one can reasonably argue are closely connected to one of the more focused ideological scales (either the British devolution scale or the Canadian social conservatism scale) *and* which consider clear-cut alternatives so that it is possible to assess confidently whether the House is considering a move from the extremes to the centre or the reverse. The set of divisions that meet these criteria is very small. I chose three divisions in the Canadian Parliament on Bill C-41.

In June 1995 the Liberal government brought Bill C-41 before the House. The bill contained general amendments to the criminal code including a controversial clause (clause 718) that sought to extend the definition of hate crimes to include crimes committed against homo-sexuals (*Debates of the House of Commons of Canada (Hansard)*, 20 September 1994, col. 5871).[15] Despite the moral overtones of this measure, the prime minister and the justice minister refused to allow a free vote on C-41, and in response Liberal backbenchers tabled several hostile amendments to the controversial clause at the report stage. Clause 718 contained two sub-clauses. The first mandated stiffer sentences for crimes 'motivated by bias, prejudice, or hatred based on race, nationality, colour, religion, sex, age, mental or physical disability, or sexual orientation of the victim' (*Debates of the House of Commons of Canada*, 22 September 1994, col. 6029). The second provided for harsher sentencing of those convicted of committing a crime while in a position of trust vis-à-vis the victim. Three proposed amendments are of concern here. The first (Motion 6) was the most extreme relative to the government's initial wording; it sought to delete entirely the sub-clause that defined groups against which hate crimes might be committed (*Debates of the House of Commons of Canada*, 13 June 1995, col. 13769). The second (Motion 7) was less extreme in that it sought to delete the list of victims' characteristics and the word 'hatred' from the first sub-clause. The third motion (Motion 8) was identical to the second, save that it proposed only to delete the list of characteristics, leaving the word 'hatred' in the bill (*Debates of the House of Commons of Canada*, 13 June 1995, p. 13770). Thus Motion 8 was the least

---

[15] The *Hansard* volumes used here are available online at www.parl.gc.ca/cgi-bin/hansard/e/hansard/master.pl.

extreme of the three motions and the one closest to the government's wording. The divisions on these motions were taken one after the other (*Debates of the House of Commons of Canada*, 14 June 1995, pp. 13837–9).

The divisions on these three amendments are excellent data on which to test the party-versus-preference hypothesis. First, the cabinet and a number of Liberal backbenchers expressed strong preferences over the content of the bill, so in a situation in which both party pressure and backbench preferences are strong, we get to see which is the more powerful force. Second, MPs' preferences over social morality are far more likely to have governed their votes in these divisions than their left–right preferences. A right-wing MP, for example, might be a libertarian who regards homosexuality as an individual's private affair, or he may be a religious conservative who balks at recognizing homosexuality in legislation. Presumably, however, the more socially conservative the MP, the more likely he or she was to have voted for the three amendments (that is, against the cabinet's position). Similarly, MPs with a liberal view of social morality should have voted against the amendments. In short, it is reasonable to assume that the social conservatism scale is a valid measure of MPs' preferences on C-41 and its associated amendments. Third, when a median agenda is employed alongside an elimination amendment procedure (the procedure used in the Canadian Parliament), legislators with single-peaked preferences have little incentive to vote strategically (Rasch 2000, pp. 16–17). A median agenda is one in which more extreme proposals are voted on before less extreme proposals. Given that the status quo in this instance is the government's original wording and that relative to this wording, the amendments are ordered from most to least extreme (i.e., there is a median agenda), voting on these three amendments should be sincere.[16] One can be fairly confident then that the preferences that governed MPs' votes in these three divisions are identical to the (presumably

[16] The bill, moreover, was not an omnibus bill of the sort encountered in the US Congress, full of sub-clauses designed to dole out particularistic benefits to MPs' constituencies. It is unlikely, then, that MPs' preferences over social morality were trumped by strategic considerations over the distribution of political pork. Nor is it possible to argue that the votes on these amendments were matters of confidence. The confidence convention in the Canadian Commons is not nearly so strong that a government would be forced to resign upon losing divisions on amendments to a bill, even an important one (see Franks 1987, p. 139).

sincere) preferences that they expressed over social conservatism in the 1993 *Canadian Candidate Survey*.

Now under a preference-driven theory of parliamentary behaviour, parties are merely agglomerations of like-minded individuals, not organizations capable of altering preferences. It follows that party affiliation should be unrelated to voting behaviour in these divisions *after one controls for MPs' social conservatism*. Thus, if MPs' votes on these three motions are regressed on their preferences on social morality and their party labels, the coefficient of the preference variable should be statistically significant, while those attached to the party dummy variables should be insignificant (Hager and Talbert 2000, p. 81). I test this hypothesis with three models of vote choice, one for each amendment. The key independent variable is an MP's score on the social conservatism dimension. This variable ranges from 0 to 1, with high scores indicating social conservatism. The Reform Party voted for the amendments while the BQ and Liberal Parties voted against the amendments, so I include party dummies for the latter two parties.[17] I also include in the model the percentage of Catholics, immigrants, and non-religious people in an MP's constituency and the MP's age; all these variables can be expected to influence MPs' views on homosexuality and hate crimes.[18]

----

[17] I omit independent, Progressive Conservative (PC), and NDP MPs from the analysis. Independents and Conservatives are excluded because it is nonsensical to talk of dissent when a member belongs to no party or when only one party member votes. The small size of the NDP (five out of nine NDP MPs voted in these amendments) severely limits its contribution to the analysis from a statistical and a substantive standpoint.

[18] The hypothesis is that younger MPs are more acceptant of alternative lifestyles. Variables such as the MP's sex and educational level did not have any impact on the models. The percentage of rural polls in a constituency, a good indicator of how urban and cosmopolitan the constituency is, also had no effect. This may be because the percentage of immigrants is already an excellent indicator of those characteristics. The general hypothesis is that a high level of immigrants and non-religious constituents is negatively correlated to votes for these amendments (both because these variables mark a constituency as cosmopolitan and also because immigrants were protected under the government's original wording). A large Catholic presence, on the other hand, should be positively correlated with support for the amendments, given the Catholic Church's opposition to homosexuality. It is conceivable, however, that the percentage of immigrants is positively correlated to support for the latter two motions. These motions attempted to remove references to sexual orientation while leaving untouched references to crimes motivated by bias and prejudice. Morally traditional immigrant or ethnic communities might well want this protection without having to recognize sexual orientation as a legitimate object of hate crimes.

There is some question about what to do with MPs who did not vote in some or all of the divisions on these three amendments. The standing orders of the Canadian Parliament do not formally recognize abstentions; if an MP wishes to abstain he or she has to miss the vote intentionally. In the abstract, abstention, like any other form of legislative behaviour, is motivated by preferences, the difference here being that the preferences of abstaining MPs over social conservatism are not strong enough to induce them to vote for or against these three amendments, but instead leave them indifferent. An MP's absence is therefore a potentially useful bit of information. Unfortunately, it is very difficult to distinguish abstention disguised as absence from absence caused by prior commitments, travel, illness, and the like. Three pieces of information afford reasonable assumptions in this area, however:

1. The twenty divisions at the report stage of C-41, including the three considered here, were held in a single afternoon (*Debates of the House of Commons of Canada*, 14 June 1995, cols. 13760–95). A division on the third reading was held the next day (*Debates of the House of Commons of Canada*, 15 June 1995, pp. 13978–9).
2. The government signalled its intention to pass C-41 before the summer break by passing a time-allocation motion a week before the report stage (*Debates of the House of Commons of Canada*, 8 June 1995, pp. 13448–9). The House also set the time and order of voting the day before the report-stage divisions were actually taken (*Debates of the House of Commons of Canada*, 13 June 1995, pp. 13760–95). The Bill's journey through the House also garnered considerable media attention.[19]
3. Four MPs whom I interviewed described intentional absenteeism as a popular means of avoiding votes on unpopular issues, with one talking about C-41 specifically, saying that many MPs left their seats and retired to the members' lounges as controversial amendments were called. One MP publicly stated that he intended to skip the third reading vote as a sign of his disapproval for the bill (*Winnipeg Free Press*, 15 June 1995).

In light of these facts it seems reasonable to count as abstaining those MPs who missed these three divisions but who voted in at least one of

---

[19] See, for example, *Globe and Mail*, 24 November 1994; *Toronto Star*, 6 February 1995; *Vancouver Sun*, 13 June 1995.

Table 4.2. *Ordered logit estimates of voting on Motions 6, 7, and 8 to Bill C-41 (Hate Crimes) in the Canadian House of Commons*

Covariate	Motion 6 (deletes entire sub-clause)			Motion 7 (deletes list of groups and 'hatred')			Motion 8 (deletes list of groups)		
	B	95% confidence interval†		B	95% confidence interval		B	95% confidence interval	
		Lower	Upper		Lower	Upper		Lower	Upper
Social conservatism	6.00***	2.98	9.03	5.73***	2.03	9.42	5.04***	1.39	8.70
Liberal MP	-5.52***	-7.61	-3.45	-5.33***	-7.47	-3.19	-4.38***	-6.14	-2.62
Bloc MP	-7.24***	-10.88	-3.59	-6.27***	-9.25	-3.28	-5.44***	-7.95	-2.93
Percentage immigrants	-.04	-.09	.01	-.02	-.06	.02	-.01	-.04	.02
Percentage Catholic	.01	-.02	.04	.01	-.02	.04	.01	-.02	.04
Percentage no religion	.08	-.03	.19	.06	-.04	.15	.04	-.04	.13
MP's age	-.05	-.13	.02	-.07*	-.14	.00	-.04	-.09	.01
Cut-point 1	-2.18	-7.19	2.82	-3.21	-8.73	2.32	-1.47	-6.32	3.36
Cut-point 2	-.79	-5.78	4.21	-2.05	-7.56	3.45	-.45	-5.31	4.41
Pseudo R²	.60			.52			.43		
N	235			235			235		

Dependent variable coding: 'no' = 0, 'absent' = 0.5, 'yes' = 1.

* 1-tail $p < .1$.

** 1-tail $p < .05$.

*** 1-tail $p < .01$.

† Multiple imputation estimates follow a t-distribution with the degrees of freedom based on the proportion of missing data.
The confidence intervals reflect these facts and are based on robust standard errors.

the twenty report-stage divisions or in the third-reading division taken the next day. These MPs were well aware that C-41 was being voted on and were in or about the House when the divisions occurred, but did not vote on the three divisions examined here. Thus I code 'no' votes as 0, absences as 0.5, and 'yes' votes as 1.[20] The results are shown in Table 4.2.

[20] I used a logistic regression to discern statistical differences between MPs who missed all report-stage motions but attended the third-reading division the following day. The dichotomous dependent variable was third-reading but not report-stage attendance (1) versus some report-stage attendance (0). The independent variables were exactly the same as those in the voting models shown in Table 4.2 plus a variable indicating the MP's parliamentary rank (whip, minister, shadow minister, etc.). These are variables that are hypothesized to lead MPs to resist the government's bill, either by voting against it or (of greater concern here) by avoiding intentionally the divisions on C-41. The only variable that even approached statistical significance was rank, with those attending only the third-reading division being of higher rank. This is sensible given that ministers and party leaders typically miss many more votes than backbenchers. With the dependent variable changed to differentiate between those who attended at least one division (i.e., my sample) and those who missed all twenty-one divisions (i.e. those dropped from the analysis), the same model found virtually no differences between the two groups. (Only the percentage of non-religious constituents approached statistical significance.) Selection bias does not seem to be a problem, then.

Finally, I altered the dependent variable so that it separated those who voted only in the third-reading division (but missed all report-stage divisions) from those who missed all twenty-one divisions (and who were dropped from the analysis). The former were included in the analysis and counted as abstaining. Given the evidence from the interviews and media it is not hard to believe that MPs who had, in fact, voted during the report stage, that is, who were demonstrably in the House the afternoon these motions were voted on, absented themselves intentionally. It is more difficult to accept that MPs who showed up only the next day for the third-reading vote did the same thing. However, the selection model not only uncovered statistically significant differences between the two groups, but showed that these differences occurred on many of the same variables that were correlated with abstention or 'yes' votes in the voting models, that is, percentage of immigrants, Catholics, non-religious people, and the MP's age. In other words, the variables that separate abstentions and 'yes' votes from 'no' votes are exactly those that separate those who voted only in the third-reading division from those who missed all twenty-one divisions on C-41. This last result in particular would seem to justify my decision to count as abstaining those MPs who missed all twenty report-stage divisions but who attended the third-reading division.

In the event, only 16 per cent of MPs missed all twenty-one divisions. A vast majority (76 per cent) of MPs voted in eleven or more of the twenty-one divisions. MPs counted as participating in the divisions on Motions 6, 7, and 8 number 235, implying that 60 MPs were excluded from the analysis either because they missed

Canadian MPs' social conservatism has a statistically significant impact on how they voted on C-41. All else equal, the more socially conservative an MP, the more likely he or she is to vote for these amendments (that is, against the Liberal cabinet's original bill). This is not to say that the MP's position relative to the Liberal–Reform cut-line had an impact on the MP's vote; it did not.[21] Party affiliation also affects MPs' voting choices. If party is little more than a voluntary agglomeration of like-minded individuals, then controlling for MPs' preferences over social conservatism should rob the party dummy variables of any explanatory power. That does not happen: Bloc and Liberal MPs were far more likely to vote against these amendments, all else (including preferences) equal.

The marginal effects of party and preferences are not obvious in these sorts of non-linear discrete-choice models. Table 4.3 shows the probability of a Liberal and Reform MP voting for or against or abstaining on Motion 7 given varying levels of social conservatism. Values of the other variables in the model are held at their medians, so what one sees are the marginal effects of party and preferences on the vote choice of an MP who represents the median constituency. Table 4.3 sets in sharp relief how much more powerful party is relative to preferences. Over 90 per cent of Liberal MPs fall between .2 and .8 on the social conservatism scale. Moving across this range sees the probability that a Liberal MP will vote against (i.e., 'no') on Motion 7 decline from 96.6 to 53.6 per cent, a shift of 43 per cent. This 43 per cent shift represents the force of preferences on the vote. The force of party on the vote can be seen by comparing the probability that a Reform MP will vote 'no' across this same range of social conservatism. Viewed in this light, party is responsible for shifts of no fewer than 52.6 percentage points (at the high end of the range), and as much as 76.3 percentage points (at the low end of the

---

all twenty-one divisions or because they were not members of one of the three major parties. The results of the divisions (including the votes of five NDP, one PC, and one independent) were as follows: Motion 6: 53 'yes', 15 'absent', 174 'no'; Motion 7: 59 'yes', 17 'absent', 166 'no'; Motion 8: 65 'yes', 21 'absent', 157 'no'. Twenty-six of 152 Liberal MPs abstained or cross-voted on at least one of these three divisions.

[21] To test this possibility I ran models (not shown) that included a dummy variable denoting the MP as being on the Liberal Party's side of the Liberal–Reform cut-line. This variable was always statistically insignificant and had no effect on the model.

Table 4.3. *The relative effects of party and preferences on MPs' votes on Motion 7 at report stage of Bill C-41 (Hate Crimes) in the Canadian House of Commons*

Social conservatism score*	Pr('no' vote) (percentages)		Pr('absent') (percentages)		Pr('yes' vote) (percentages)	
	Liberal MP	Reform MP	Liberal MP	Reform MP	Liberal MP	Reform MP
0	98.5	39.6	1.0	20.7	0.5	39.8
.2	96.6	20.3	2.3	18.6	1.2	61.1
.4	91.4	8.0	5.6	11.5	3.0	80.5
.6	78.2	2.8	13.5	5.1	8.3	92.1
.8	53.6	1.0	23.9	2.0	22.5	97.0
1.0	29.7	0.4	24.3	0.8	46.6	98.8

Liberal Party (i.e., cabinet) position = 'no'; Reform Party position = 'yes'.
Constituency variables (percentage immigrants, percentage Catholics, percentage non-religious) and MP's age are set at medians.
* Higher scores indicate greater social conservatism.

range). Among Reform MPs voting 'yes,' this party-preferences comparison is even more heavily weighted in favour of party.

These results drive home two points. First, while MPs' voting behaviour is influenced by their ideological preferences, their positions relative to coalitional cut-lines in the chamber are irrelevant. This suggests that dissent is not about joining with the opposition to secure a more congenial policy. Second, party provides a strong constraint on MPs' behaviour. This suggests, first, that parties are more than agglomerations of like-minded individuals and second, that parties (demonstrably) have the capacity to rein in the effects of ideological differences among party members.

The voting behaviour of defectors

In all of the above tests MPs' preferences are estimated from their survey responses. In light of this, one might well argue that the above results are due to measurement error or that the policy preferences tapped by the surveys and those that guide MPs' voting decisions are two entirely different things. An MP could, for example, privately believe that abortion should be legal and say so on the survey. Nevertheless, given years of correspondence with his constituents the MP may be acutely aware of the fact that a large majority of his constituents oppose legalized abortions, and hence he may vote against it in the division lobbies. In other words, the surveys may tap MPs' sincere policy preferences while their votes are guided by their electorally induced preferences. Under these circumstances, it would not be surprising to find little connection between MPs' preferences and their voting behaviour; one has simply measured the wrong preferences.[22]

One way to respond to this argument is to examine the voting behaviour of MPs who left their parties either to join another party or to sit as independents. The test is simple: MPs' voting behaviour prior to their departure is compared to their voting behaviour after their departure. If party is simply a label rather than an organization capable of altering preferences, then pre- and post-departure voting records should be very similar (Cox 2000, p. 182).[23] The advantage of this test relative to the others is that it does not rest on any survey data whatsoever. Thus, worries about the discrepancies between MPs' sincere and induced preferences, the temporal distance from the application of the candidate surveys to the act of voting in the division lobbies, the inherent measurement error of survey instruments, and any doubts about the multiple imputation of missing survey responses are all addressed by this simple test. Table 4.4 shows the percentage of votes that eight party-leavers in my sample cast for (i.e., with) and against their original parties before and after their departure.[24] The table also shows the percentage of divisions missed by the MP and the number of votes on which these percentages are based.

The results are striking. In every single case there is a marked change in voting behaviour. The within-country and overall means indicate that party-leavers are far less likely to vote for their original parties (65.4 per cent to 8.5 per cent on the overall mean) and were far more likely to miss divisions altogether (31.2 per cent to 66.1 per cent on the

---

[22] The argument and the example were suggested by an anonymous referee.

[23] Whether the MP leaves or is expelled is moot. In either case, the null hypothesis is that a change in party affiliation does not lead to a change in voting behaviour.

[24] There is nothing exceptional about these eight MPs, save that they were the Canadian and British MPs who left their parties during the 1993–7 Parliament and 1992–7 Parliament, respectively.

Table 4.4. *Voting patterns of party defectors in the 1993–7 Canadian House of Commons and 1992–7 British House of Commons before and after leaving their parties*

MP (Party)	Before defection				After defection			
	For	Versus	Absent	N	For	Versus	Absent	N
Canadian MPs								
Nunziata (Liberal)[4]	50.7	18.8	30.6	144	13.4	7.9	78.7	164
Brown (Reform)[1]	61.3	1.3	37.3	150	2.2	0.0	97.8	137
Leblanc (Bloc)[1]	42.7	1.1	56.1	260	8.7	2.2	89.1	46
Mills (Liberal)[2]	43.9	3.4	52.7	262	0.0	2.2	97.8	46
British MPs								
Body (Cons.)[2]	59.5	0.0	40.5	37	27.8	0.0	72.2	18
Howarth (Cons.)[3]	82.4	2.9	14.7	34	0.0	71.4	28.6	21
Nicholson (Cons.)[3]	82.4	0.0	17.6	34	0.0	61.9	38.1	21
Thurnham (Cons.)[3]	100.0	0.0	0.0	36	15.8	57.9	26.3	19
Canada mean	49.7	6.2	44.2		6.1	3.1	90.9	
Britain mean	81.1	0.7	18.2		10.9	47.8	41.3	
Overall mean	**65.4**	**3.1**	**31.2**		**8.5**	**15.1**	**66.1**	

Cell entries denote percentage of votes cast for, against, etc. MP's party.
1 = Left to sit as an independent
2 = Resigned whip temporarily
3 = Defected to another party
4 = Expelled

overall mean) after their departures.[25] It is hard to square these results with a model in which behaviour is unaffected by party.[26]

[25] The means are just the simple means across members; they are not weighted by the number of divisions. Within countries, the simple and weighted means are very similar.

[26] One might argue that MPs simply changed their preferences. This could happen, for example, if MPs' preferences are electorally induced and their electorate undergoes a significant change during the parliamentary term. This hypothesis can, in fact, be rejected. A substantial redistribution of constituency boundaries was conducted in Britain in 1995, and Butler and Kavanagh (1997, p. 258) record an index of change measuring the inflow and outflow of voters relative to the size of a constituency's electoral base. If changes to MPs' electorates motivate changes in their behaviour, then one would expect to see relatively large indices of change for the electorates of the four British party-leavers. This is not the case. The average index of change among Conservative constituencies was 25; among the

Discussion

Preferenceship raises the possibility that parties (and the associated paraphernalia of preferment, discipline, and socialization) are not necessary for cohesion. Party unity could be driven solely by the preferences of individual parliamentarians. From this perspective, the only way in which parties might matter is via the screening of prospective candidates so as to more or less effectively exclude individuals with uncongenial policy preferences. The results here suggest that this null model (as far as parties are concerned) can safely be rejected. It is not just that MPs' policy preferences have only a partial influence on their voting behaviour, but that parties appear to have the capacity to contain divergent policy preferences: MPs do not dissent as much as one would expect on the basis of their policy preferences, and party affiliation trumps ideological preferences as a predictor of MPs' voting behaviour. Of course, the mechanisms by which parties exert control over their members are not set out here, but one is pushed back on to the results of the previous chapter: dissent is correlated with declining levels of party identification, dwindling party popularity, and limited career advancement opportunities in the party. These results cannot be written off as due to the shifting of policy preferences over time or across countries. Note also that just as in the LEADS model, backbench dissent is unconnected to the MP's ideological position relative to other voting coalitions in the chamber. Dissent is instead triggered by the MPs' ideological distance from the party's policy position, implying (as per the LEADS model) that it is less a parliamentary tactic than an electoral tactic designed to appeal to the MP's constituents. Assessing this possibility, the first step in corroborating the LEADS at the micro-level, is the next chapter's task.

defectors, only Body's constituency experienced greater than average change (62) – and his behaviour changed the least. I also compared the defectors to six loyal Conservatives whose constituencies experienced large changes. The pre- and post-redistribution voting patterns (in the same divisions) of these six MPs were almost identical: pre-redistribution, 70.5 per cent 'for', 0.7 per cent 'versus', 29.2 per cent 'absent'; post-redistribution, 69.4 per cent 'for', 0.0 per cent 'versus', 30.7 per cent 'absent'. In addition, the political impact of the redistribution was similar across both defectors' and loyalists' constituencies.

5 | *Dissent, constituency service, and the personal vote in Great Britain and New Zealand*

Introduction

A central assumption of the LEADS model is that dissent insulates the MP from the electoral effects (i.e., lost votes) of unpopular party policies. The qualitative evidence of Chapter 2 suggests that MPs believe that dissent has this capacity, but is there broader empirical evidence to that effect? In this chapter I show that there is. Using data from the UK and New Zealand, I demonstrate that dissent provides MPs with two valuable resources: increased name recognition and higher approval ratings. These effects are independent of MPs' constituency service efforts – though as the British data make clear it is not accurate to think of dissent and constituency service as mutually exclusive activities. On the contrary, British MPs appear to use dissent and constituency service as complementary vote-winning strategies. The New Zealand data are more provocative, however. Dissenting New Zealand MPs enjoyed higher approval ratings among their constituents than loyal MPs and they were able to translate that advantage into an electoral return of 2.2 per cent at the 1993 election. What is especially striking, however, is that the approval effect is driven largely by the positive reaction of non-partisan and weakly partisan voters to dissent. This evidence not only establishes that MPs can use dissent to build up a personal vote that is independent of their parties, it provides a compelling individual-level link between electoral dealignment and parliamentary dissent.

Could dissent generate a personal vote?

There is an extensive literature on the personal vote in these four countries (e.g., Anagnoson 1987; Cain *et al.* 1987; Bean 1990; Ferejohn and Gaines 1991; Norris *et al.* 1992; Norton and Wood 1993; Heitshusen *et al.* 2005), and the claim that dissent wins MPs votes runs against the grain of much of this work. A central result of this literature is that the personal vote in these countries is primarily a function of MPs' constituency service efforts, not of their parliamentary activities or policy stances (Cain *et al.* 1987, pp. 188–93; Norton and Wood 1993, p. 141). Indeed, looking specifically at the electoral impact of dissent, McAllister and Studlar (2000) show that British Conservative MPs who broke ranks on European issues did no better at the 1997 general election than their more loyal colleagues. This sort of evidence comports with Norton and Wood's (1993, p. 38) view that British MPs 'compartmentalize' their parliamentary and constituency roles. In other words, MPs separate their parliamentary and constituency roles so that they can appeal to voters through constituency service even while they toe the line on party policies that may not sit well with their constituents. It is because of compartmentalization that what an MP does in Parliament (e.g., supports or opposes a given policy) has little impact on the MP's electoral performance.

In effect, this previous research sets up a triangular barrier to the claim that dissent contributes to a personal vote. Two sides of this triangle are empirical results (the primacy of constituency service and the irrelevance of parliamentary action), while the base is a theoretical proposition (the compartmentalization thesis). Evidence can be brought to bear against the empirical parts of this structure. Pattie *et al.* (1994), for example, demonstrate that the populist stances that some British Conservative MPs took on a variety of free votes in the 1987–92 Parliament boosted their performance at the 1992 election. One can also legitimately complain that judging the electoral efficacy of dissent by comparing the aggregate vote shares of rebellious and loyal MPs ignores the possibility that dissenting MPs are likely to be those in the most difficult and vulnerable electoral (or preselection) circumstances to begin with. This situation could easily lead to an ecological fallacy in which the aggregate data always show a negative relationship between dissent and electoral performance regardless of the direction of the individual-level relationship between dissent and the vote.

The central issue here, however, is the structure's theoretical base, the compartmentalization thesis itself. Demonstrating that voters react to dissent helps to falsify this thesis, but in the absence of a theoretical counter-argument to compartmentalization there is no reason to go further and interpret any such evidence as supporting my contention that dissent generates personal votes. So why, as a matter of first principles, is compartmentalization a compelling theory? Equally important, what first-principles arguments might be arrayed against compartmentalization and in support of my counter-claim?

Three major arguments exist in favour of compartmentalization. First, compartmentalization could simply reflect a state of the world in which voters rationally ignore MPs' parliamentary actions in response to the fact that few MPs can fashion legislation or dispense pork in the ways that representatives in presidential systems can. Second, as Norton and Wood (1993, p. 38, pp. 146–8) argue, compartmentalization allows MPs to avoid being caught up in conflicts between their parties' policies and their constituents' preferences. Lastly, in so far as party leaders view constituency service as anodyne and parliamentary dissent as subversive, constituency service would seem to be a safer career-building strategy for the MP than dissent.

Compartmentalization is not without logical weaknesses, however, and an equally compelling case can be made for MPs having incentives to link their parliamentary and constituency roles. To the extent that compartmentalization is a strategic choice that MPs make rather than a state of the world in which voters ignore MPs' parliamentary activities, it is not clear why it is in MPs' interests to maintain a system that forces them to rely solely on constituency service to win personal votes. As a vote-winning strategy constituency service certainly has advantages: it allows MPs to earn personal votes without antagonizing party leaders, and it may also provide MPs with a sense of satisfaction (Searing 1994). That said, constituency service also has corresponding disadvantages relative to dissent, to wit:

1. *Labour intensity and opportunity costs.* Constituency service is labour intensive, winning voters over one at a time and pulling MPs away from parliamentary and party activities. In economic terms, constituency service lacks an economy of scale and as such involves high opportunity costs to the MP. These opportunity costs should not be understated. British MPs who fail to receive a promotion in their first term of office are less than half as likely to achieve a ministerial position during their careers than colleagues who receive early promotion (see Chapter 9). If promotion depends on being active in parliament and the parliamentary party, the opportunity

cost of constituency service is potentially very high and the career implications of constituency service and dissent not as dissimilar as one might think.[1]

2. *Efficiency and economies of scale.* In contrast to constituency service, dissent offers the MP an economy of scale. Dissent, because it is typically well publicized, reaches many voters at once. Thus, even if dissent is less effective than constituency service at convincing a voter to vote for the MP, it may still be a more efficient strategy, because it reaches many more voters than can possibly be reached by constituency service directly.

3. *Effectiveness.* The relative effectiveness of dissent and constituency service is actually an open question. Compartmentalization assumes that voters blame the party rather than the MP for uncongenial policies (Norton and Wood 1993, p. 146). Whether constituents respond in this fashion is partly an empirical issue, but it is not clear why voters should automatically draw a distinction between the MP and the party solely on the basis of the MP's constituency service. Dissent, at least, provides voters with an observable signal that their MP is not a party cipher – and indeed, public opinion research informs us that many voters (in these and in other parliamentary systems) want their parliamentary representatives to behave more independently (e.g., Paltzelt 2000).[2] To the extent that dissent feeds this popular desire, it could be quite effective in providing the MP with an electoral advantage.[3] How effective it

---

[1] Searing and Game's (1977) work on the recruitment of party whips details the heavy parliamentary demands that are placed on MPs advancing up the parliamentary career ladder.

[2] Responses to the 1993 *New Zealand Election Study* (NZES) are illustrative of this phenomenon. One question asked respondents whether MPs should be allowed more freedom to vote against party policy in parliament: 80 per cent of respondents thought that this idea was definitely or probably desirable. Less than 5 per cent of respondents saw this idea as undesirable. Furthermore, when asked to pick from a list the single most important group or entity for the MP to listen to, 42.9 per cent of New Zealand voters said 'the majority in the MP's electorate', 24.2 per cent said the 'majority in the country', and 16.2 per cent said 'the MP's personal judgement'. Again, less than 5 per cent of respondents thought that MPs should give much weight to their parties' views. These figures are computed from Vowles *et al.* (1994).

[3] Voters might react positively to their MP's dissent for a variety of reasons (though the survey evidence recommends a desire for independently minded MPs as the most plausible). My point, however, has less to do with the precise causal path by which dissent influences voters than the fact that there are good reasons to expect dissent to be as effective as constituency service in generating electoral support for the MP.

might be likely depends on the level of party identification in the electorate. If most voters are strongly partisan, electoral behaviour will be structured almost entirely by voters' affective ties to a specific party, and dissent will be ineffective. As party identification weakens, however, and these affective connections lose their grip over electoral behaviour, the door opens for the MP to use dissent to win personal votes.

The upshot of these arguments is that constituency service cannot be assumed to dominate dissent as a vote-winning strategy. On the contrary, given the different costs and benefits of dissent relative to constituency service, at least some MPs will want to use dissent in place of or in addition to constituency service. This is only feasible, however, if MPs *do not* compartmentalize their parliamentary and constituency activities. That being the case, compartmentalization is unlikely to be self-enforcing; whilst MPs might wish to commit to a strategy of compartmentalization and constituency service, when pushed to the electoral margin, they have strong incentives to use parliamentary dissent to win votes and to make their constituents aware of their dissent.

Five hypotheses about dissent, constituency service, and the personal vote

One can, then, draw a contrast between two possible parliamentary worlds. In the compartmentalized world, MPs' parliamentary and constituency activities are orthogonal. MPs construct their personal votes primarily on the basis of constituency service, with the intensity of their constituency service efforts determined by their electoral security and parliamentary career status (with longer-serving frontbench MPs typically offering less constituency service than less experienced backbenchers (Norton and Wood 1993)). Parliamentary dissent is not an effective vote-winning strategy in this compartmentalized world, and so even when MPs are desperate for votes they do not augment their constituency service efforts with dissent.

The other parliamentary world is not compartmentalized. MPs' parliamentary and constituency activities are related to one another; while MPs still construct their personal votes primarily on the basis of constituency service, they augment constituency service efforts with dissent when electoral conditions warrant it. Existing research indicates that most voters are ignorant of or unresponsive to individual MPs' policy positions (Cain *et al.* 1987, p. 193; Norton and Wood 1993, p. 139), so it is unlikely that dissent works by signalling MPs' policy positions to voters. A more likely alternative is that dissent simply raises an MP's public profile because of the media attention that it receives. To the extent that dissent does this, it provides the MP with a valuable electoral resource. A second, more complex, possibility is that dissent directly elicits a positive reaction from voters. This may be because dissent satisfies a popular desire for more independently minded MPs (survey evidence certainly backs up this interpretation), but voters may reward dissent for other reasons.

Regardless of precisely why voters might respond positively to dissent, one should observe different responses from strongly partisan voters and non-partisan voters. By definition, strongly partisan voters have strong affective ties to one party or another – and these strong affective ties should blunt the impact of dissent on the voters' opinions or behaviour.[4] In more direct terms, voters who strongly identify with the dissenting MP's party may prefer that the MP toe the party line, but will nevertheless support the MP because of the MP's party affiliation; dissent will have only a small marginal impact on the opinion or behaviour of these voters. Voters who strongly identify with another party, on the other hand, are unlikely to be swayed by the MP's actions, precisely because of the MP's party affiliation. Again, the marginal impact of the MP's dissent on these voters' opinions and behaviour is likely to be minimal. Non-partisan voters, in contrast, lack strong affective ties to a party, and should therefore be more open and responsive to political cues like dissent.

These arguments suggest five hypotheses about the relationships between constituency service, parliamentary dissent, and the personal vote. If the compartmentalization thesis is correct, then:

Hypothesis 1. Constituency service and parliamentary dissent are independent activities. In other words, how much constituency service an MP offers is unrelated to whether the MP dissents in parliament.

Hypothesis 2. Voters do not respond to their MP's parliamentary dissent.

[4] This is, of course, the Michigan school definition of party identification (Campbell *et al.* 1960), that is, the idea that partisanship is an affective rather than cognitive attachment to party.

On the other hand, if parliamentary politics is not compartmenta-lized, one should observe that:

Hypothesis 3. Constituency service and parliamentary dissent are related vote-winning strategies (i.e., knowing how much an MP dissents informs one about how much constituency service that MP offers and vice versa).

Hypothesis 4. Dissenting MPs are more widely recognized by voters than loyal MPs.

Hypothesis 5. Voters respond positively to their MP's dissent, but voters with weak partisan attachments respond more positively than voters with strong partisan attachments.

Only one set of hypotheses should withstand testing. Hypotheses 1 and 2, for example, imply a compartmentalized world in which Hypotheses 3–5 cannot be true. Similarly, if Hypotheses 3–5 survive empirical testing, then Hypotheses 1 and 2 must be false.

Are dissent and constituency service related activities?

In determining whether constituency service and dissent are indepen-dent or related activities, it is helpful to adopt an economic analogy and think of MPs as firms that produce constituency service in exchange for votes. The supply curve (i.e., how much constituency service the MP offers) in this shadow market for votes is determined by three factors:

1. *The shadow price in votes of constituency service.* In standard economic treatments, a firm's production and supply increase as the market price for its goods rises. In this analogy, the price of constituency service is reflected in the marginal value of votes to the MP, with MPs in precarious electoral positions placing a higher marginal value on votes than MPs who are assured of re-election. Thus, MPs' constituency service efforts should intensify as their re-election prospects worsen.

2. *The demand curve facing the MP.* A high volume of letters and phone calls from constituents signals that demand for constituency service is high. In equilibrium, supply meets demand and so the

more requests the MP gets asking for help, the more constituency service the MP offers.

3. *The opportunity cost of inputs to constituency service.* The chief input to constituency service is the MP's time, implying that there is an opportunity cost to constituency service. Thus, as the MP takes on greater parliamentary responsibilities (as tends to happen over the course of an MP's career or as the MP climbs the parliamentary career ladder), the opportunity cost of constituency service rises and the amount of constituency service that the MP offers declines.

Once these variables are held constant, one can ask whether MPs who dissent produce more or less constituency service than shadow market conditions would predict. If dissent is negatively related to constituency service, parliamentary dissent is being used as a substitute for constituency service, that is, MPs are switching to dissent to win votes as the costs of constituency service rise. Alternatively, if dissent is positively related to constituency service, it is being used as a complement to constituency service. This result would fit a story of MPs who are desperate for re-election using every available strategy to win votes. In a compartmentalized world, however, there should be no relationship between how much an MP dissents and how much constituency service the MP offers.

Data and methods

Data come from two sources. The 1992 *British Candidate Study* (BCS) (Norris and Lovenduski 1992) provides data on MPs' constituency service efforts and demands; Philip Norton and Philip Cowley's *Dissension in the House of Commons* data set (Norton and Cowley 1999) (supplemented by issues of *Dod's Parliamentary Companion*) provides information on MPs' parliamentary ranks, electoral situations, and dissent. The dependent variable (the MP's constituency service production) is the natural logarithm of the number of hours per week that the MP devotes to constituency service.[5] Constituency demand is measured by the number of letters from constituents and

[5] The semi-log specification accords with the economic analogy being used here and also corrects the right skew in the distribution of hours per week devoted to constituency service.

others (e.g., interest groups) received by the MP per week.[6] The timing of the 1992 *BCS* means that incumbent MPs were being asked to reflect on their pre-1992 experience. Thus, 'market' conditions were assessed over the previous (1987–92) parliamentary term. Parliamentary demands are measured by the MP's rank in the last year of the 1987–92 Parliament and the number of years the MP has sat in the House prior to 1992, with the square of the number of years' service added to allow constituency service efforts to rise and then fall over the course of an MP's career.[7] Electoral demand is measured by the MP's party's standardized mean vote share in the constituency at the 1983, 1987, and 1992 elections. In other words, the party's mean vote share at each of these elections is divided by the standard deviation across those three vote shares. This provides a compact measure of how secure the MP was given the electoral volatility commonly encountered in the constituency. This measure incorporates information on the MP's 1992 (i.e., future) electoral performances because it is likely that MPs condition their vote-winning behaviour not just on their past electoral performance, but also on their expectations (informed by polls, projections, and instinct) of how they are likely to do at the upcoming election. Finally, dissent is measured as the number of dissenting votes that the MP cast over the course of the 1987–92 Parliament.

Results

The results are presented in Table 5.1. The basic dynamics follow predictions: higher demand for constituency service and electoral inse-curity (i.e., a smaller standardized vote share) spur MPs to devote more

[6] The survey does not ask MPs to detail what percentage of their correspondence is from private constituents asking for constituency service. Thus, it is possible that one MP's correspondence is composed entirely of letters from private constituents whereas another MP's correspondence comprises only letters from national-level interest or lobby groups. The implicit assumption behind this measure, then, is that the proportion of letters from constituents asking for constituency service is roughly the same across MPs.

[7] I also control for the MP's party affiliation, in effect, his position in government or opposition, because the opportunity costs of being away from Parliament tend to be lower for opposition MPs, who tend not to have as many official duties. MPs' parliamentary ranks are measured on an ordinal scale: 1 = backbencher; 2 = select committee chair; 3 = parliamentary private secretary; 4 = whip; 5 = under-secretary or opposition spokesperson; 6 = minister of state or principal opposition spokesperson; 7 = cabinet minister or shadow cabinet minister.

Table 5.1. *OLS regression model of constituency service effort (in constituency service hours per week) by British Labour and Conservative MPs in the 1987–92 Parliament*

Covariate	B
Party	.067
	(.050)
Parliamentary rank	−.032*
	(.017)
Parliamentary experience	−.037***
	(.014)
Parliamentary experience^2	.001***
	(.0005)
Demand for constituency service	.001***
	(.0002)
Standardized mean vote share, 1983–92	−.002***
	(.0006)
Dissenting votes cast, 1987–92	.007**
	(.003)
Constant	3.101
	(.122)
R^2	.248
N	183

Figures in parentheses are Huber-White standard errors.
* $p < .10$
** $p < .05$
*** $p < .01$

time to constituency service. Also in line with predictions and prior research, constituency service efforts decline with higher parliamentary rank. The key variable, though, is the number of dissenting votes cast by the MP over the course of the 1987–92 term. This coefficient is positive and statistically significant, with each additional dissenting vote associated with a 0.7 per cent increase in the number of hours the MP devotes to constituency service efforts.[8] This is not to say that dissent

---

[8] This interpretation of the marginal effects follows from the model's semi-log specification.

increases constituency service, but rather that dissent and constituency service increase in lockstep.

More nuanced analyses of these data corroborate additional observable implications of my argument, but the simple regression set out in Table 5.1 is sufficient to make my main point: MPs' parliamentary dissent is not compartmentalized from their constituency activities. On the contrary, constituency service and dissent appear to be complements, with MPs using whatever strategies are at their disposal to earn votes. The logical implication of this complementarity is that dissent, like constituency service, is employed by MPs as a vote-winning strategy.

Parliamentary dissent and name recognition in Great Britain

If MPs are using parliamentary dissent as a complement to constituency service, the next question to ask is what electoral benefit does dissent generate for the MP? One possibility (Hypothesis 4) is that dissent simply gains the MP notoriety among voters. Name recognition is a valuable electoral asset: MPs spend money during campaigns to achieve it and it is effective in winning votes (Cain *et al.* 1987, pp. 179, 186, 193). Dissent is still rare enough in these countries that it attracts media attention, and so voting against the party line, especially on important policies, is an inexpensive way for the MP to develop a public profile. The more dissenting votes the MP casts in parliament, the more likely, then, that a voter knows who the MP is.

Data and methods

I test this idea with data from the 1997 *British Election Study* (Heath *et al.* 1999). The dichotomous dependent variable indicates whether the survey respondent correctly recalled the name of his or her incumbent Labour or Conservative MP. (Districts held by minor party incumbents or those for which the incumbent Labour or Conservative did not seek re-election are excluded from the analysis.) The key independent variable is the number of dissenting votes cast by the MP during the previous (i.e., 1992–7) parliamentary term. Obviously, a number of other variables are likely to affect the MP's level of name recognition and need to be controlled. These include:

1. *The respondent's level of political knowledge.* Respondents vary in how much they know (or care to know) about politics. Clearly, more politically knowledgeable respondents are more likely to recall their MP's name, and as this effect is quite independent of anything that the MP says or does, it needs to be controlled. I use a common measure of political knowledge, the number of correct answers the survey respondent gave to a battery of factual political questions, as the control variable.

2. *The MP's parliamentary status.* Long-serving MPs have had time to build reputations, whilst frontbench members, especially those on the government side of the House, enjoy more media exposure than backbenchers. Consequently, I control for the MP's (a) parliamentary experience (*ln* years in Parliament), (b) government or opposition status, and (c) membership in the cabinet or shadow cabinet.

3. *The constituency environment.* It is probably easier for MPs representing rural districts to achieve high levels of name recognition than for MPs representing urban districts. The lower levels of social mobility and denser social networks of a rural district make it easier for rural MPs to build local reputations. Moreover, unlike urban MPs, who have to compete for media attention, rural MPs enjoy a default celebrity status. I measure urban–rural status of the district by the natural logarithm of the population density (persons per hectare) of the respondent's census area.

4. *Constituency service.* Finally, MPs' constituency service efforts may have boosted their name recognition. (Indeed, this is one of the objectives of constituency service.) I capture this effect by controlling for whether the respondent recalled being contacted directly by their MP during the previous term.

Results

Table 5.2 presents five specifications of the model, two taking in both Labour and Conservative MPs, the remainder focusing on Labour and Conservative MPs separately. The first specification contains only the control variables and as such serves as a baseline. The respondent's level of political knowledge, the population density of the district, and prior contact between the MP and the constituent (my proxy for constituency service) all help to fix the MP's name in the respondent's mind. The second specification adds the number of dissenting votes that the MP

Table 5.2. *Logit model of name recognition of British Labour and Conservative MPs at the 1997 election*

Covariate	All MPs		Labour	Conservative	
	1	2	3	4	5
Respondent's political knowledge	.36***	.36***	.33***	.41***	.42***
	(.03)	(.03)	(.03)	(.04)	(.04)
Population density of district (*ln* persons per hectare)	−.12***	−.12***	−.11***	−.13***	−.13***
	(.03)	(.03)	(.04)	(.04)	(.04)
MP's parliamentary experience (*ln* years)	.13*	.11	−.01	.19*	.23**
	(.07)	(.07)	(.10)	(.10)	(.10)
Frontbench MP	.14	.17	.11	.26	.21
	(.12)	(.13)	(.17)	(.19)	(.19)
Government MP	.11	.13	–	–	–
	(.08)	(.09)			
Respondent contacted by MP	1.08***	1.08***	1.33***	.82***	.83***
	(.15)	(.15)	(.22)	(.21)	(.21)
N dissenting votes cast by MP, 1992–7	–	.003	−.006	.021***	–
		(.003)	(.004)	(.007)	
N dissenting votes cast on Maastricht Treaty	–	–	–	–	.41***
					(.13)
Constant	−1.22***	−1.21***	−.79*	−1.47***	−1.56***
	(.29)	(.30)	(.42)	(.41)	(.41)
Pseudo R^2	.10	.10	.09	.11	.11
N	2,663	2,663	1,422	1,241	1,241

Column entries are logistic regression coefficients followed by Huber-White standard errors in parentheses.
* $p < .10$
** $p < .05$
*** $p < .01$

cast over the course of the previous parliamentary term, but this has no impact on the model whatsoever. The third and fourth specifications divide Labour and Conservative MPs into separate samples. Again, dissent has little impact on the name recognition of Labour MPs. For Conservative MPs, however, dissent significantly increases the probability of the respondent correctly recalling the MP's name, every dissenting vote boosting that probability by about 0.5 per cent. The more rebellious Conservative MPs cast between ten and fifteen dissenting votes in this Parliament (with about two dozen exceeding twenty-five), figures that translate into levels of name recognition among voters between 5–8 per cent higher than those enjoyed by their more loyal colleagues.

The fact that the dissent affects only Conservative MPs' levels of name recognition likely reflects the fact that Conservative infighting, especially over the European Union, dominated the 1992–7 Parliament. Eurosceptic Conservative MPs conducted a highly public campaign to derail the government's attempt to ratify the Maastricht Treaty (see Major 1999, pp. 342–85). The defining moment of this rebellion took place on 22 July 1993, the rebels first voting in favour of a Labour amendment to accept the treaty's social chapter (for which Major had secured an opt-out) and then contributing to the government's defeat on the Treaty's ratification in the subsequent division. If the argument is that parliamentary dissent boosts MPs' names' recognition (and further, that the political environment in the 1992–7 Parliament was such that only Conservative MPs could secure this advantage), then the Eurosceptics' dissent in these two highly publicized divisions should certainly have increased their public profiles.[9] The fourth specification addresses this issue directly. It drops the total number of dissenting votes that the Conservative MPs cast in the 1992–7 Parliament and substitutes in its place the number of dissenting votes that Conservative MPs cast in these two divisions (0, 1, or 2).[10] A typical Conservative backbencher who toed the line in these two divisions could expect voters

---

[9] With Labour voting as a unified bloc in these divisions, Labour MPs never had the chance to use this episode to boost their profiles in the same manner.

[10] I coded an MP's failure to vote in one of these divisions as half a dissenting vote. Only MPs who were listed on the division lists for one of these two divisions were coded in this fashion, as it is clear that these MPs were available to vote, but decided to abstain ostentatiously. Indeed, several Conservative MPs advertised in the media that they intended to abstain in one or the other of the divisions.

to recall her name correctly with a probability of .48. One dissenting vote in these divisions boosted that probability to .58, and a second dissenting vote to .67.[11] These results suggest, first, that the asymmetry between the Labour and Conservative results reflects the Conservatives' much greater disunity over Europe, and second that Eurosceptic MPs secured higher levels of name recognition by dissenting.

One might suggest that all of this merely reflects an endogeneity problem: MPs with very high public profiles have the political capacity to engage in dissent without worrying about punishment from party leaders. This counter-argument can, in fact, be dismissed. The results from the previous analysis (Table 5.1) make clear that electoral insecurity drives constituency service – and dissent increases in tandem with constituency service. Thus, it appears more likely that dissent and constituency service are reactions to electoral insecurity and reflect the MP's need for voter recognition.

Dissent, approval, and partisanship in New Zealand

Dissent may do more than just boost an MP's profile; it may also directly improve the MP's standing among voters. Any positive electoral reaction to dissent likely flows from a broad popular desire for more independent parliamentary representation. However, regardless of their source, the reactions of non-partisan voters are hypothesized to be stronger than the reactions of strongly partisan voters.

Data and methods

I test this hypothesis with data from the 1993 *New Zealand Election Study (NZES)* (Vowles *et al.* 1994). The 1993 *NZES* contained a very direct measure of voters' evaluation of their MPs, asking respondents, 'Overall, do you approve or disapprove of the way in which your local MP has been handling his or her job over the last three years?'[12] The

---

[11] The probabilities are computed with the MP's parliamentary experience, the respondent's political knowledge, and the district's population density held at the sample means. There was assumed to be no prior contact between the MP and the respondent. The 90 per cent confidence intervals for these point estimates are, respectively, (.45, .51), (.53, .64), and (.59, .77).

[12] Respondents could strongly (dis)approve, (dis)approve, or neither approve nor disapprove of the local MP's performance. Note that at this time New Zealand still operated under a single-member plurality electoral system.

respondent's answer to this question, rather than their vote, is my dependent variable. The respondent's vote is likely to reflect a variety of considerations beyond the respondent's evaluation of the MP, e.g., the relative attractiveness of the parties' manifestos and the strategic situation in the district; the respondent's approval of the MP is less likely to be contaminated by these forces. There is no reason, for example, for the respondent to answer the question strategically. The hypothesis is that an MP's approval rating should increase with the MP's dissent, but that this relationship should also be modified by the strength of the voter's party identification.

Alternative forms of dissent

The New Zealand data also provide an opportunity to examine alternative forms of dissent, in particular, dissent in the media. I collected media dissent data for all MPs in the 1990–3 New Zealand Parliament using reports from the country's two major papers, the *New Zealand Herald* and the *Dominion* (Wellington). I define media dissent as a direct or indirect quotation from an identified MP in which that MP criticizes party leaders, attacks a policy endorsed by the party leadership, or threatens to vote or speak against party policy. This definition excludes anonymous threats or complaints, second-hand reports of critical speeches, or remarks without direct or indirect quotation.[13]

One might complain that dissenting media statements are not the hard, easily measured data that dissenting parliamentary votes are, or that they do not affect the parliamentary game in the way that dissenting votes do. Party leaders consider media dissent to be a serious breach of party discipline, however (Crowe 1983, pp. 914–15; Docherty 1997, p. 168). Moreover, in so far as the mass media is the principal link between citizens and their elected representatives – and the aim here is to show how dissent influences this linkage – it is sensible and important to take account of media dissent as well as parliamentary dissent. There are, then, three measures of a New Zealand MP's dissent: (1) the number of dissenting votes cast by the MP in the 1990–3 Parliament, (2) the number of dissenting media statements made by the MP between 1990–3, and (3) the combination of the MP's dissenting votes and

---

[13] Appendix 3 offers some examples of media dissent.

media statements.[14] The MP's approval rating should increase in all three measures.

Party identification

The impact of dissent on approval should be attenuated by the voter's party identification, with strongly partisan voters responding less positively than non-partisan voters. However, there is also the direct effect of party identification to consider, to wit, that voters who strongly identify with the MP's party are likely to approve most strongly of the MP. Party identification has to be specified to account for both effects. To accomplish this I created three variables:

1. *Party identification vis-à-vis MP.* This variable classified respondents as non-partisans (coded as 0), or weak (1), moderate (2), strong (3), or very strong (4) party identifiers. Respondents identifying with their MP's party received positive scores on this scale (i.e., 1, 2, 3, 4), whereas respondents identifying with another party received negative scores (i.e., -1, -2, -3, -4). This variable should be positively related to approval.
2. *Strength of party identification.* This variable is simply the respondent's party identification vis-à-vis the MP squared. Thus, the more strongly the respondent identified with *any* party, the higher their score on this variable.
3. *Dissent–strength of party identification interaction.* Interacting the MP's dissent with the strength of the respondent's party identification allows strong identifiers to react differently to dissent than weak identifiers and non-partisans. The coefficient on this interaction should be negative, i.e., it should lessen the impact of dissent on approval.

It should be noted that the 1990–3 New Zealand Parliament saw several National Party MPs defect to sit independently or as members of newly formed minor parties. Respondents' party identification is coded with respect to their MP's *original* party affiliation. That is, if the

---

[14] The correlation between dissenting votes and media dissent is not so strong ($r = .54$) as to make the MP's overall dissent (i.e., votes and media dissent) a redundant measure. Some New Zealand MPs dissent in the media, but do not follow through by voting against their parties in Parliament; others cast dissenting votes without saying too much in the media.

respondent identified with the National Party and his or her MP defected from the Nationals to sit independently, the respondent's party identification is still coded as matching the MP's (i.e., as positive). The justification for this coding decision is that respondents cannot have formed long-standing affective ties to newly formed parties or to independent MPs – and it is this affective connection to a given party that is hypothesized to blunt the impact of the MP's dissent.

Defection and policy distance

Obviously, some control for this pattern of defection has to be established. I take two steps to deal with this matter. First, a dummy variable marking the MP as having defected during the parliamentary term is added to the model. (Note that a defecting MP could still have engaged in dissent *prior* to leaving his or her party.) Second, I include in some models the respondent's assessment of the ideological proximity between themselves and their MP's current party (i.e., party at the 1993 election on a seven-point left–right scale).

Constituency service and name recognition

Logic suggests that the happier constituents are with the MP's constituency service efforts on their behalf, the more likely they are to approve of the MP. Furthermore, there is every reason to believe (given its direct effect on the vote) that name recognition boosts the MP's approval. I use two variables to account for these effects. The first is the respondent's satisfaction with the MP's constituency service.[15] The second is a dummy variable indicating whether the respondent correctly recalled their MP's name. With these two controls in place, the model estimates the impact of dissent on approval net of the MP's constituency service efforts *and* the publicity-boosting effects of dissent that were apparent in the British data examined above.

---

[15] Respondents to the 1993 *NZES* were asked whether they had had any contact with their MP and if so, how satisfied they were with this interaction. Respondents could respond that they were very (dis)satisfied, (dis)satisfied, or neither satisfied nor dissatisfied. Respondents who had no contact with the MP in the three years previous to the 1993 election were coded as being neither satisfied nor dissatisfied with the MP's constituency service.

Results

Table 5.3 presents the results of a multiple regression of New Zealand MPs' approval ratings on these independent variables. Approximately 700 respondents failed to locate either themselves or their MP's party on the left–right scale, making it impossible to estimate the ideological distance between these respondents and their MP's current party. In light of the attrition generated by this variable, I run two specifications for each measure of dissent, one controlling for the respondent's ideological distance from their MP's current party, the other omitting this control. This has little effect on the general result, however: dissenting MPs enjoy higher approval ratings than their more loyal colleagues, even after accounting for the MP's constituency service and level of name recognition and the respondent's party identification and (where possible) ideological proximity to the MP's party. Moreover, just as predicted, the rate at which dissent translates into approval diminishes as the respondent's party identification grows stronger.

These dynamics come through in the graphs set out in Figure 5.1. The solid line in each graph traces out the marginal effect of dissent conditional on the respondent's party identification for each specification in Table 5.3. The dashed lines bracketing the solid lines set out the corresponding 90 per cent confidence intervals. All specifications of the model save the first show statistically significant effects. The marginal effect of dissent peaks at the zero-point on the party identification scale (i.e., for non-partisans) and falls away in either direction as the respondent's party identification strengthens. The effect is largest for dissenting votes (Specification 2), topping out at .06. Obviously, this has no impact on the electoral performance of loyal MPs, but for the more rebellious New Zealand MPs (those who committed four or more dissenting acts) this coefficient translates into a .25–1.2 point increase on the five-point approval scale. By comparison, the approval ratings offered by voters who very strongly identified with their MP's party were approximately one point higher on average than those offered by voters who very strongly identified with a different party. In other words, the impact of dissent on approval was potentially as large as that of party identification.[16]

---

[16] This assumes, of course, that the MP remained a member of his or her party long enough to enjoy the boost in approval; defection substantially undercut the benefits of dissent (see Specification 6).

Table 5.3. *OLS regression model of New Zealand MPs' approval ratings*

	Dissenting votes		Media dissent		Overall dissent	
	1	2	3	4	5	6
Defecting MP	.107	-.389	.012	-.113	-.170	-.518*
	(.185)	(.289)	(.132)	(.222)	(.198)	(.273)
Ideological distance to MP's party	—	-.131***	—	-.127***	—	-.127***
		(.023)		(.024)		(.023)
Correctly recalled MP's name	.104**	.102	.102*	.123	.103*	.117
	(.053)	(.084)	(.053)	(.084)	(.053)	(.084)
Satisfaction with MP's constituency service	.319***	.318***	.313***	.324***	.316***	.322***
	(.032)	(.041)	(.032)	(.042)	(.031)	(.041)
Party identification vis-à-vis MP	.110***	.083***	.110***	.084***	.110***	.084***
	(.011)	(.017)	(.011)	(.017)	(.011)	(.017)
Strength of party identification (i.e., party ID vis-à-vis MP)^2	.017***	.022***	.020***	.020***	.020***	.022***
	(.005)	(.007)	(.005)	(.006)	(.005)	(.007)
Dissenting votes, 1990–3	.016	.059***	—	—	—	—
	(.011)	(.017)				
Media dissent, 1990–3	—	—	.040***	.031	—	—
			(.012)	(.020)		
Overall dissent (votes + media), 1990–3	—	—	—	—	.024***	.036***
					(.008)	(.010)

	(1)	(2)	(3)	(4)	(5)	(6)
Dissenting votes × strength of party identification	-.001	-.006***	—	—	—	—
	(.001)	(.002)				
Media dissent × strength of party identification	—	—	-.005***	-.004***	—	—
			(.001)	(.002)		
Overall dissent × strength of party identification	—	—	—	—	-.002**	-.003***
					(.001)	(.001)
Constant	1.958***	2.167***	1.960***	2.147***	1.943***	2.129***
	(.109)	(.161)	(.108)	(.162)	(.108)	(.161)
R^2	.143	.201	.150	.197	.148	.202
N	1,983	1,154	1,983	1,154	1,983	1,154

Cell entries are OLS regression coefficients with robust standard errors in parentheses.

* $p < .10$
** $p < .05$
*** $p < .01$

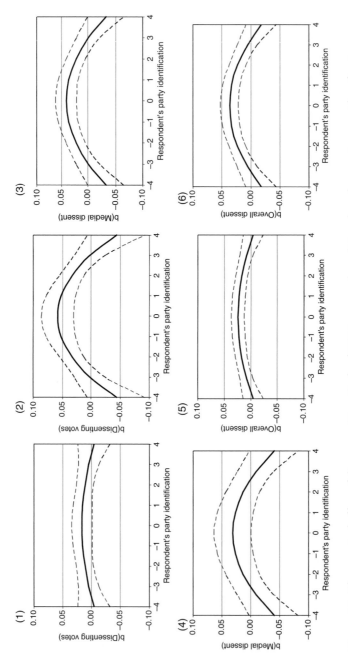

Figure 5.1 The marginal effect of dissent on New Zealand MPs' approval conditional on the voter's party identification

Table 5.4. *Logit model of vote choice at the 1993 New Zealand election*

Covariate	B
Party identification vis-à-vis MP	.469***
	(.072)
Current support for MP's party	1.479***
	(.162)
Ideological distance to MP's party	−.391***
	(.091)
Correctly recalled MP's name	.956***
	(.349)
Approval of MP	.819***
	(.158)
Satisfaction with MP's constituency service	.065
	(.163)
Overall dissent	−.003
	(.020)
Constant	−6.866***
	(.883)
Pseudo-R^2	.616
N	1,090

Column entries are logistic regression coefficients with robust standard errors in parentheses.

*$p < .10$
**$p < .05$
***$p < .01$

Effects: individual and aggregate, direct and indirect

The results so far show that dissent provides MPs with two valuable electoral resources, name recognition and public approval. Whether MPs are able to translate these resources into votes and how these individual-level effects aggregate to produce electoral outcomes remain open questions. A model of vote choice at the 1993 New Zealand election helps to provide answers to both questions. Table 5.4 sets out the results of this model. The dichotomous dependent variable identifies respondents as having voted for their incumbent MP at the 1993 election or not. All but one of the independent variables, the respondent's current level of support for the MP's party (on a five-point scale), come from the approval analysis just presented.[17]

Party and partisan effects – the respondent's party identification vis-à-vis the MP, the respondent's current support of the MP's party and policy distance from the MP's party – dominate vote choice. However, even after these partisan forces have been accounted for, recognition of the MP's name and approval of the MP apart from the party make the respondent more likely to have voted for the MP. Constituency service and dissent, on the other hand, have no direct impact on the vote itself.

The indirect effect of dissent on approval is more than strong enough to generate votes, however. Table 5.5 maps this individual model of vote choice on to an aggregate electoral outcome in a hypothetical New Zealand constituency. Using the distribution of party identifiers in the national sample as a template, the second column of Table 5.5 sets out the number and percentage of each group of party identifiers that one could expect to find among the 35,000 voters of the average 1993 New Zealand electoral district. In other words, on average, a New Zealand MP could expect 1,360 voters in the district (3.9 per cent of the electorate) to very strongly identify with another party. The third column estimates the voter's approval of the MP from the sixth specification in Table 5.3 conditional on the voter's party identification and no dissent by the MP. The fourth column uses these approval levels and the coefficients from the voting model in Table 5.4 to generate probabilities that a voter in that particular group votes for the MP. Thus, a voter who very strongly identifies with an opposing party has just a 6.8 per cent chance of voting for the MP. The fifth column uses these predicted probabilities to project the number of votes that the MP could expect to gain from each group of party identifiers. For example, only 92 (i.e., 6.8 per cent) of the 1,360 strongly partisan opponents are expected to vote for the MP.[18] The last three columns repeat the exercise on the assumption that the MP had committed five dissenting acts over the course of the previous parliamentary term.[19] The bottom line of

---

[17] The question was: 'Regardless of what their chances were at the 1993 election, how do you feel about these political parties?' Respondents could answer on a five-point scale, ranging from 'strongly support' to 'strongly oppose'.

[18] These figures are based on the assumption that turnout is independent of partisanship, i.e., that weak partisans are as likely to vote as strong partisans.

[19] The mean number of dissenting acts in the 1990–3 Parliament was 2.6; the maximum was 29. Five acts of dissent would put the MP at the ninetieth percentile of MPs.

Table 5.5. *The aggregate impact of dissent on vote choice at the 1993 New Zealand election*

Respondent's party identification vis-à-vis MP	Estimated N voters in district from national sample (percentage)	MP does not dissent			MP commits five dissenting acts		
		Expected value (MP's approval)	Pr(voted for MP) in percentage	Projected N votes from group	Expected value (MP's approval)	Pr(voted for MP) in percentage	Projected N votes from group
-4 (Very strongly against)	1,360 (3.88)	3.08	6.8	92	3.33	8.1	110
-3	3,055 (8.73)	3.01	9.7	296	3.24	11.4	348
-2	2,207 (6.31)	2.98	14.2	313	3.20	16.3	360
-1	2,112 (6.03)	3.00	21.1	446	3.20	23.6	498
0 (Non-partisan)	11,533 (32.95)	3.06	30.9	3,564	3.24	33.7	3,887
1	3,119 (8.91)	3.17	43.8	1,366	3.33	46.5	1,450
2	3,711 (10.60)	3.32	58.5	2,171	3.47	60.6	2,249
3	6,031 (17.23)	3.51	72.4	4,366	3.64	73.8	4,451
4 (Very strongly for)	1,872 (5.35)	3.75	83.4	1,561	3.87	84.1	1,574
Total	35,000			14,176 (40.50%)			14,927 (42.65%)

this simulation is that five acts of dissent earn the MP 751 votes, a 2.15 per cent boost in the MP's vote share.

One of the hallmarks of electoral dealignment is the decline in both the extent and intensity of party identification among voters. The electoral ramifications of this decline are evident in Table 5.5. Most of the votes (321 or 42.7 per cent) generated by the MP's dissent come from non-partisan voters, the most pliable and largest group of voters. In contrast, the votes of strong identifiers are not really in play here. Strong partisans are so overwhelmingly likely to vote for or against the MP that dissent has only a small marginal impact on their behaviour. In addition, voters who strongly identify with the MP's party start out with higher approval ratings of the MP to begin with, and this effect passes on to the vote. Dissent therefore appears as an ideal response to de-alignment: it effectively secures the votes of non-partisans, the largest and growing segment of the electorate, without adversely affecting the voting behaviour of strong partisans. By implication, the incentives that MPs have to engage in dissent must increase as electoral dealignment sets in.

Conclusion

MPs do not inhabit compartmentalized worlds where their parliamentary activities are isolated from their constituency service efforts and electoral results. On the contrary, the results here suggest that MPs use their parliamentary dissent as a complement to constituency service in their efforts to secure a personal vote. Dissent does this effectively, but not directly. Instead, dissent operates indirectly, providing rebellious MPs with two valuable electoral resources, name recognition and approval, that they can translate into votes. The indirect electoral impact of dissent is not large, but at 2.2 per cent of the vote it is roughly equal to what previous research suggests an MP earns via constituency service – and it is earned in a far more time-efficient fashion.

This result answers the chapter's opening question and provides empirical verification of a central assumption of the LEADS model. There is more here than the bottom-line result of 2.2 per cent more votes, however. Dissent is an effective vote-winning strategy primarily because it alters the opinions and voting behaviour of non-partisan and weakly partisan voters. This is a key finding, providing an individual-level explanation for one of the main cross-national patterns set out in

Chapter 3, to wit, that the frequency and extent of parliamentary dissent increases as party identification in the electorate weakens. It is no coincidence, then, that dealignment and parliamentary dissent proceed in lockstep: as the party system dealigns and party identification weakens, dissent becomes a more effective and worthwhile electoral strategy.

6 | *The cost of dissent to the party*

Introduction

The previous chapter showed that dissent can provide MPs with name recognition and votes; in this chapter, I explore the cost of dissent to the party. The party whips and MPs quoted in Chapter 2 suggested that any reward reaped by dissident MPs came at the party's expense. By dissenting, an MP weakens the authority and credibility of party leaders, places colleagues in the difficult position of having to explain away their loyalty to their own constituents, and undermines the party's image as a unified and coherent political force. This characterization of the situation casts party discipline as an archetypal prisoner's dilemma in which MPs, left to their own devices, defect from the party line to secure the benefits of independence and leave their colleagues to bear the burden of supporting unpopular party policies. The result of this myopically self-interested behaviour is to leave the party unable to sustain any collective effort that goes against its members' short-run interests.

This description of intra-party politics provides a tidy functionalist explanation for the institutions that are commonly taken to underpin party discipline (e.g., candidate selection rules, whips, patronage, etc.). Even so, one can point to arguments and evidence that contradict the theoretical assertion that there exists a collective action problem at the heart of intra-party politics. Richard Lucy (1985), for example, identifies several instances in which Australian Liberal MPs and Senators had their party's tacit approval to rebel against the party line on matters of local importance precisely because that strategy left both the rebels and the party better off. Lucy argues that:

For this minimal cost, the Liberals achieved a degree of flexibility to respond to local pressures which ran counter to government policy. It helped them be all things to all electorates (like the American congressional Democrats). It may well be good electoral politics for a Tasmanian MHR [Member of the House of Representatives] to be seen to be attacking the national government and prime minister in defence of the interests of Tasmanians. Hodgman's 'rebellion' doubtless strengthened his (and the government's) hold on office. He proved electorally unassailable even when challenged by Ken Wriedt – a former Labor senate leader and future leader of the state parliamentary party. Hodgman's activities in the House were part of his campaign to convince his electorate that he was their determined champion. (Lucy 1985, p. 360)

Powell and Whitten (1993) report the more general empirical result that in political systems where party cohesion is low, incumbent governments incur milder electoral sanctions for poor economic conditions. They hypothesize that the lack of cohesion obscures responsibility for economic conditions, and thus voters do not blame the incumbent government entirely for the economic situation. The mechanisms identified by these authors are different (a capacity for political flexibility or a blurring of the lines of accountability), but in each case the argument and evidence is that a modicum of disunity works to the party's advantage. From this perspective, party discipline is (or can be) a positive-sum game in which all players benefit rather than a zero-sum situation where one side's gains come at the other side's expense.

It is not immediately obvious, then, that disunity necessarily damages the party or its leaders. The qualitative evidence from Chapter 2 points to the existence of a zero-sum collective action problem at the heart of party discipline, and certainly much of the rational choice literature on political parties (e.g., Aldrich 1995) takes this position as its starting assumption. It may be, however, that this collective action perspective on party discipline is a theoretical construct without much empirical grounding. There is also the question of mechanism to consider. If dissent does harm the party, how does this happen? There are a number of possibilities, but the result that emerges here is that dissent presents informational barriers to voters that undercut the party leadership's capacity to sell their policies to the electorate. The chapter starts by returning to the cross-national data used in Chapter 3 to determine whether there exists a relationship between the aggregate level of dissent experienced by a party at any point in time and its performance at the subsequent election. The results suggest that it is the salience rather than the frequency or amount of dissent that damages a party. This result is reinforced by individual-level survey data from British elections showing that voters tend not to vote for parties they perceive to be disunited. Finally, the exact nature of this relationship is explored in more detail in an examination of British voters' reaction to the Labour Party's disunity over the invasion of Iraq in 2003.

Cross-national evidence on the cost of dissent

The cross-national data employed in Chapter 3 can be used to evaluate the hypothesis that party disunity is a zero-sum game. To do so, I use dissent as an independent variable to predict a party's performance at the subsequent election. On this test, a party confronts a collective action problem in maintaining party discipline only to the extent that its level of dissension during a parliamentary term is negatively related to its vote share at the subsequent election. A null or positive relationship between a party's dissent and its subsequent electoral performance, on the other hand, suggests that there is no such conflict of interest between MPs and party leaders.

Data and methods

The data employed here are exactly the same as those employed in Chapter 3, though they are analysed in a different fashion. The dependent variable is the vote share a party secures in a given election. The central independent variable is the percentage of divisions in the preceding parliamentary term in which the party experienced dissent, i.e., the frequency of dissent. I also included a lagged dependent variable (i.e., the party's vote share at the previous election) in the model to control for any serial correlation. All specifications also include fixed effects for the political party with the result that the statistical comparison drawn is with respect to that party's relative electoral performance across time. A dummy variable marking the party as the incumbent governing party accounts for the fact that incumbent governments tend to lose votes and seats upon seeking re-election (Powell and Whitten 1993).

Results

Table 6.1 contains the results of this analysis. The initial specification of the model shows that a 1 per cent increase in the frequency of dissent experienced by a party is associated with a 0.2 per cent decline in the party's vote share at the subsequent election. The effect just reaches the 0.1 level of statistical significance, but this is actually quite impressive given that the lagged dependent variable and fixed effects soak up almost all the variance in the data (note the very high R-squared

Table 6.1. *Parties' vote shares and the frequency of dissent, 1945–2005*

	Vote share at subsequent election		
	1	2	3
Percentage dissenting divisions in previous term	−.20*	(.12)	−.09
	(.11)	−.12	(.10)
N MPs defecting from party in previous term	–	–	−.47***
			(.18)
Party popularity in month before election	–	.32***	.32***
		(.07)	(.06)
Vote share in previous election	.50***	.43***	.44***
	(.10)	(.08)	(.08)
Incumbent governing party	−3.24***	−2.75***	−2.92***
	(.96)	(.88)	(.85)
Fixed effects	Included	Included	Included
N†	132	132	132
R²	.98	.99	.99

Column entries are OLS regression coefficients followed by robust standard errors in parentheses.

*p < .10
**p < .05
***p < .01

† Whilst the data analysed here are identical to those used in Chapter 3, the lagged nature of the independent variables means that ten observations, one at the start of each party's time series, are lost to the analysis.

statistic).[1] The worry with this result is less its statistical significance, however, than the possibility that it reflects a spurious relationship between a party's dissent and its electoral performance, both variables merely reflecting the party's popularity or lack thereof. If this is true, controlling for the party's level of popularity as indicated in opinion polls conducted just prior to the election should wipe out any connection between a party's dissent and its electoral performance. The second specification of the model shows that this is exactly the case, a result that reinforces the point made in Chapter 3, to wit, that the causal arrow

---

[1] The result is in fact stronger ($b = -.35$, $s.e. = .19$, $p = .07$) if one uses the party's seat shares rather than their vote shares as the measure of electoral performance.

flows from unpopularity to dissent rather than from dissent to unpopularity. This null result remains in place irrespective of whether one uses the frequency, depth, or extent of dissent as the measure of a party's disunity.

At this stage, one would have to conclude that dissent is at worst a parliamentary nuisance to parties. It may result in the defeat or alteration of a few bills, but it rarely threatens a government's survival in office, and – on these results – has little or no direct electoral impact. Arguments that party discipline exists to resolve a zero-sum collective action problem among MPs and party leaders thus appear to be overdrawn. It may be, however, that the electoral impact of dissent hinges on its visibility. If dissent involves only a handful of mavericks voting against their party on obscure matters that are not widely reported in the media, then there is no reason to expect the dissent to affect the party's electoral performance. To test this idea, the third specification of model includes the number of MPs defecting from the party in the parliamentary term to sit as independents or as members of another party. Defections are relatively rare events, and consequently tend to receive a fair degree of media coverage.[2] The results provide some support for this argument: even after accounting for the party's popularity just prior to the election, the number of MPs defecting from a party adversely affects its vote share at the subsequent election, every defection costing the party .47 per cent of the vote.[3]

Vote choice and perceptions of party unity at British elections

This last result hints that it is less the frequency of dissent (or, for that matter, its depth or extent) that harms the party as much as it is voters'

---

[2] The mean number of defections per term is 2.1 MPs. Bear in mind that this number includes several outright party splits, as when twenty-eight British Labour MPs broke away from the party in 1981 to establish the Social Democratic Party (SDP). Indicative (though hardly comprehensive) evidence of how highly publicized defections are is the fact that a Lexus-Nexus search of the names of the MPs who defected from the British Conservative Party to the Labour Party between 1995 and 2005 returned the following number of hits: Alan Howarth 726; Shaun Woodward 536; Peter Temple-Morris 131; Robert Jackson 62. By comparison, a typical British backbench MP might receive twenty to thirty hits per year.

[3] This result is robust to the omission from the analysis of the Labour–SDP split, the largest defection in the data.

awareness or perception of the party as disunited. To test this hypothesis, I examine the extent to which British voters altered their voting choices contingent on how united or disunited they thought a party was. Every *British Election Study* (*BES*) from 1983 onward has asked voters whether they viewed each of the major political parties as united or disunited. To be sure, there is a clear difference between a party actually being disunited and being perceived as disunited. A single highly publicized dispute between party leaders and MPs may create a public impression of disunity notwithstanding the fact that the party manages to maintain cohesion in the division lobbies. That said, how voters cast their ballots is what determines election outcomes, and if voters' choices are driven principally by their perception of a party as united or disunited, then that perception matters. The test, then, is whether the voter's perception of the party's unity or disunity made them more or less likely to vote for the party, or had no impact on that decision.

Data and methods

The challenge in working with a large number of election surveys which do not all employ identical questions is to present a sufficiently well-specified model of vote choice that relies on only a few variables that are common to all of the surveys. This strategy allows one to apply the same statistical model to each survey, greatly aiding comparability. In light of these requirements, I do not control for voters' attitudes on election-specific issues or events (e.g., the respondent's views on the invasion of Iraq at the 2005 election). Nor do I include a measure of voter–party proximity based on a generic left–right spectrum (the 1987 *BES* did not include the 0–10 left–right self-placement scale that is typically part of the *BES*).[4] Instead, I rely on three principal controls: the respondent's party identification (*Party ID*), evaluation of the party leader (*Leader*), and retrospective evaluation of the national economy (*Economy*). Other factors inform voters' choices at the ballot box, of course, but these three variables are central determinants of vote choice in Britain

---

[4] I have also omitted the respondent's social class from the model. Whether this omission is conspicuous or immaterial and whether the nature of social class has itself evolved over time are very much subjects of running debates in British political behaviour (e.g., Butler and Stokes 1969; Crewe *et al.* 1977; Heath *et al.* 1985, 2001; Clarke *et al.* 2004). My omission is intended to avoid these issues.

(e.g., Butler and Stokes 1969; Heath *et al.* 1985; Crewe and King 1994; Clarke *et al.* 2000; Clarke *et al.* 2004).

For each survey wave I estimate two probit models of vote choice, one predicting the voter's decision to vote for the Conservatives, the other, the voter's decision to vote for Labour:

$$Pr(Conservative\ Vote = 1) = \Phi(\beta_0 + \beta_1 Unity + \beta_2 PartyID$$
$$+ \beta_3 Leader + \beta_4 Economy) \qquad [6.1]$$

$$Pr(Labour\ Vote = 1) = \Phi(\beta_0 + \beta_1 Unity + \beta_2 PartyID$$
$$+ \beta_3 Leader + \beta_4 Economy) \qquad [6.2]$$

In both cases, the voter's alternative choice is to vote for another party, i.e., non-voters are excluded from the analysis.[5] The *Unity* variable is coded so that a positive sign on β_1 signals that voters are more likely to vote for parties they perceive as united (1) and less likely to vote for parties they perceive to be disunited (−1).[6] In other words, if and only if $\beta_1 > 0$ would one characterize party discipline as a zero-sum game.

Results

The results of the analysis appear in Table 6.2. With each *BES* from 1983 to 2005 providing two estimates of vote choice and the 1992–7 *BES* Panel providing additional estimates of vote intentions for 1994 and the spring and winter of both 1995 and 1996, there are twenty-two regressions in total. The control variables in each regression behave as expected: the voter's party identification and evaluation of the party's leader are positively related to the decision to vote for the party; economic evaluations are positively related to the decision to vote for the governing party (identified by the emboldened 'party' label) and negatively related to the decision to vote for the opposition party. In so far as perceptions of party unity are concerned, two things immediately stand out from Table 6.2. First, in every case, the coefficient on the party unity variable is positive: unity attracts votes, disunity repels them. Second, this effect is statistically significant at the .05 level in sixteen out of

---

[5] Non-voters are excluded on the grounds that the decision to participate in the election or to abstain is driven by other causal processes and variables (e.g., Clarke *et al.* 2004).

[6] The question also allowed respondents to report that they saw a party as neither united nor disunited (coded 0).

Table 6.2. *British voters' perceptions of party unity and their impact on vote choice, 1995–2005*

	Unity	Party ID	Economy	Leader	Constant	Impact of disunity (percentage)	Percentage dissenting divisions	N	Pseudo R^2
2005									
Conservative	.34**	1.38***	−.29***	.20***	−.70***	−23.2	9.2	1,442	.65
	(.14)	(.06)	(.07)	(.03)	(.22)				
Labour	.35***	1.15***	.19***	.16***	−1.84***	−23.8	21.0	1,620	.58
	(.10)	(.05)	(.06)	(.02)	(.20)				
2001									
Conservative	.06	1.49***	−.19***	.12***	−.89***	−4.7	12.7	1,390	.67
	(.10)	(.07)	(.06)	(.03)	(.16)				
Labour	.07	1.25***	.09*	.18***	−.97***	−5.5	7.5	1,684	.59
	(.06)	(.05)	(.05)	(.03)	(.13)				
1997 (1992–7 panel)									
Conservative	.26	1.33***	.32***	.36***	−.73***	−19.6	14.10	1,369	.64
	(.16)	(.06)	(.06)	(.06)	(.19)				
Labour vote	.37***	1.17***	−.21***	.19	−.08	−27.2	23.20	1,277	.50
	(.11)	(.05)	(.06)	(.13)	(.20)				
Winter 1996									
Conservative	.30***	1.53***	.10	.64***	.97***	−16.9	4.60	979	.75
	(.09)	(.12)	(.11)	(.11)	(.35)				
Labour	.19***	1.52***	−.21	.54	1.80	−14.4	11.1	894	.73
	(.08)	(.08)	(.09)	(.11)	(.30)				

Table 6.2. (*cont.*)

	Unity	Party ID	Economy	Leader	Constant	Impact of disunity (percentage)	Percentage dissenting divisions	N	Pseudo R²
Spring 1996									
Conservative	.14 (.10)	1.43*** (.08)	.14* (.08)	.53*** (.07)	.70*** (.27)	−8.3	4.60	1,424	.72
Labour	.23*** (.06)	1.29*** (.06)	−.28*** (.07).	.42*** (.09)	1.54*** (.25)	−18.4	11.1	1,321	.63
Winter 1995									
Conservative	.33*** (.07)	1.48*** (.08)	.21*** (.07)	.37*** (.06)	.24 (.23)	−20.1	7.9	1,474	.72
Labour	.14** (.06)	1.33*** (.06)	−.20*** (.06)	.42*** (.07)	1.49*** (.19)	−11.4	8.8	1,365	.63
Spring 1995									
Conservative	.23** (.09)	1.56*** (.09)	.13* (.07)	.45*** (.07)	.45*** (.25)	−12.1	7.9	1,672	.72
Labour	.07 (.06)	1.28*** (.05)	−.10* (.05)	.45*** (.07)	1.30*** (.17)	−5.7	8.8	1,569	.60
1994									
Conservative	.00 (.07)	1.42*** (.06)	.02 (.07)	.57*** (.06)	1.02*** (.22)	.0	7.4	1,933	.69
Labour	.19*** (.05)	1.38*** (.05)	−.02 (.05)	.62** (.25)	.62*** (.15)	−15.2	4.4	1,631	.62

Table 6.2. (*cont.*)

	Unity	Party ID	Economy	Leader	Constant	Impact of disunity (percentage)	Percentage dissenting divisions	N	Pseudo R^2
1992 (1992–7 panel)									
Conservative	.18***	1.39***	.26***	.31***	−.99***	−13.1	12.2	2,687	.67
	(.05)	(.04)	(.04)	(.05)	(.09)				
Labour	.09**	1.32***	−.19***	.24***	.08	−6.9	8.4	2,696	.61
	(.04)	(.04)	(.03)	(.04)	(.07)				
1987									
Conservative	.15***	1.09***	.06***	.45***	−1.92***	−11.9	16.2	2,703	.63
	(.05)	(.04)	(.02)	(.04)	(.15)				
Labour	.23***	1.22***	−.08***	.34***	−1.24***	−16.2	6.7	2,349	.66
	(.05)	(.05)	(.03)	(.03)	(.18)				
1983									
Conservative	.20***	1.06***	.22***	.14***	−1.33***	−14.0	12.1	3,303	.48
	(.04)	(.03)	(.04)	(.02)	(.10)				
Labour	.11**	1.23***	−.28***	.14***	−.81***	−6.0	12.3	3,327	.51
	(.05)	(.05)	(.04)	(.02)	(.09)				

Column entries are probit regression coefficients followed by robust standard errors in parentheses.
Party label in bold denotes the governing party at the time.
* $p < .10$
** $p < .05$
*** $p < .01$

twenty-two cases, far greater than random chance would suggest. Only the 2001 election runs wholly against this pattern. The substantive effect of the voter's views of the party as disunited rather than united is to reduce the voter's probability of voting for the party by an average of 13.4 per cent, an impact that is about equal to that of retrospective economic evaluations, something widely accepted as influencing voting behaviour.

Party disunity and informational barriers: Blair and Iraq

The most obvious shortcoming of the above analysis concerns the validity of the party unity variable. What exactly this variable measures is not at all clear. One possibility is that the voter's assessment of a party as united or disunited is wholly perceptual in nature, perhaps rooted in a general disdain for parties and organized politics. This would not alter the variable's empirical relationship to the vote, but it would leave one uncertain about whether that relationship was relevant for gaining an understanding of the underlying nature of party discipline. The argument that disunity damages the party would be more convincing if one could demonstrate some causal connection between the voter's assessment of parties' unity and actual parliamentary events.[7]

There are a number of means by which disunity might lead voters to withdraw their support from a party, but the hypothesis that I explore here is that dissent impairs the party leadership's capacity to sell the party's policies to the electorate. This may be because dissent makes voters sceptical about the party's leadership and policies, prompting them to ask themselves why they should accept a leader's claims when even the leader's own supporters dispute these claims. Alternatively, voters may be confused by disunity. The party label is a key informational heuristic, one that not only informs voters about what the party stands for, but also how to evaluate and position themselves on political issues (Popkin 1994; Aldrich 1995, pp. 48–50). By definition, however, a party that is divided on policy lacks a clear policy position. The informational value of the party's label is commensurately diminished,

---

[7] There is a correlation of $r = .45$ ($p = .06$) between the coefficients on the party unity variable and the party's observed level of dissent, but absent some sort of causal mechanism linking these two variables, it is not clear how to interpret this correlation.

and in consequence voters may have difficulty drawing the appropriate connections between parties and policies and their own preferences and votes.

Blair, Iraq, and Labour's disunity

From the time of George W. Bush's State of the Union address in January 2002, in which the president identified Iraq as a direct threat to international security, to the parliamentary vote committing British troops to the invasion on 18 March 2003, Tony Blair faced increasing resistance from his own MPs (Cowley 2005). Initially, the government was able to use its control of the parliamentary agenda to forestall debate on Iraq and thus limit opportunities for open rebellion. Blair's tabling of the intelligence dossier that claimed Saddam Hussein's regime possessed weapons of mass destruction on 24 September 2002, however, gave fifty-six Labour MPs the chance to signal their displeasure with the cabinet's handling of the Iraq issue by supporting an adjournment motion (Cook 2003, pp. 214–15; Seldon 2004, p. 582; Cowley 2005, pp. 107–8). Another group of forty-four Labour MPs then presented another critical motion in January 2003. The next major debate on Iraq, on 26 February 2003, saw 121 Labour MPs voting for a motion asserting that the government's case for military action was not yet proven. This was, at the time, the largest backbench rebellion in the British House of Commons since 1886. Less than a month later, on 18 March 2003, with Blair's premiership at stake, this historic mark was outstripped when 139 Labour MPs voted for a hostile amendment to Blair's motion to join the American-led invasion of Iraq (Seldon 2004, pp. 596–7; Cowley 2005, pp. 123–5). Three ministerial resignations, among which that of Robin Cook, leader of the House of Commons and former Foreign Secretary, amplified the dissent (*The Economist*, 18 March 2003). A number of Conservative MPs also defied their party and voted against the motion, but the Liberal Democrats were, as Blair remarked scathingly in the debate, 'unified, as ever, in opportunism and error' (*Debates*, 18 March 2003, col. 761) in their opposition. Within months, questions began to emerge about the factual basis of the dossier that Blair had tabled in Parliament, and whether Blair had knowingly misrepresented its contents to Parliament. Iraq, Seldon (2004, p. 602) concludes, 'profoundly damaged [Blair's] relationship with the Labour Party, and the media, and further sullied his reputation with the electorate as someone who could be trusted and tarnished Labour's electoral prospects'.

Did Labour's disunity matter?

The question, then, is whether Labour's highly public split on Iraq contributed to the public's scepticism about the government's policy on Iraq or confused voters as to where the party stood on the issue. These are not mutually exclusive possibilities, of course. Labour's disunity may have left poorly informed voters confused as to what the government's position was on Iraq, whereas highly informed voters may have grown sceptical of Blair's pro-invasion position precisely because they were aware that many Labour MPs disagreed with the prime minister's stance. Even if this makes it difficult to disentangle voters' scepticism from their confusion, it is clear that an evaluation of these hypotheses must hinge on more than just the voters' perception of the party's unity or disunity. Some additional evidence must be presented to show that voters' reactions were due to their knowledge (as opposed to their perceptions) of Labour's disunity. For example, it is not sufficient to show that voters who perceived Labour as disunited were less approving of involvement in Iraq than voters who perceived the party as united; both the voters' perception of Labour as divided and their disapproval of involvement in Iraq might reflect a general dislike of the Labour Party. If, however, one observed that disapproval of the invasion of Iraq was concentrated primarily among highly informed Labour Party identifiers who admitted their party's disunity (i.e., voters who generally supported the party, but knew that it was disunited), there would be some basis for asserting that disunity generates scepticism among voters.

Data and methods

To test these possibilities, I use data from the 2005 *British Election Study* to measure the relationship between British voters' perception of party unity, party leadership, and policy. The survey asked voters to identify each of the major parties as united or disunited, to assess the trustworthiness of each party leader, and to express their approval or disapproval on Britain's involvement in Iraq. The latter two variables are probably endogenous to one another, especially in Blair's case. It is likely, in other words, that voters who strongly disapproved of Britain's involvement in Iraq were inclined to see Blair as very untrustworthy, whilst those who saw Blair as very untrustworthy were similarly inclined to strongly disapprove of the country's involvement in Iraq. I adopt a standard solution to this situation and model voters' views on British involvement in Iraq and their assessments of Blair's trustworthiness as a set of simultaneous equations estimated via two-stage least squares. The method requires exogenous predictors for each endogenous variable, and I use voters' left–right self-placement, that is, their ideologies, as an instrument for their positions on Iraq and their retrospective evaluations of the economy and general trust in politicians to help estimate voters' assessments of Blair's trustworthiness.

The role of party identification and information

Party identification is another obvious exogenous variable, but its role here is substantive rather than merely statistical. If the argument is that Labour's disunity on Iraq sent voters mixed signals about where the party stood on the issue, then Labour party identifiers, who continued to rely on party identification as a cue for how to position themselves on the Iraq issue, should find themselves distributed randomly on either side of the issue. In contrast, the Liberal Democrats' unity on Iraq theoretically offered a clear signal to voters as to the party's stance on the issue. Thus, if Liberal Democrat identifiers relied on party identification to develop their own views on Iraq, one should observe a strong relationship in the data between Liberal Democratic party identification and disapproval of Britain's involvement in Iraq. How can one be sure that any such difference between Labour and Liberal Democratic party identification does not merely reflect Labour voters being as deeply divided on Iraq as Labour MPs, and Liberal Democrat voters being as united against Iraq as Liberal Democrat MPs? One cannot entirely rule out this possibility, but two patterns in the data would run against that counter-argument. First, the existence of a statistically significant relationship between voters' ideological positions and their positions on Iraq among Labour identifiers who saw the Labour Party as disunited *but not among those who saw the party as united* would suggest that voters who were aware of the parliamentary situation did not view the Iraq issue through a (misleading) partisan lens. Second, if the above pattern were also stronger among highly informed voters (whose assessments of

Labour's disunity are presumably accurate) than among poorly informed voters (whose assessments of Labour's disunity are presumably less accurate, if not inaccurate), it would further suggest that party disunity presents an informational barrier to voters. No such patterns should be visible among Liberal Democrat identifiers, however, because their party was united on the Iraq issue. Indeed, if the structure of Liberal Democrats' attitudes toward Iraq is the same as Labour attitudes, one would have to attribute the results to voters' inaccurate perceptions of the parties' unity, as only one party (Labour) was divided.[8]

The voters' levels of political information and party identification are therefore important conditioning variables in the model. I measure a voter's level of political information as the number of correct responses the voter gave to the battery of (eight) factual questions contained in the 2005 *BES*. Party identification is measured on a scale that ranges from strong Labour identification (+3) to strong Liberal Democratic identification (−3). The fact that the main opposition party, the Conservatives, was also divided on Iraq dulls the contrast between Labour disunity and Liberal Democrat unity, and so I omit all Conservative identifiers from the analysis.

Results

The results of the analysis are presented in Table 6.3. The first comparison to draw is with respect to the impact of party identification on the policy attitudes of Labour identifiers, on the one hand, and Liberal Democrat identifiers, on the other. In Specifications 2–4, setting out the relationship between voters' opinions on Iraq and their assessment of Blair's trustworthiness among Labour identifiers, party identification has no impact on the respondent's stance on Iraq (i.e., strong Labour identifiers are no more likely to approve or disapprove of British involvement in Iraq than weak identifiers). This result is not an artefact of limiting the analysis to Labour identifiers and restricting the variance of

---

[8] Indeed, this was not just true for Iraq, it was true of the Labour Party throughout the 2001–5 Parliament (Cowley 2005); the Liberal Democrats were, by comparison, a paragon of cohesion. British voters appear to have been aware of these facts because 67.3 per cent of respondents to the 2005 *BES* saw the Labour Party as disunited, whereas only 14.8 per cent saw the Liberal Democrats as disunited.

Table 6.3. *Two-stage least squares estimates of British voters' approval or disapproval of British involvement in Iraq*

Approve of Britain's involvement in Iraq[†]

	Labour and Liberal Democrat identifiers and non-partisans	Labour identifiers			Liberal Democrat identifiers and non-partisans	
	1	2	3 High info.	4 Low info.	5	6
Blair: trustworthiness (instrumented)	.12*** (.02)	.15*** (.03)	.14*** (.04)	.16*** (.04)	–	–
Kennedy: trustworthiness (instrumented)	–	–	–	–	.13*** (.05)	.13** (.05)
Respondent's party identification	.00 (.20)	–.02 (.05)	.01 (.06)	–.05 (.09)	–.15** (.07)	–.13* (.07)
Labour disunited	–.14 (.25)	–.06 (.33)	–.80 (.72)	.42 (.60)	–.12 (.59)	–
Liberal Democrats disunited	–	–	–	–	–	.38 (.62)
Respondent's left–right position	–.01 (.02)	–.02 (.02)	–.04 (.03)	.01 (.04)	.10 (.07)	.01 (.04)
Respondent's political information	.06** (.02)	.08*** (.03)	–.06 (.07)	.13* (.08)	–.06 (.06)	–.00 (.03)
Labour disunited × Respondent's political information	–.03 (.03)	–.06 (.04)	.01 (.10)	–.10 (.11)	–.09 (.08)	–
Labour disunited × Respondent's left–right position	.04 (.03)	.05 (.04)	.09** (.05)	–.01 (.06)	.07 (.06)	–
Liberal Democrats disunited ×	–	–	–	–	–	–.04

Table 6.3. (*cont.*)

Approve of Britain's involvement in Iraq[†]	Labour and Liberal Democrat identifiers and non-partisans	Labour identifiers			Liberal Democrat identifiers and non-partisans	
	1	2	3 High info.	4 Low info.	5	6
Respondent's political information						(.08)
Liberal Democrats disunited ×	–	–	–	–	–	–.03
Respondent's left–right position						(.09)
Constant	.28	.08	1.11**	–.32	.26	.16
	(.22)	(.28)	(.53)	(.49)	(.54)	(.38)
RMSE	.81	.80	.73	.89	.91	.93
N	1,126	661	384	277	458	422

* $p < .10$
** $p < .05$
*** $p < .01$
[†] Dependent variable is respondent's approval or disapproval of Britain's involvement in Iraq: 0 = strongly disapprove; 1 = disapprove; 2 = approve; 3 = strongly approve

party identification, because the initial specification, which takes in the whole sample, shows the same null result. In contrast, the fifth and sixth specifications, which are limited to Liberal Democratic identifiers and non-partisans (and conditioned on the trustworthiness of Charles Kennedy, the Liberal Democrat leader), show a statistical relationship only between party identification and the respondent's approval or disapproval of Iraq: strong Liberal Democrat identifiers tend to express stronger disapproval of involvement in Iraq, consistent with their party's position. Indeed, assessments of the parties' unity or disunity were entirely and sensibly irrelevant for Liberal Democrat identifiers:

their own party's unity provided them with a clear signal on the Iraq issue, and given this clear signal, Labour's disunity was an irrelevant piece of information.

This pattern of results is one indication that Labour's disunity confused Labour voters, but (as discussed above) the possibility remains that the lack of any relationship between Labour identification and Iraq merely reflected the fact that Labour's electoral base was as divided over Iraq as Labour MPs. The interaction terms cast doubt on this interpretation. The first interaction term in the second specification is between the respondent's perception of the Labour Party as disunited and the respondent's level of political information. Calculating the conditional standard errors of the *Labour disunited × Respondent's political information* interaction (from the second specification) shows that Labour disunity was related to disapproval of involvement in Iraq *among Labour identifiers with above-median levels of political information*. The relationship comes through clearly in Figure 6.1, which shows the marginal effect of Labour's disunity when modified by the voter's level of political information. Once the voter's level of political information exceeds a score of five (i.e., the voter answered at least five of eight factual questions correctly), both 90 per cent confidence bounds (the dashed lines) are below zero, indicating a statistically significant, negative relationship. The second interaction term is between the respondent's level of political information and their ideological position on the left–right spectrum. Once Labour identifiers are separated into those with above- and below-median level of political information (labelled high and low information voters, respectively), this interaction is statistically significant, *but again only among highly informed Labour identifiers.*[9] This indicates that highly informed Labour identifiers saw the Iraq issue in ideological rather than partisan terms, *but only if they saw the Labour Party as disunited.* The evidence, then, suggests that the

---

[9] For highly informed Labour identifiers the marginal effect is $b_{R's\ L-R\ position}$ + $b_{Labour\ disunited\ \times\ R's\ L-R\ position} = -.035 + .094 = .059$. The associated standard error is .034, providing a t-statistic of 1.71. Splitting the sample in this fashion is not as statistically efficient as incorporating a triple interaction term (i.e., *Labour disunity × R's left–right ideological position × R's political information*) into the model, but the results are far easier to interpret. Of course, splitting the sample in this fashion truncates the variance on the political information variable and hence, for this quite predicable reason, the *Labour disunity × R's political information* interaction is statistically insignificant in the third and fourth specifications.

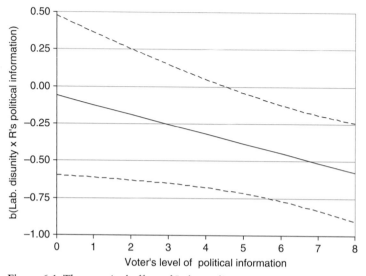

Figure 6.1 The marginal effect of Labour disunity on voters' views on Iraq by levels of political information

Labour Party's disunity contributed to both scepticism and confusion among the party's core voters. In the absence of a clear partisan cue, less politically informed Labour identifiers chose their positions on Iraq randomly. Only highly informed Labour identifiers who saw the party as disunited conditioned their stance on Iraq on their own ideological positions, and the net effect of their doing so was to lead them to disagree with Blair's stance on Iraq, all else equal.

Conclusion

These last results provide some confidence that voters' assessments of parties' unity or disunity are rooted, at least partly, in real parliamentary events. They also suggest that party disunity tends to present informational barriers to voters, and in particular to the disunited party's core supporters. This, in turn, bolsters one's confidence that the results presented in Table 6.2 are, in fact, a valid indication that a party's parliamentary unity or disunity has electoral consequences. It is equally true that disunity is not automatically damaging to political parties; the critical factor appears to be how salient or visible the party's disunity is to voters. If the party's disunity is publicly visible, however, the party finds itself in a difficult situation, one in which the party leadership's capacity to communicate with the party's core voters in the country at large is undercut by the actions of dissident MPs, whose dissension earns them the support of non-partisan voters in their districts.

7 | *Demotion and dissent in the Canadian Liberal Party, 1991–1997*

Those who have not witnessed the making of a government have reason to be happier than those who have. It is a thoroughly unpleasant and discreditable business in which merit is disregarded, loyal service is without value, influence is the most important factor and geography and religion are important supplementary considerations.

The Borden Ministry was composed under standard conditions, and was not, therefore, nearly as able, honest, or as industrious an administrative aggregation as could have been had from the material available ... There were some broken hearts – in one instance, literally. In others, philosophy came to the rescue, but the pills were large and the swallowing was bitter.

Paul Bilkey[1]

Introduction

One of the main predictions of the LEADS model is that, all else equal, dissent increases as office benefits became less available within the party. The aggregate-level results of Chapter 3 comport with this theoretical proposition, showing a negative relationship between the frequency and extent of dissent in the party and the relative size of the party's front bench. This chapter provides the individual-level analogue to this aggregate result. At the start of the 1993–7 Parliament, Jean Chrétien, the new Liberal prime minister, withheld government appointments from a large number of incumbent MPs. These demoted incumbents then went on to cast more dissenting votes in the Parliament than their colleagues. Electoral insecurity also contributed to Liberal MPs' dissension, but there is little evidence to indicate that the dissent was due to ideological disaffection, poor socialization, or a prior history of rebellion. Thus, what emerges from these data is a tight causal connection between the loss of career advancement and dissent. The

---

[1] As quoted in Ward (1987, p. 204).

150

results suggest that the distribution of preferment in the form of career advancement opportunities is the primary bulwark of party unity in the short run; when party leaders withhold or cannot provide their members with advancement, their ability to compel loyalty is diminished.

The Liberals' return to power

The 1993 election brought the Liberals into government with a substantial majority (177 of 295 seats). The victory ended nine years in opposition and came just two and a half years after Jean Chrétien succeeded John Turner as party leader. Chrétien did not make extensive changes to the shadow ministry when he took over the party, instead waiting until after the election and using his first governmental appointments to settle scores and pay off debts. John Nunziata, for example, had also contested the leadership when Turner stood down, but he had not had the foresight to throw his delegates behind Chrétien. The consequences, a long-serving Liberal MP noted, were predictable: 'Nunziata was not going to get into Cabinet, not in a hundred years. Remember, he was a leadership candidate against Chrétien.'[2] Many other Liberals who were in the House when Chrétien took over from Turner also found themselves pushed off the front bench.

Not all of this was purposive. Not every loyalist could be promoted, not every opponent punished. A convention of ensuring broad regional representation at the cabinet table and a promise to not repeat past excesses (previous Conservative cabinets had contained upward of forty ministers) constrained Chrétien's personnel decisions. Chrétien was also limited by the lack of experience within the parliamentary party. A significant majority (108 of 177) of Liberal MPs were neophytes, only six of whom had previously served in a provincial legislature.[3] Chrétien's dilemma was not simply that ministerial talent was thin, but that he had to forge a disciplined party from a group of people, two-thirds of whom were unfamiliar with the inner workings of the Canadian Parliament.

---

[2] I interviewed six Liberal MPs in November 1999.

[3] Another nine Liberal MPs entered Parliament later in the session via by-elections, all of whom are included in this analysis. Four other MPs were dropped, two because of their appointment to the Senate, two because they took on the relatively non-partisan offices of the Speaker and Deputy Speaker of the House, respectively.

The new Liberal government also confronted a challenging political environment. The country's dire fiscal situation forced the cabinet to pass several austere budgets and retract a promise to repeal the Goods and Services Tax (GST), policies that ran against the grain of the Liberal's economic instincts. Controversial bills on gun ownership, hate crimes, and pension reforms recognizing same-sex relationships were also pushed through the Commons to fulfil electoral promises. The overall policy agenda upset many Liberal backbenchers. Left-leaning Liberal MPs looked askance at the cabinet's budgetary policies, while MPs on the right of the party (many of whom had been elected only because the right-wing vote in their constituencies had been split between the Reform and Progressive Conservative Parties), questioned the cabinet's social policy agenda.

Not coincidentally, Chrétien presided over one of the more fractious Liberal governments in recent memory. Liberal MPs dissented on 16 per cent of divisions in the 1993–7 Parliament, and they did so in numbers, an average of between five and six Liberal MPs dissenting at a time. The dissent never jeopardized the government's majority, but by the end of the Parliament 97 of 177 (54.8 per cent) Liberal MPs had voted against the party at least once, and the dissension – and Chrétien's harsh response to it – was highly publicized. The contrast with how Liberal MPs had behaved in the previous Parliament was marked. Only 46 of 976 divisions in the 1988–93 Parliament (4.7 per cent) had witnessed Liberal MPs voting against their party, with no evidence to suggest that Chrétien's takeover of the party in and of itself incited dissent. It is this stark before-and-after dimension that makes this case a useful one. To the extent that one can isolate an individual-level variable that is not just correlated with Liberal MPs' dissent, but which also changed alongside the party's move to government, one can say that one has identified a *cause* of intra-party dissension.

Explaining the surge of Liberal dissent

The difficulty, of course, is that a number of factors changed alongside the Liberals' transition to government, and in consequence several possible explanations for the party's dissension might be advanced. While discriminating among contending hypotheses is ultimately an empirical exercise, the LEADS model provides a theoretical framework for constructing and evaluating alternative explanations for the

Liberals' dissent. The model serves, first, to encourage explanations that focus on the constraints that amplify MPs' incentives to dissent or blunt the impact of advancement or discipline and second, to evaluate the logical consistency of these arguments.

Policy constraints

One plausible explanation for the surge in dissent centres on the policy constraints under which the Liberal government operated. The country's poor financial situation dictated the government's economic policy, while manifesto pledges committed the cabinet to enacting a series of progressive yet controversial social policies. Chrétien himself had repeatedly stressed the inviolability of the Liberal's 'Little Red Book' (as the manifesto was known), so while it might have been possible to backtrack on these campaign promises, it would have been politically costly to do so.[4] As a result of these policy constraints the cabinet found itself wedged between left-wing Liberal MPs who opposed the cabinet's economic agenda and right-wing Liberals who resisted its social policies.

As accurate a description of the party's situation as this might be, the LEADS model warns against casting these policy constraints as a direct cause of the Liberals' dissension. The comparative statics of the model demonstrate that this sort of policy rigidity does not in and of itself generate dissent. Instead, policy constraints amplify existing incentives to dissent and force leaders to rely more heavily on advancement and discipline to make up for the fact that they cannot compromise on policy. These latter effects are the more likely causes of the Liberal dissension.

Sharpened electoral incentives to dissent

Electoral incentives to dissent were certainly present. While the Liberals remained broadly popular throughout their first term of office, the party's support was not evenly distributed.[5] Liberal plans to establish

---

[4] Indeed, Nevitte *et al.* (2000) show that breaking their promise to repeal the GST was the main reason for the Liberals' loss of some twenty seats in the 1997 election.

[5] The Liberals averaged an approval rating of 50.8 per cent in the opinion polls over their first term.

a firearms registry, for example, were highly unpopular in rural areas. Liberal MPs who had won in traditionally conservative districts also had cause to worry about what would happen at the next election if the Conservative and Reform parties were to resolve their differences and field a single, stronger, right-wing candidate. There was, in addition, a scheduled redistribution of district boundaries with which to contend. The redistribution threatened to force MPs into nomination (i.e., pre-selection) battles against other sitting Liberal MPs or push them into electoral battles against incumbents from other parties.[6] Liberal MPs caught in these nomination battles could too easily burnish their credentials as local champions by taking a run at the national party.[7] All of these electoral pressures generated incentives for Liberal MPs to distance themselves from the party and might well have been the root cause of the internal dissension.

A problematic reliance on advancement and discipline

The policy constraints would have forced Chrétien back on advancement and discipline to maintain unity. Both of these tactics were problematic under the circumstances. The basic problem as far as advancement was concerned was that the Liberal caucus was too large given the limited number of cabinet positions available. Expanding the cabinet while slashing budgets and preaching austerity to the country was politically infeasible, so Chrétien reacted instead by demoting a number of senior

---

[6] In Canada, redistributions ('redistricting', as Americans call it) are carried out by an independent electoral commission. MPs could not, therefore, manipulate constituency boundaries to avoid intra-party selection battles. This did not prevent Liberal MPs from trying to impede the passage of the redistribution legislation through the House. The redistribution actually caused only a few preselection battles, but the attention that the enabling legislation received from Liberal MPs suggests that they were quite worried about its consequences at the time.

[7] Canadian electoral law gives party leaders veto power on use of the party label. That said, a deeply ingrained tradition of local control of nominations severely limits the leader's ability to determine who will be the party's candidate in any given riding, and this makes it more likely than not that a sitting MP will side with the local rather than the national party in any sort of policy dispute (Sayers 1999, pp. 4–5). Certainly, several Liberal MPs faithfully reflected the socially conservative proclivities of their constituency associations in the division lobbies. One of these MPs, Roseanne Skoke, was involved in a spirited (but ultimately unsuccessful) renomination battle against another incumbent MP.

Liberal MPs from the front bench. Demotion was not fatal to these MPs' parliamentary careers, but as Appendix 4 shows, the farther they fell down the parliamentary career ladder, the less likely it was that they would be able to climb back to a frontbench position. Regaining a cabinet post would also take time, forcing these demoted MPs to further discount the value they attached to promotion and leaving them with commensurately less incentive to toe the party line.

Hemmed in on policy and with little advancement to distribute, Chrétien's only other option was to use discipline to control his MPs. The large influx of neophyte Liberal MPs blunted the effectiveness of this strategy. These neophytes had not been in Parliament long enough to become firmly attached to norms of party loyalty, to discover the limits of political independence in a parliamentary system, or to learn how to resolve their grievances within the party's private channels of communication. This lack of socialization left Chrétien reliant on a harsh and public brand of discipline that involved sacking several rebellious MPs from their committee positions and expelling another (John Nunziata) from the party altogether for voting against the budget. While this sort of summary discipline marginally dampened the scope of the dissension (see Chapter 8), it made Chrétien appear dictatorial. A more sociological hypothesis, then, is that the principal cause of Liberal disunity was a lack of socialization among the large cohort of parliamentary newcomers, which raised the marginal cost to Chrétien of imposing discipline.

These arguments suggest three hypotheses about the cause of the surge in Liberal dissension:

Hypothesis 1.   The dissent was generated by the electoral insecurity of Liberal MPs.

Hypothesis 2.   The dissent was due to Chrétien's demotion of a number of senior Liberal MPs.

Hypothesis 3.   The dissent was caused by unsocialized parliamentary neophytes.

Each of these hypotheses accords with a subset of the facts at hand and so there is no reason to privilege one of them over the others. Indeed, these arguments are not mutually exclusive. The surge in backbench dissent could, for example, be the result of actions by both demoted incumbents and poorly socialized neophytes. That said, each hypothesis identifies a different variable as the *chief* source of dissent. The first explanation roots the dissension in the electoral insecurity of Liberal MPs: the more precarious the MP's electoral or nomination position, the more likely the MP should be to dissent. The second hypothesis identifies Chrétien's personnel decisions as the cause of Liberal disunity, and it implies a clear link between demotion and dissent. The third explanation pinpoints a lack of socialization as the source of dissent, and it suggests that the dissidents were mainly (unsocialized) parliamentary neophytes.

Data and methods

I rely on a count model of the number of dissenting votes cast by Liberal MPs over the 1993–7 parliamentary term to adjudicate between these three hypotheses.[8] The analysis encompasses whipped divisions, that is, divisions in which MPs were under formal instructions to vote the party line, and divisions on private members' bills.[9] (Free votes are excluded by definition.) Divisions on private members' bills are not formally whipped, but are included because the mechanics of voting in the Canadian Parliament make the cabinet's position quite clear to government backbenchers. Canadian MPs do not vote by passing through division lobbies as in Britain, but rather by rising in their seats and stating their position, party leaders rising and voting first, backbenchers following row by row (*Annotated Standing Orders of the House of Commons* 1989, p. 150). A dissident Liberal noted the system's effects: 'A last minute flash of terror hits you when the prime minister turns in his chair and looks at you as you stand and vote against him' (*Winnipeg Free Press*, 15 June 1995). (In fact, Liberal MPs were so sensitive to these dynamics that later in the session they tried to change the pattern of voting so that the backbenchers voted before the frontbenchers!) The Chrétien cabinet, moreover, frequently took additional steps to control voting on private members' business. For example, the deputy prime minister circulated a pamphlet attacking C-216, a private member's bill to make negative-option billing of cable television services illegal, and

---

[8] To be precise, the model is a negative binomial count model.
[9] Dissent was not restricted to private members' business. The Liberals experienced dissent on 12.8 per cent of whipped divisions (versus 16 per cent of all divisions). All told, Liberal MPs cast 1,278 dissenting votes; of these, 523 (41 per cent) were cast in whipped divisions.

warning Liberal MPs not to vote for it (*Globe and Mail*, 25 September 1996).

The independent variables in the model are: (1) the MP's ideological position on economic and social issues; (2) the importance the MP attaches to party loyalty; (3) the MP's parliamentary experience; (4) the number of ranks that the MP was promoted or demoted; (5) the age at which the MP first entered Parliament; and (6) a set of variables measuring the MP's electoral security. Liberal MPs' ideological positions on economic and social policy issues are taken from Chapter 4, with lower scores on these ideological dimensions corresponding to left-wing positions. The ideological variables are primarily controls here, but according to the narrative above, Liberal MPs' dissent should be correlated to economic liberalism (i.e., a negative coefficient) and social conservatism (i.e., a positive coefficient).

The second and third variables measure an MP's exposure to parliamentary socialization. I estimate the MP's attachment to party loyalty with data from the 1993 *Canadian Candidate Survey* (CCS), the same data used in Chapter 4 to estimate Canadian MPs' ideological positions. Respondents to the 1993 CCS were asked to rate how important various tasks were to an MP's job. A factor analysis identified three tasks as key components of party loyalty: (1) supporting the party leader; (2) voting the party position in the House of Commons; and (3) defending party policy. MPs' scores on these items were rescaled and added to give a score between zero and three, higher scores indicating that the MP attached greater importance to party loyalty. Multiple imputation techniques were then used to deal with non-responses.[10]

In theory, the MP's attachment to these social norms results from a long-term process of socialization. Continued membership in the parliamentary party is the most obvious avenue of socialization. In other words, the longer the MP is a member of the parliamentary party, the more firmly norms of loyalty and solidarity become entrenched and the more strongly they constrain the MP's actions (Crowe 1986, pp. 168, 177). To capture this socialization effect, I enter the loyalty variable directly into the model and as an interaction with the MP's parliamentary experience, on the assumption that the effect of loyalty grows stronger over the course of an MP's career.

---

[10] I used *NORM 2.2 for Windows* to generate five imputation data sets.

The fourth and fifth variables measure the expected utility the MP attaches to a ministerial career. The number of ranks that the MP was promoted or demoted measures the deterioration (or improvement) in the probability of the MP building a ministerial career. This variable was calculated by coding parliamentary ranks and then subtracting the rank an incumbent MP held in the 1988–93 Parliament from the rank that he or she was appointed to in the 1993–7 Parliament.[11] (Neophyte MPs received scores of zero because, by definition, they could not have lost status.) Thus, the further down the parliamentary career ladder the MP slips, the more frequently he or she should dissent. In contrast, the MP's entry age should be positively related to the value that the MP places on career advancement. Entering the House at a young age marks the MP as a career politician (King 1981, pp. 262–3). Having forgone non-political careers, these MPs should prize a ministerial career more highly than MPs entering Parliament later in life and so should be warier of defying the party whip.

MPs who hold ultra-safe seats are unlikely to worry about the electoral effects of party policy and hence have little incentive to dissent. The MP's majority at the 1993 election is an obvious indicator of electoral safety (and one that should be negatively related to dissent), but as I have indicated above, it does not tell the whole story. The Liberals' 1993 electoral victory was partly due to the Reform and Progressive Conservative (PC) parties splitting the right-wing vote and so the safety of any Liberal MP's majority was contingent on the extent to which right-wing support in the riding was divided. The more even the Reform and PC vote shares, the more vulnerable a Liberal majority would be to a coalescence of the right at future elections. To capture this dynamic, I include in the model the fractionalization of the Reform and PC parties' vote shares.[12] *Ceteris paribus*, the greater the

---

[11] I coded parliamentary ranks as follows: cabinet ministers and shadow ministers = 6; junior ministers, opposition critics for minor portfolios, chief whips, and House leaders = 5; parliamentary secretaries and deputy opposition critics = 4; deputy whips = 3; committee chairs = 2; and backbenchers = 1. So, for example, an MP who was a shadow minister in the 1988–93 Parliament but who was left on the back bench in the 1993–8 Parliament would receive a score of –5. Other coding schemes did not substantially change the results.

[12] Fractionalization was computed as $1/(Reform\ \%^2 + PC\ \%^2)$, where *Reform %* and *PC %* are the Reform and PC proportions of the combined Reform and PC vote share in the MP's constituency. Fractionalization ranged between 1 and 2, higher figures indicating a more even split of the right-wing vote.

fractionalization of the right, the more electorally insecure the MP, and the more likely he or she should be to dissent.

Re-election was not the only challenge to Liberal MPs' political careers. Liberal Party rules normally protect incumbent MPs from nomination challenges, but the scheduled redistribution promised to force nomination battles between a few Liberal MPs. I measure MPs' vulnerability to a nomination challenge with two variables, the number of challengers that the MP faced for the nomination (this was almost always zero for incumbent MPs) and the dollar amount of 1993 campaign contributions. A large number of nomination challengers indicates a permeable local party that is vulnerable to branch-stacking and infiltration by single-issue groups (Sayers 1999, p. 35). These sorts of associations cannot be counted on to provide the solid core of supporters required to win a nomination battle.

There are two reasons to think that a high level of campaign contributions reflects an MP's ability to fend off nomination challenges. First, because the average individual contribution is only about $200, a high level of contributions signals that a constituency association has a large membership, and this is in and of itself a barrier to challengers. Second, the loopholes in Canadian campaign finance law that existed at the time allowed MPs to translate campaign contributions into unregulated financial resources that they could use for a variety of political activities outside of the campaign period, including nomination battles.[13] An MP's dissent, then, should increase the number of nomination challengers faced and decrease the amount of campaign contributions received.

I also control for the number of dissenting votes the MP cast in the previous Parliament (set to zero for new MPs). An argument can be made that any correlation between demotion and dissent in the 1993–7 Parliament is spurious, merely reflecting the fact that both variables are

---

[13] On average, private campaign contributions cover 95 per cent of candidates' campaign expenses, so the public reimbursement (for 50 per cent of expenses) leaves most candidates with a large surplus: the more money raised and spent, the greater the reimbursement and final surplus. Candidates must dispose of these surpluses by handing them over to the national party *or* their constituency associations (CAs), but as the Canada Elections Act (1974) does not regulate CAs, most candidates transfer their surplus to their CAs – whereupon all public accountability ends. The CAs' funds are then used in a way 'that is likely to be politically beneficial to the MP' (Stanbury 1993, p. 102).

functions of past dissent. Controlling for past dissent eliminates this possibility. The final control in the model is a variable counting the number of months that the MP held ministerial office in the 1993–7 Parliament. Ministers must maintain collective responsibility, and being on the government's 'payroll' is clearly an incentive to loyalty.

Results

The results of the model are presented in Table 7.1. I ran two versions, the first based on all Liberal MPs, the second on incumbent Liberal MPs only. This helps to locate the source of dissent in the party and to reveal similarities and differences in behaviour between neophytes and incumbents. Two main differences between the two groups of MPs are visible. The first difference revolves around preselection competition. The number of preselection opponents has no impact on incumbent MPs' propensity to dissent. The initial version of the model, on the other hand, has every additional preselection opponent increasing Liberal MPs' dissent by 21 per cent ($e^{.19} = 1.21$). This effect is driven by the inclusion of new MPs in the sample; these were the MPs who had just fought and won nomination battles.

Second, when all Liberal MPs are included, dissent has an ideological dimension. The more left-wing the MP, the more frequently he or she dissented. This ideological dimension disappears when the sample is restricted to incumbents because incumbents as a group were further to the right than new Liberal MPs and hence more comfortable with the cabinet's economic policies. The ideological diversity of the large Liberal majority appears, therefore, to have been one source of dissent. That said, the marginal effect of ideology on dissent is not large, every unit shift to the left on the ideological scale increasing an MP's dissent by about 5 per cent. Given the range of ideology in the parliamentary Liberal Party, this means that very left-wing Liberals (.25 on the left–right scale) cast only two more dissenting votes during the parliamentary term than very right-wing Liberals (6.5 on the scale).

Evidence in favour of the electoral hypothesis is stronger. Dissent has clear roots in MPs' electoral insecurity, increasing alongside fractionalization of the right-wing vote and decreasing in campaign contributions. MPs in ridings in which the Reform and PC Parties evenly split the vote (and in which Liberal majorities were therefore more fragile) cast 35 per cent more dissenting votes than colleagues facing a consolidated

Table 7.1. *Negative binomial regressions of Liberal MPs' dissenting votes*

Covariate	Expectation	All MPs 90% confidence interval			Incumbents 90% confidence interval		
		B	Lower	Upper	B	Lower	Upper
Loyalty	–	.02	–0.10	0.14	.01	–0.20	0.22
Parliamentary experience	–	–.01	–0.07	0.05	–.01	–0.07	0.06
Loyalty × parliamentary experience	–	.00	–0.03	0.03	.00	–0.03	0.03
Left–right position	–	–.05**	–0.10	0.00	–.05	–0.16	0.06
Social conservatism	+	.10	–0.10	0.30	.12	–0.05	0.29
Change in parliamentary status	–	–.12***	–0.19	–0.05	–.14***	–0.23	–0.05
Entry age	+	–.01	–0.02	0.00	–.01	–0.02	0.01
Log(campaign $)	–	–1.01***	–1.70	–0.32	–1.34***	–2.18	–0.50
N pre-selection opponents	+	.19***	0.09	0.29	.10	–0.10	0.30
1993 majority (percentage)	–	–.01	–0.01	0.00	.01	0.00	0.02
Fractionalization of Reform, PC vote in 1993	+	.30**	0.05	0.55	.31*	–0.09	0.71
Months in ministry	–	–.01***	–0.02	–0.01	–.01***	–0.02	0.00
Dissent in 34th Parliament	+	.06***	0.02	0.10	.06***	0.02	0.10
Constant		6.19***	2.87	9.51	7.43***	3.38	11.48
ln(α)		–1.10***	–1.41	–0.79	–1.46***	–1.99	–0.93
Pseudo R²		.06			.11		
N		181			68		

Cell entries are negative binomial coefficients. Multiple imputation estimates follow a t-distribution with the degrees of freedom based on the proportion of missing data. The displayed confidence intervals reflect these facts and are calculated on the basis of robust standard errors.

One-tailed *p*-values:

* *p* < .10

** *p* < .05

*** *p* < .01

right. The amount of campaign funds raised by the MP's riding association also affected the MP's willingness to dissent: the richer the association, the more loyal the MP. The marginal effect of campaign contributions was quite large, especially among incumbents. Incumbents in the bottom decile of fund-raising cast 8.1 dissenting votes on average, those in the top decile 5.4 on average, a reduction of 33 per cent.[14] An appropriate interpretation of this result is, I would argue, that campaign funding reflects a combination of a local party's electoral strength, organizational capacity, and size. Hence, a wealthy riding association indicates that the MP possesses a large and solid base of political support and is therefore insulated from both nomination and election challenges.

The impact of electoral security on dissent is, nevertheless, dwarfed by the impact of changes in MPs' parliamentary status. An MP who climbed three ranks, from the back bench to a parliamentary secretary-ship, for example, is predicted to cast approximately 4.5 dissenting votes. Demote an MP three ranks, however, and the number of dissenting votes that the MP is predicted to cast over the parliamentary session rises to 9.5. The overall effect of a change in status of this scale (i.e. a promotion of three ranks versus a demotion of three ranks), then, is to double the number of dissenting votes that an MP casts – and the magnitude of this career-related effect is substantially larger than the effects generated by other variables. It is worth noting that this effect is driven by the behaviour of incumbent Liberal MPs, MPs whose status was altered by the reshuffle. Thus, we can infer that the surge in dissension was not due to a general shortage of advancement in the party as much as it was to the fact that the reshuffle pushed on to the back bench a number of veteran MPs who now had little personal stake in toeing the party line.

In contrast to the strong evidence supporting the electoral insecurity and career advancement hypotheses, there is no evidence favouring the sociological hypothesis. The MP's attachment to a loyalty norm appears unconnected to his or her propensity to dissent, and time in the House neither alters this propensity nor magnifies the effect of loyalty.[15] In short, there is no evidence that norms or socialization constrain parliamentary behaviour.

---

[14] These figures are computed with all other variables held at their median values.

[15] The interaction was tested as per Friedrich (1982) and Brambor *et al.* (2005).

Root causes of promotion and demotion

These results do not reveal the extent to which an MP's past behaviour influenced Chrétien's decision to promote or demote the MP. In light of this, it is worth pushing the investigation back in time and asking what factors influenced Chrétien's personnel decisions. Doing so reveals that changes in incumbent MPs' parliamentary status depended on two factors, support of Chrétien's leadership and political influence. These results provide a clear picture of the Liberal Party's internal politics, revealing a close connection between an MP's failure to support Chrétien's leadership bid, the MP's subsequent demotion, and finally her dissent.

The organizational dimension

The challenge in modelling Chrétien's personnel decisions is to separate political motives for an MP's promotion and demotion from natural organizational dynamics that lead to personnel changes. Older members inevitably step back from leadership roles because of weariness, poor health, electoral defeat, etc. and they must be replaced. This cannot be done entirely randomly; some attention has to be given to ambition, talent, and experience. Ambition and talent are difficult to measure, but the former tends to be correlated with a youthful entry to Parliament, and this variable is in turn closely correlated with career advancement (MacDonald 1987). Electoral success signals political talent, though it almost certainly picks up other factors, too. If, for example, the leadership views promotion as an investment in the party's human resources, they are unlikely to promote MPs in marginal electoral circumstances. To some extent, however, whether leaders discriminate against marginal MPs because of a perceived lack of talent or risk aversion is moot. The important thing is to control for such discrimination, if only to dismiss the alternative hypothesis that connection between dissent and demotion is entirely electoral in nature. I measure an MP's electoral security with the same variables used in the previous analysis, the MP's majority and the fractionalization of the right-wing vote. The MP's majority should be positively correlated with changes in the MP's rank; the fractionalization of the right-wing vote should, in contrast, be negatively related to such changes.

The MP's parliamentary experience is also important to consider. Although Canadian parties do not operate seniority systems, experience does play a role in the advancement and decline of MPs' careers. Few Canadian MPs move directly to the front bench upon entering the Commons (Docherty 1997, pp. 217–19). That said, an early start on the parliamentary career ladder is vital if one is to achieve a ministerial career. The effect of experience is curvilinear, then, aiding advancement at the start of a career, hindering it later on. To reflect this dynamic, the model includes the MP's parliamentary experience and its square.

Finally, MPs possess characteristics that make them more or less appealing to the party; sex, race, religion, language, region, and the like. Of these the MP's region is the most important to control.[16] First, it speaks to the fact that Canadian prime ministers must ensure regional representation in the cabinet. Second, region is a useful proxy for language and religion; even today most Quebec MPs are francophone and Catholic. I use three dummy variables to identify MPs as being from the West, Quebec, or Atlantic Canada. Ontario is left as the reference category because with the Liberals winning all but one of the province's ninety-nine seats, the province's overrepresentation in the Liberal caucus was a potential barrier to Ontario MPs' chances of promotion.

The political dimension

The organizational and representational constraints of cabinet-building in Canada are burdensome, but Chrétien still had room to manoeuvre. Government appointments could be used to repay debts, settle scores, and secure his leadership of the party. I use three variables to assess the political motivations of Chrétien's personnel decisions: the MP's support of Chrétien's leadership, the amount of campaign contributions received by the MP's riding association, and the MP's past dissent.

The first political variable is a dummy variable marking the MP as having supported Chrétien's leadership bid.[17] The Canadian Liberal

---

[16] The small number of MPs from some of the provinces makes it impossible to control for the MP's province; controlling for region is the best that can be done. Other variables, such as the MP's sex, educational level, language, and ideological orientation were tested, but had no effect.

[17] I assigned MPs into leadership camps based on the assessment of Professor Peter Regenstrief and the Liberal MPs with whom I spoke. Factional affiliation had no impact on how often MPs cast dissenting votes.

Party does not have formal factions, but it has identifiable camps of MPs. These camps are only weakly ideological, as the Canadian Liberal Party is intensely pragmatic, and are better seen as teams of MPs formed around prominent personalities for the purpose of securing the leadership. Who an MP supports for the leadership is incredibly important: MPs who back losing leadership contenders or who themselves head losing leadership bids are likely to be exiled to the back bench. (Recall the anecdote about Nunziata.)

The second political variable is the amount of campaign contributions received by the MP's riding association during the 1993 election. As I argued above (see footnote 13), loopholes in Canadian campaign finance law provide a strong basis for assuming a positive relationship between campaign contributions and the amount of financial resources available to the MP for unregulated inter-election activities. There are reasons to think that MPs could translate such assets into parliamentary influence. First, a wealthy riding association can serve as a political base from which to contest the party leadership; MPs possessing these sorts of resources are too dangerous to leave on the back bench, unencumbered by collective responsibility and free to foment rebellion. Second, Chrétien's two recent bids for the party leadership (in 1984 and 1990) had cost the prime minister approximately $4 million dollars (Stanbury 1993, p. 99). MPs could respond to Chrétien's resulting financial needs either by funnelling contributions to their local associations through the central party organization (thereby allowing the central party to take a percentage), or they could wait until the unregulated inter-election period and contribute to the leader's trust fund directly.[18] It is not unreasonable therefore to imagine that MPs who are particularly effective fund-raisers would (a) exert influence in the party at large and (b) be rewarded for their efforts.

The final variable in the model is the number of dissenting votes the MP cast in the 1988–93 Parliament. This variable is obviously included in the hope of dismissing outright the possibility that past dissent drove demotion (which, in turn, drove dissent in the 1993–7 Parliament). However, the substantive argument here is worth spelling out and it is that leaders punish dissent with demotion in order to discourage further rebellion. Certainly, this was how Liberal MPs to whom I

---

[18] The Liberal Party traditionally operated an unregulated trust fund for the party leader, to be used for a variety of activities (Stanbury 1993, p. 103).

spoke interpreted Nunziata's isolation on the back bench and eventual expulsion from the party.

Results

Table 7.2 presents the results of a regression model of promotion and demotion. The dependent variable is the number of ranks the MP lost or gained in Chrétien's reshuffle.[19] The sample is restricted to the sixty-eight incumbent Liberal MPs (because neophytes, by definition, could not have experienced a change in their parliamentary status).

The main control variables – the MP's parliamentary experience, age at entry into the House, and electoral performance – have no discernable effect on promotion or demotion. Nor does it appear that past dissent had any effect on the MP's career path. This null result is important in so far as it establishes that the effect of demotion on dissent in the 1993–7 Parliament was not spurious. On the contrary, this result clearly demonstrates that an MP's demotion at the start of the 1993–7 Parliament sparked his or her subsequent dissension.

The explanatory power of the model rests squarely on the variables designed to assess the political motivations for the personnel changes. Supporting Chrétien's leadership and possessing financial resources clearly offered the MP a better shot at advancement in the reshuffle. On average, Chrétien supporters emerged from the reshuffle one rank ($b = 1.12$) higher than MPs who had supported other leadership contenders. Financial resources exerted a greater marginal effect on MPs' career fortunes. With campaign contributions ranging from \$20,000 to \$135,000, financial resources could potentially move the MP up three rungs on the parliamentary career ladder. However, given the skewed distribution of MPs' campaign contributions, the average impact of financial resources was more modest, amounting to a promotion of between one and two ranks.

Conclusions and implications

The opening quotation from Bilkey is an accurate summary of these results – at least in part. Loyal service – if that is defined as toeing the

---

[19] To be clear, the dependent variable is $MP's\ rank_{35th\ Parliament} - MP's\ rank_{34th\ Parliament}$.

Table 7.2. *Multiple regression model of incumbent Liberal MPs'*
changes in status

Covariate	Expectation	B
Chrétien supporter	+	1.12**
		(.55)
Log(campaign $)	+	3.17**
		(1.55)
Dissent in 34th Parliament	–	.05
		(.06)
Entry age	–	.03
		(.03)
Parliamentary experience (years)	+	–.07
		(.22)
Parliamentary experience^2	–	.01
		(.01)
1993 majority (percentage)	+	–.02
		(.02)
Fractionalization of Reform, PC vote in 1993	–	.09
		(.89)
West		–.45
		(.85)
Quebec		1.57
		(1.21)
Atlantic		–.19
		(.85)
Constant		–16.94**
		(7.97)
R^2		.18
N		68

Cell entries are OLS regression coefficients with robust standard errors in parentheses.
*$p < .10$
**$p < .05$
***$p < .01$

party line – appears to be without value. Influence – in the form of
financial assets – is a far more important factor in career advancement,
rivalled only by demonstrated support for the PM. To be sure, this sort
of support is one way to define and think of loyalty, but it is not a
sociological one; it has little to do with the internalization of norms and

appears more as a patron–client relationship between a party leader and his or her supporters.

Indeed, one sees in the causes and consequences of Chrétien's prime ministerial appointments the terms of a fairly explicit agreement between party leaders and MPs: support in leadership campaigns is exchanged for advancement and advancement for support. When one side of this arrangement breaks down, so does the other. This conclusion rests on the quasi-experimental nature of the research design. We observe Chrétien demoting a set of incumbent MPs almost solely on the basis of their opposition to his leadership or their lack of political influence. These demoted incumbents then cast more dissenting votes in the subsequent term than their more fortunate peers. In addition, there is *no evidence* that these MPs were demoted because of past dissent. On the contrary, demotion was not a consequence of their dissent, but its principal cause.

The surge in Liberal dissent was also driven by MPs' electoral incentives. Thus, what fractured the Liberals' unity was a combination of professional frustration and electoral insecurity. Conversely, ideology appears to have exerted only a weak influence on MPs' behaviour and social norms no apparent influence. This does not imply that ideological tension or social forces play no role in intra-party politics. The ideological tension within the Liberal Party was necessary for dissent to occur – just not sufficient. Only when constraints on policy and preferment limited Chrétien's ability to fashion compromises within the party and amplified MPs' electoral incentives to dissent did rebellion break out. These constraints were clearly more binding on the prime minister – hence more immediate causes of the Liberals' dissent – than those relating discipline and socialization. Bear in mind, also, that the evidence here speaks to the short-run effects of demotion on MPs' parliamentary behaviour. Whether these demoted MPs reined in their dissension in the long run in response to increased discipline or social pressure remains an open question.

8 | *Discipline and dissent in the Australian Coalition, 1996–1998*

We're a bit more tolerant now. Expulsion is very messy anyway, and as a result it's counter-productive.

> ALP shadow minister commenting on party discipline, July 1999

Party discipline never prevented anyone from rebelling.

> British MP quoted in Jackson (1968, p. 187)

Introduction

Advancement may be the immediate bulwark of party unity, but it is not the only means that party leaders have of compelling their MPs to toe the party line. In the LEADS model, for example, the leader shifts from advancement to discipline as the cost of distributing preferment increases. Imposing discipline is costly, however: publicly punishing or threatening dissidents advertises the party's internal discord, and leaders who discipline dissidents too harshly may be seen as dictatorial. In the model, these costs are offset by lower levels of dissent. This chapter examines the extent to which discipline is in fact effective at suppressing dissent. I assess the efficacy of party discipline by studying the relationship between media dissent, party discipline, and parliamentary dissent in the Australian Coalition during the 1996–8 term. I show that by publicly disciplining some of the MPs who were engaged in media dissent, the Coalition leadership slowed the rate at which these rebels engaged in parliamentary dissent. This is an important result, because Coalition media dissidents were overwhelmingly MPs who lacked ministerial futures. A similar test conducted on the Canadian Liberal Party shows parallel results. We see in this chapter, then, how party leaders use discipline to control members after they have made clear that promotion is not forthcoming.

The Coalition in the 1996–8 Australian Parliament

The 1996–8 Parliament of the Commonwealth of Australia opened on 30 April 1996, the Liberal–National Coalition occupying the government benches for the first time since 1983. John Howard, the new prime minister, planned an ambitious legislative programme aimed at reining in trade unions, privatization, restricting Native Title (i.e., Aboriginal land claims), and, after a shooting tragedy in Tasmania, firearms registration. While the Coalition's massive lower House majority (the Liberal Party on its own held 75 of 149 House of Representative seats; the National Party contributed a further 19) provided the means to initiate all this legislation, there were soon indications of trouble. The Senate posed the most obvious obstacle: the Coalition's thirty-seven seats left the government one seat shy of a Senate majority and therefore reliant on the two independents who held the balance of power in the upper House. There was also internal opposition to the cabinet's policies, much of it highly public. Over the course of the term, thirty-one Coalition MPs explicitly attacked their own government in the media and threatened to vote against the party's policies unless there were amendments.[1] This media dissension did not pass unnoticed. Howard (or his ministers) reprimanded a number of the dissidents. On occasion, the discipline was formal, with Howard stripping some Coalition MPs of their committee assignments, intervening in preselections, or banning them from party conferences. This discipline appeared to be effective: only eight of the thirty-one media dissidents went on to dissent on the parliamentary floor.

Discipline or policy compromise?

There are, of course, competing explanations of why only a few of the media dissidents actually carried through with their threats. The Coalition leadership, knowing that it could do little to restrain the media dissidents, may simply have capitulated to the dissidents' policy demands. This counter-argument, while plausible, can be ruled out on logical grounds. On many issues the Howard government was pressured by two groups, a disparate set of disgruntled Coalition back-benchers and opponents in the Senate. In so far as elements of these

---

[1] Another eight Coalition MPs made veiled threats.

groups sometimes wanted policy to move in different directions, it is difficult to determine precisely with whom Howard was compromising. In the 1996–8 Parliament, for example, Howard's plan to limit Aboriginal land claims was criticized by both moderate and right-wing elements on the Coalition back bench, the former warning Howard not to extinguish Aboriginal claims, the latter demanding that he do exactly this.[2] In addition to these intra-party and intra-coalitional pressures, Howard required the vote of independent Senator Brian Harradine to pass the legislation through the upper house. Harradine was openly sympathetic to the Aboriginals' position, and he demanded, first, that time limits must not be placed on Aboriginal claims and second, that the legislation be made subject to the terms of the Racial Discrimination Act (*Sydney Morning Herald*, 2 December 1997). Howard acceded to Harradine's demands, ultimately removing from the bill the sunset clause on land claims and putting in another establishing the primacy of the Racial Discrimination Act – but he did so only after several Coalition moderates (including some senators whose votes were just as pivotal as Harradine's) urged him to negotiate with Harradine.[3] Thus, the first problem with the policy compromise explanation is that it is not clear whether Harradine or the Coalition moderates should be credited with forcing the compromise. The second problem is that Howard's compromise with Harradine (or the moderates) did nothing to assuage the concerns of the Coalition MPs who wanted Native Title eliminated.

The logical difficulties of the policy compromise explanation recommend a closer look at the effectiveness of the leadership's disciplinary efforts. There are two pertinent questions to ask of the relationship between discipline and dissent:

1. *Who was disciplined?* If the high level of unity ultimately achieved by the Coalition was in fact due to the leadership's ability to discipline the media dissidents, it has to be the case that the media dissidents were targets of disciplinary action. If they were not, it is hard to argue that these members altered their course of action because of party pressure.

---

[2] See, for example: *Sydney Morning Herald*, 23 October 1997; *Sydney Morning Herald*, 20 March 1997.
[3] *Sydney Morning Herald*, 18 June 1998; *Sydney Morning Herald*, 4 July 1998.

2. *Was the discipline effective?* Discipline could be effective in two obvious ways. It could act as a direct brake on rebel MPs, making them less likely to continue their dissension, or it might act as a party-wide deterrent to dissent, making other MPs aware that the leadership is prepared to punish insubordination. If discipline does not do either of these things, then one cannot maintain that party discipline changes how MPs behave.

Targeting dissidents

Taking up the first question, one can note that Coalition leaders disciplined ten MPs either formally (e.g., by stripping them of committee assignments, banning them from party meetings, or moving against them at preselection meetings) or informally (e.g., by threatening formal reprisals if the dissent continued or simply by telling them to shut up and toe the party line).[4] Only one of the ten MPs disciplined had not engaged in explicit dissent in the media. This means that twenty-two media dissidents were not disciplined. However, the disciplinary explanation does not require that the party discipline every dissident or that it respond to every incident of media dissent with an act of discipline. If party leaders' overriding concern is with portraying an image of unity to the public, then engaging in a highly public game of tit-for-tat can be counter-productive. Moreover, just as the police do not need to ticket every speeder to deter speeding, party leaders may not need to discipline every dissident to deter dissent. Nevertheless, there should be a positive relationship between dissent and discipline. A logistic regression of a dummy variable indicating whether or not an MP was disciplined on the number of critical media comments made by the MP provides a simple estimate of the probability of discipline:

$Pr(\text{MP is disciplined} = 1)$

$$= [1 + exp - (-3.17 + .38COMMENTS)]^{-1} \qquad [8.1]^5$$
$${-8.02} \quad {2.52}$$

Psuedo $R^2 = .19$
$N = 133$

---

[4] Appendix 2 describes the collection and coding of media dissent and disciplinary incidents.

[5] Figures in italics are z-statistics for the logistic regression coefficient estimates above.

These parameter estimates imply that there was just a 4.3 per cent chance that an MP who had not explicitly dissented from the party in the media would be disciplined.[6] However, an MP who made three publicly critical comments, about the average number made by media dissidents, stood a 12.6 per cent chance of being disciplined. It seems fair to conclude then, that the party targeted media dissidents for discipline.

Was the discipline effective?

Was the discipline at all effective in reining in media dissent? Qualitative evidence suggests that it was not. Of the nine media dissidents who were disciplined, only two dissented less frequently in the media after being disciplined, and in the case of Bob Katter, the most outspoken dissident, this was only because party leaders disciplined him just prior to the 1998 election leaving him no time to engage in further dissent during the parliamentary term. The far more common pattern was for the dissidents to continue or even accelerate their criticism of Howard and his government after being disciplined. Wilson 'Iron-bar' Tuckey, for example, began the parliamentary term by writing a public letter criticizing Prime Minister Howard's decision to allow the Australian High Court to rule on the coexistence of pastoral leases and Aboriginal land claims:

There is a disturbing rumour circulating that Cabinet has agreed that it is too hard to resolve the problem of pastoral leases extinguishing Native Title and it has decided to 'leave it to the courts.' I trust this rumour is incorrect. It would be an understatement for me to say I would be devastated to learn I am now part of a governing party that so lacks the commitment and intestinal fortitude that it is prepared to abdicate its legislative responsibility to our courts (*Sydney Morning Herald*, 11 May 1996).

Tuckey later went further and was quoted as calling the prime minister's tactics toward Native Title 'gutless'. This earned Tuckey a reprimand from the prime minister reminding him that the proper place to voice concerns with Coalition policy was in the privacy of the party room, not the media (*Sydney Morning Herald*, 22 May 1996). This did

---

[6] This could occur because an MP's dissent was unobserved, while the consequent discipline was reported publicly. My coding rules do not permit me to infer dissent in these situations.

not deter Tuckey in the least. The following month he described changes that cabinet made to the tax code without consulting its backbenchers as reflective of 'executive arrogance' and a 'callous disregard' for the role of MPs (*Sydney Morning Herald*, 14 June 1996). The month after that Tuckey urged state governments to ignore the restrictions on gun ownership that cabinet was introducing into law (*Sydney Morning Herald*, 11 July 1996). Throughout the remainder of the term Tuckey continued to attack Howard's approach to Aboriginal land claims. Most of the other media dissidents who were disciplined, even those who earned far more serious reprimands than Tuckey, behaved in a similar fashion.

It does not appear, then, that the Coalition's attempts at discipline were all that successful. At one level, this is not surprising. In the media dissidents, the Coalition leadership faced a group of MPs who had strong incentives to dissent. Many of the media dissidents were under electoral pressure because of Coalition policies. As Tuckey's comments illustrate, Howard's unpredictable handling of Native Title issues, limitations on gun ownership, and the removal of sugar tariffs were unpopular, especially in rural areas of Queensland and West Australia. These areas were also hotbeds for the nascent One Nation Party, a potential competitor to the National Party.[7] Howard's ability to respond to these electoral pressures was limited. When he tried to adopt a harder line toward Aboriginal land claims, for example, he was attacked by social moderates like Peter Nugent, a Liberal MP from the Melbourne area. Perhaps the media dissident in the worst situation was Paul Zammitt. Zammitt represented a very marginal electorate in Sydney, right next door to Howard's electorate of Bennelong. Aircraft noise was a huge issue in Sydney at the 1996 election, and immediately upon his election, Howard had the take-off and landing approaches to Sydney airport diverted from the skies over Bennelong, placing them directly over Zammitt's constituency. Zammitt's very electoral survival thus came to depend on verbally attacking his own prime minister.

There is probably no other MP in my entire sample for whom the trade-off between career advancement and electoral survival was as oppressive as it was for Zammitt. However, the career prospects of

---

[7] One Nation made no inroads at the 1998 federal election, but the threat was very real, especially in Queensland, where the party showed well at the state elections that took place in the middle of the parliamentary term.

most of the other media dissidents were also dim. Tuckey, for example, had been Andrew Peacock's lieutenant (Peacock's 'numbers man', as Australian MPs would say) when Peacock usurped Howard's leadership in 1987.[8] Bob Katter, an incorrigible National Party rebel who represented the rural Queensland electorate of Kennedy, arrived in the House at the relatively late age of forty-eight with commensurately poor prospects of advancement. Nugent had been demoted from the front bench by Howard when the latter took over the party from John Hewson after the 1993 election. Don Randall, an outspoken West Australian Senator, was a client and ally of Noel Crichton-Browne, an erstwhile Senator and a sworn factional enemy of John Howard's. The list goes on. In sum, the Coalition leadership faced a classic end-game problem with the media dissidents: the media dissidents had strong electoral incentives to dissent from the party line, and having already sent these MPs signals about their bleak professional prospects, the Coalition leadership appears not to have had the means to suppress dissension.

This situation thus begs the larger question of how party leaders control MPs after MPs' career prospects decline. The answer, at least on the basis of the qualitative evidence presented so far, is that the party cannot. Appearances may be deceptive, however. It might have been the case that media dissidents were simply so disaffected that no amount of discipline would get them to stop publicly attacking their own party's policies and leaders, but that by disciplining these MPs Coalition leaders could dissuade other backbenchers from engaging in such behaviour. Alternatively, while the discipline might not have stopped media dissidents from continuing to speak out in the media, it might have stopped them from taking their dissent a step further and acting against the party in Parliament (e.g., by voting against the party, abstaining ostentatiously, or defecting altogether).

It is very difficult to test the first hypothesis. After all, we know from Equation 8.1 that the more media dissent an MP engaged in, the more likely it was that he or she would be disciplined. The account of Wilson

---

[8] Tuckey's stay on the back bench was actually not a long one, and he returned to the front bench as minister for forestry and conservation in the following Parliament. Tuckey's case is a reminder that the relationship between dissent and demotion is not ironclad (see Piper 1991). It should be noted, however, that Tuckey was not a typical backbench MP, but a factional heavyweight whom Howard could not easily shunt aside.

Tuckey's dissent also indicates that media dissent is the independent variable here: MPs are disciplined because they dissent in the media; they do not, at least in the first instance, dissent because they are disciplined. Tuckey's story was not exceptional in this regard. Given these facts, showing that Coalition MPs who were not disciplined dissented less frequently in the media than MPs who were disciplined does not establish that the Coalition's disciplinary efforts were a deterrent to media dissent. This interpretation mixes up cause and effect. The correct interpretation of this sort of evidence would have to be that MPs who dissent less frequently in the media are less likely to be disciplined.

The second hypothesis is testable, however. Media dissent tended to precede dissent in Parliament. MPs would publicly threaten to act against the party on the floor of the House or Senate and then they would either carry through on these threats or not.[9] One can, therefore, sensibly cast media dissent as the initial (hence exogenous) step in a sequence of events that ultimately ended on the floor of the House with the MP dissenting or toeing the line, as the case may be. In theory then, if one regresses the number of acts of parliamentary dissent (i.e., dissenting votes, ostentatious abstentions, and defection) that an MP committed on the number of explicit anti-party media remarks that he or she made, one can estimate the rate at which media dissent translated into parliamentary dissent. One can add to this model a dummy variable marking the application of discipline to the MP and an interaction between this dummy variable and the number of acts of media dissent the MP committed. Of these two variables, the interaction is more important, because it informs one whether the rate at which disciplined MPs' media dissent translated into floor dissent was different from that of non-disciplined media dissidents. There are three possible results, each with different theoretical implications:

1. The interaction could be positive, indicating that the media dissent of disciplined MPs led to more floor dissent than the media dissent of non-disciplined MPs. There is not much that one could take from such a result. A positive interaction might indicate that discipline deterred non-disciplined media dissidents from engaging in parliamentary dissent, or it may be that the discipline simply exacerbated

---

[9] See, for example: *Sydney Morning Herald*, 27 March 1997; *Sydney Morning Herald*, 6 March 1997; *Sydney Morning Herald*, 29 October 1997; *Sydney Morning Herald*, 30 October 1997.

the relationship between rebel and party and fuelled an escalation in the cycle of dissent and discipline.

2. On the other hand, the interaction might be negative. This result would indicate that the application of discipline slowed the rate at which the media dissent of disciplined MPs, *and only disciplined MPs*, turned into parliamentary dissent. These results would suggest that party discipline is an effective but limited method of leadership. Discipline might solve a leader's immediate problems with a couple of dissidents, but would be difficult to use to quell widespread or chronic backbench rebellions.

3. Finally, the interaction term might turn out to be statistically indistinguishable from zero. This would indicate that the leadership's disciplinary efforts had no discernible effect on the rate at which media dissidents went on to engage in floor dissent. This result would imply that disciplining MPs is counter-productive: it publicizes the party's in-fighting without quelling it.

Data and methods

The dependent variable is the number of acts of parliamentary dissent committed by the MP. This includes ostentatious abstentions (n = 3) and defections (n = 3) as well as dissenting votes (n = 13). The key independent variables are the number of explicit anti-party media statements made by the MP (coding described in Appendix 3), a dummy variable for discipline, and an interaction term. The remaining variables control for additional factors that alter MPs' incentives to dissent, notably the MP's parliamentary rank, attachment to party loyalty, and ideological distance from the cabinet.[10] The latter two variables were generated from MPs' responses to the 1993 and 1996 *Australian Candidate Surveys* (*ACS*) (McAllister *et al.* 1994) and were constructed in precisely the same fashion as the ideological and party loyalty scales used in Chapters 4 and 7 (see pages 79 and 157). Appendix 2 provides further details on the content and construction of these measures.

Variables tapping district characteristics and electoral security are obvious additions here, but they need to apply in a valid fashion to

---

[10] Parliamentary ranks were coded just as in the previous chapter: backbencher = 1; committee chair = 2; assistant whip = 3; parliamentary secretary = 4; junior or non-cabinet minister = 5; cabinet minister = 6.

House of Representatives members and to senators. Members of the Australian House of Representatives are elected in single-member districts by the alternative vote. Australian senators, however, represent entire states and are elected via proportional representation from a state-wide party list.[11] Thus, while it is easy to identify district characteristics and measures of electoral security for representatives, it is not obvious how these measures apply to senators. I employ three variables:

1. *Electoral security.* For representatives this is just their first-preference vote share at the most recent election divided by 100 to give a measure between zero and one. For senators, I define electoral security as: [*party's quota at election* – (*senator's list position* – 1)]/ *party's quota at election.* Thus, for a senator at the top of the party's list (i.e., first on the list), electoral security is 1, implying that re-election is a certainty – and with the Coalition earning 2.67 quotas on average (and never less than 1), the top-listed senator is indeed assured of re-election. As the senator falls down the list, the electoral security score declines. This measure turns out to provide a similar distribution of scores across senators and representatives.[12]

2. *Agricultural labour force.* For representatives this is the percentage of the district's labour force engaged in agriculture. Senators receive state-wide averages of this variable. In so far as Howard's policies on Aboriginal title and firearms restrictions were unpopular in rural areas, this variable measures the electoral pressure on the MP as a result of specific party policies.

3. *Electorate–cabinet ideological distance.* Representatives have readily identifiable electoral constituencies, namely the voters and party supporters that live in the district. Senators have electoral constituencies too, though because these constituencies tend to be sectoral (e.g., business groups, farmers, etc.) in nature, they are harder to identify and characterize. I use two left–right placement questions from the *ACS* to address this problem. The 1996 *ACS* asked

---

[11] Formally, Australian senators are elected by single transferable vote. In practice, however, upward of 95 per cent of voters vote 'above the line', that is, for the list as set by the party.

[12] Representatives' electoral security scores ranged from .28 to .70 with a mean of .52. Senators' scores ranged from .25 to 1 with a mean of .70. This seems accurate as the top two spots on the party list are generally assured of re-election, but with an average quota of 2.67, the third candidate on the list is at risk. The main threat is that senators will lose their spots on the list at selection time.

respondents – House and Senate candidates – to place themselves and their electorates on a 0–10 left–right scale.[13] I take the mean self-placement responses of ministers as the cabinet's ideological position. I then use the absolute distance between the cabinet's position and the respondent's placement of their electorate as a measure of the ideological distance between the cabinet and member's electorate. This provides a more precise measure of electoral pressure for senators.

Results

The results of the Poisson regression model are shown in Table 8.1. Expectations for the variables are set out in the second column of the table. Thus, ideological deviation by the member or the member's electorate is predicted to incite dissent, whereas electoral security and normative attachment to party loyalty should suppress it. The first regression is run on all non-cabinet members. (Cabinet ministers are excluded on the grounds that they tend to be the ones meting out discipline, not receiving it.) The second and third regressions are run on subsets of Coalition members to ensure that the results are stable. The marginal effects of the variables are not immediately clear from these results as the model is not a linear one, so let me make some general points about the dynamics of the model before moving on to a simulation of the results. Few of the controls are significant, though there is evidence that dissent was partly driven by electoral insecurity. The results also show a strong positive relationship between media dissent and floor dissent – exactly as one would expect. Disciplining the MP disrupted this relationship entirely, however ($b_{MEDIA\ DISSENT} - b_{MEDIA\ DISSENT \times DISCIPLINE} = .83 - .85 = -.02$). In other words, if one takes acts of explicit media dissent as indicative of the MP's dissatisfaction with the front bench's policy or performance, then the dissatisfaction of disciplined MPs turned into floor dissent at a slower rate than did the dissatisfaction of non-disciplined MPs. This suggests that the media rebels reacted to discipline by curbing their propensity to engage in floor dissent.

The second and third regressions test the robustness of this general result. One worry here is that the interaction in the first regression is

---

[13] Survey items B7 and B8.

Table 8.1. *Poisson regression model of the relationship between parliamentary (floor) dissent, media dissent, and discipline in the Australian Coalition, 1996–8*

Covariate	Expectation	All non-cabinet members			Media dissidents			Media dissidents minus Katter		
		B	90% confidence interval† Lower	Upper	B	90% confidence interval Lower	Upper	B	90% confidence interval Lower	Upper
N incidents explicit media dissent	+	.83**	.10	1.56	.94*	−.04	1.92	.90**	.13	1.68
Disciplined	−	.57	−5.29	6.44	5.02	−4.68	14.71	3.93	−3.62	11.48
Explicit media dissent × disciplined	−	−.85*	−1.74	.05	−.88*	−1.80	.05	−1.24**	−2.37	−.12
Loyalty	−	−4.21	−10.55	2.13	−.02	−8.17	8.13	−1.44	−8.63	5.76
MP's left–right position§	+	1.87	−.68	4.41	1.48	−1.21	4.17	1.15	−1.17	3.46
Electoral security	−	−.86**	−1.64	−.08	−.48	−1.57	.60	−1.25	−7.01	4.51
Percentage agricultural labour force	+	−.72	−1.28	−.17	−.45	−1.06	.16	–		
Electorate's left–right position§	+	−.38	−2.37	1.62	−.54	−2.16	1.08	−.66	−2.49	1.17
Parliamentary rank	−	−.17	−1.20	.86	−.26	−.93	.42	−.50*	−1.04	.05
National MP		4.68**	1.46	7.90	.53	−4.84	5.89	−4.20	−9.15	.75
Constant		7.04	−4.04	18.13	−2.76	−21.25	15.72	−1.25	−15.77	13.26
Pseudo R^2		.75			.72			.58		
N		119			39			38		

Cell entries are Poisson regression coefficients.

One-tailed *p*-values:

* *p* < .10

** *p* < .05

*** *p* < .01

† Multiple imputation estimates follow a t-distribution with the degrees of freedom based on the proportion of missing data. The displayed confidence intervals reflect these facts and are based on robust standard errors.

§ These variables are expressed as deviations from the cabinet's mean position on a 0–10 left–right scale.

driven more by mean differences between disciplined and undisciplined media dissidents and loyal MPs (who neither spoke out nor voted against the party) than by any individual-level relationship between discipline, media dissent, and floor dissent.[14] If this were the case, however, the interaction effect should vanish once loyal MPs are dropped from the sample. This is done in the second regression, which is run using just the thirty-nine Coalition members who engaged in veiled or explicit media dissent. The interaction term is only slightly affected by this change ($b_{MEDIA\ DISSENT} - b_{MEDIA\ DISSENT \times DISCIPLINE} = .94 - .88 = .06$), and it remains statistically significant. Of course, in a small sample like this, statistical outliers can exert undue influence. Bob Katter, for example, committed twenty-two acts of explicit media dissent and cast seven dissenting votes (by far the most of any Coalition member) before he was finally disciplined near the end of the term. (It is unlikely that disciplining Katter earlier would have done much good; he was described to me by colleagues as 'mad as a cut snake' or 'the mad Katter'.) To ensure Katter's behaviour and subsequent discipline were not the only factors driving the results I ran the second regression again without Katter in the sample.[15] The results are

[14] One way to think about this is to imagine a scatter plot with media dissent on the *x*-axis and floor dissent on the *y*-axis. Coalition members are clustered in three areas of this plot. Members who engaged in neither media dissent nor floor dissent fall at the origin. Disciplined MPs (almost all media dissidents) fall in the upper-right quadrant of the graph; they had the highest mean levels of floor dissent according to the first regression results. Undisciplined media dissidents are located in the middle of the graph, albeit below the disciplined MPs and a bit off-centre towards the *y*-axis. In no group is there a relationship between media dissent and floor dissent (i.e., there are just three random clusters of MPs). The best-fit line is going to run through the group of loyal MPs near the origin and undisciplined media dissidents near the centre of the scatter plot. Similarly, the best-fit line that describes the effect of discipline on this basic relationship (i.e., the interaction term) runs through the loyal MPs and the disciplined media dissidents in the upper-right quadrant. This second best-fit line is, therefore, flatter than the first. One cannot take away from this result the fact that discipline slowed down the rate at which media dissidents committed acts of floor dissent; by definition, there is no relationship between media and floor dissent in any subgroup of MPs. The slope of the interaction is reflective only of mean differences between groups. Indeed, this would be quickly recognized if the loyal MPs were omitted from the regression because the relationship between media dissent and floor dissent would vanish once one controlled for discipline (i.e., the mean level of floor dissent among disciplined and non-disciplined MPs).

[15] A degrees of freedom limitation meant that the agricultural labour force variable had to be dropped from the third regression.

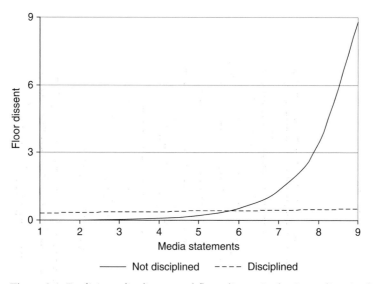

Figure 8.1 Explicit media dissent and floor dissent in the Australian Coalition, 1996–8

actually cleaner with Katter omitted, though the overall fit of the model to the data is not as good. These are important results because they indicate that the relationship between discipline, media dissent, and floor dissent is not spurious: discipline actually appears to have slowed the rate at which media dissidents committed acts of floor dissent.

The marginal effects of media dissent and discipline come through more clearly in a simulation. To show the effect of discipline on dissent I simulate the behaviour of a typical National Party backbench representative (not a senator). The effects of discipline on this National backbencher are traced out in Figure 8.1 using the coefficients from the second regression in Table 8.1 with the control variables held near their mean values for the set of MPs who engaged in media dissent.[16] The rate at which media dissent is translated into dissent on the floor of Parliament is very slow at first, but once the member moves beyond six acts of media dissent, the number of acts of floor dissent escalates rapidly. If the leadership fails to rein in the MP at this point, floor

---

[16] The precise values of the control variables are: loyalty = 2; MP's left–right position = 1; electoral security = .5; agricultural labour force = 4; electorate left–right position = 1.

dissent accelerates so that by eight acts of media dissent, the undisciplined MP is predicted to commit approximately three acts of floor dissent. Discipline, however, puts a complete brake on the rapid increase in floor dissent.

The strategy of party discipline

What does all this tell us about the strategy of discipline? It suggests, first, that the application of discipline is not random. Indeed, as I noted above, the distribution of media dissent is not equal across disciplined and non-disciplined media dissidents. Disciplined MPs were disciplined precisely because they criticized the leadership so frequently. Discipline also appears to have been effective. By intervening at a critical point, the Coalition leadership appears to have avoided a surge in floor dissent among media dissidents. This does not automatically make discipline a dominant strategy (i.e., one that is always worthwhile for the leadership to play), however. In the first place, there are costs to enforcing discipline, including a public image of disunity, the danger of appearing dictatorial, and the personal costs of facing down a colleague. (The fact that leaders tend to use informal rather than formal discipline and do not impose discipline in response to every act of dissent is indicative of these high costs.) In the second place, discipline has no effect on the party as a whole: it slows the rate at which the disciplined MP, and only the disciplined MP, dissents on the floor. There is no evidence that it has a wider deterrent effect. In this respect, discipline appears to be an effective, albeit inefficient, means of achieving party cohesion: it may be usefully employed to rein in a handful of mavericks, but the costs of disciplining wide sections of a parliamentary party almost certainly outweigh the potential benefits.

Alternative explanations

An alternative hypothesis to all this is that disciplined MPs, with their higher mean levels of media and floor dissent, may simply have hit a point at which there were diminishing returns to further dissent. One can imagine, for example, that the first few times that an MP publicly criticizes the leadership he or she makes headlines. Each additional outburst becomes less newsworthy, however, and so less valuable in terms of establishing the MP's reputation for independence. Indeed, in the LEADS model it is precisely at this point that the MP curbs her dissent – and quite irrespective of the leadership's actions. Thus, the MP's high level of dissent may have invited discipline, but this has nothing to do with the changes in the MP's behaviour and merely creates the illusion that discipline limited the translation of media dissent into floor dissent.

This counter-argument is not easily dismissed. Its weakness, it seems to me, is that dissent in the Australian Parliament is so low. If dissent were as frequent or extensive in Australia as it is in Canada and Britain, one could imagine MPs being at a point at which further dissent neither enhanced their reputation for independence nor helped them stand out from other MPs. In the 1996–8 Australian Parliament, however, only nine MPs dissented on the floor of Parliament. Moreover, the average number of acts of explicit dissent per media dissident was low, about four per dissident. It is plausible that there are diminishing marginal returns to media dissent, but it is hard to imagine that any Coalition MPs actually reached this point.

Replication: dissent and discipline in the Canadian Liberal Party

There are, however, two other points of concern. First, with only a few media dissidents taking the extra step to parliamentary dissent, variance in the data is limited, and this generates wide confidence bounds on the behavioural predictions set out in Figure 8.1. Second, media dissent statements are not hard data in the way that acts of floor dissent are. MPs either vote the party line or dissent, remain party members or defect. Media dissent, on the other hand, is based on what is ultimately the subjective assessment of newspaper stories. Although I have taken pains to stick to the coding criteria outlined in Appendix 3, it is possible that my results reflect the vagaries of my coding decisions rather than consistent behavioural patterns. Both problems imply that the results shown above may not be reliable.

As a reliability check, I replicate the analysis using the data on Canadian Liberal MPs. The first step is to determine if Canadian Liberal dissidents were targeted for discipline. A logistic regression model of disciplinary action on the number of explicitly rebellious media comments made by an MP indicates that they were:

$$Pr(\text{MP is disciplined} = 1) = [1 + exp - (-3.18 + 1.01COMMENTS)]^{-1}$$
$$-8.60 \quad 3.69 \qquad [8.2]^{17}$$

Psuedo $R^2 = .30$
$N = 181$

Thus, in both the Australian and Canadian cases, engaging in media dissent made it more likely that the MP would be disciplined.

The second step in the replication is to construct a model similar to the one in Table 8.1 to test the impact of discipline on dissent in the Canadian Liberal Party. If the relationship between media dissent, floor dissent, and discipline in the Canadian Liberal Party was also substantially the same as it is in the Australian Coalition, it would be difficult to dismiss the Australian results as a one-off occurrence. The Canadian model is not identical to the Australian one used above because some measures employed in Australia have no ready application or parallel in Canadian politics. However, just like the Australian dissent-and-discipline model, the Canadian model controls for an MP's ideological preferences vis-à-vis the cabinet (on the moral conservatism and left–right scales employed in Chapters 4 and 7), normative attachment to party loyalty and electoral and preselection situation. The variables used to assess the MP's electoral and preselection circumstances are exactly the same as those used in the previous chapter, namely,(1) the MP's margin of victory (percentage), (2) the fractionalization of the right-wing parties' vote at the 1993 Canadian election, (3) the number of contestants the MP had to overcome to secure the party nomination, and (4) the logarithm of campaign contributions the MP received at the 1993 election. The central variables in the analysis are, of course, the number of explicit acts of media dissent committed by the MP, a dummy for discipline, and an interaction between the two. The dependent variable is the number of times the MP voted against the Liberal Party on whipped divisions in the 1993–7 Parliament.

The results of the Canadian model are shown in Table 8.2. The main effects of media dissent and discipline and (most importantly) the interaction between the two variables run in exactly the same direction as

---

[17] Figures in italics are z-statistics for the logistic regression coefficient estimates above.

Table 8.2. *Poisson regression model of the relationship between parliamentary (floor) dissent, media dissent, and discipline in the Canadian Liberal Party, 1993–7*

Variables	All non-cabinet Liberal MPs	Liberal MPs engaged in media dissent				
		90% confidence interval[†]			90% confidence interval	
	B	Lower	Upper	B	Lower	Upper
N incidents explicit media dissent	.24***	.15	.33	.16***	.05	.27
Disciplined	.90***	.62	1.18	.81***	.41	1.22
Explicit media dissent × disciplined	−.19***	−.30	−.07	−.14**	−.26	−.01
ln(campaign $)	−.28	−.84	.28	.26	−.61	1.13
1993 election margin	.00	.00	.01	.01	.00	.01
Right party fractionalization	.26*	−.01	.53	.25	−.15	.65
N nomination opponents	.06	−.03	.15	.02	−.11	.14
Left–right position vis-à-vis cabinet[§]	−.06	−.14	.02	−.07	−.18	.04
Social conservatism vis-à-vis cabinet[§]	.08	−.10	.25	.17	−.07	.40
Loyalty	.03	−.13	.18	.02	−.12	.16
Time on government 'payroll'	−.01*	−.02	.00	−.02***	−.03	−.01
Constant	2.64	.01	5.26	.29	−16.52	17.11
Pseudo R^2		.24			.34	
N		150			54	

Cell entries are Poisson regression coefficients.
One-tailed *p*-values:
* $p < .10$
** $p < .05$
*** $p < .01$
[†] Multiple imputation estimates follow a t-distribution with the degrees of freedom based on the proportion of missing data. The displayed confidence intervals reflect these facts and are based on robust standard errors.
[§] These variables are expressed as deviations from the cabinet's mean position on a 1–7 left–right scale.

they did in the Australian Coalition (albeit at different levels), and they are all statistically significant. Just as in Australia, discipline appears to have caused Canadian Liberal MPs to curb the rate at which their media dissent led to floor dissent.[18] This relationship remains in place (though the interaction shrinks in magnitude from –.19 to –.14) even after the sample is restricted to the fifty-four Canadian Liberals who engaged in media dissent. In short, the Canadian results parallel the Australian results, a fact that certainly shores up my confidence in the statistical results and the reliability of the media dissent data.

There is, however, one point of difference between the Australian and Canadian results that deserves comment. Discipline in the Canadian Liberal Party only partially constrains the translation of media dissent into floor dissent (b MEDIA DISSENT $- b$ MEDIA DISSENT × DISCIPLINE = .24 – .19 = .05). The Canadian estimates suggest, then, that it is more accurate to see discipline as limiting floor dissent rather than suppressing it entirely. In so far as the confidence bounds surrounding the Canadian estimates are far tighter than those around the Australian estimates, it seems reasonable to adopt this more conservative view about the impact of discipline on dissent.

Conclusions and inferences

My inferences here are based on three pieces of evidence. First, Wilson Tuckey engaged in uninterrupted media dissent, Howard's public rebukes and veiled threats notwithstanding. Tuckey's behaviour was not exceptional. Thus, media dissent seems to be the exogenous variable in the relationship: it invites discipline. Second, statistical results show that disciplined Coalition MPs turned their media dissent (my proxy for their dissatisfaction with Coalition leaders) into floor dissent at a slower rate than non-disciplined MPs. Third, the same dynamic occurs in the Canadian Liberal Party, implying that the relationship is both reliable and general. Taken together, these pieces of evidence suggest that party discipline leads media dissidents to curb the rate at which they commit

---

[18] Not too much should be made of the mean differences between media and floor dissent in the two countries. This likely reflects a more crowded Canadian media market, one in which an MP's criticism of her party is relatively less newsworthy, rather than a systemic difference in the relationship between discipline and dissent in the Australian Coalition, on one hand, and the Canadian Liberals, on the other.

acts of floor dissent. Party discipline is an effective tool, it appears, for controlling the odd backbench rebel, but the lack of any deterrent effect beyond the targeted MP and the cost involved in applying discipline harshly or to many MPs at once still make it an inefficient means of forging and maintaining cohesion. Leaders have to employ discipline in a strategic and focused fashion.

9 | Career trajectories, socialization, and backbench dissent in the British House of Commons

Introduction

There is much truth to Enoch Powell's maxim that all political lives end in failure. Indeed, the vast majority of MPs never attain a cabinet position. Even the lucky few who do stand a good chance of finishing their careers on the back bench, their time as ministers cut short by reshuffles, leadership changes, or simply age. This points to an inherent end-game problem with relying solely on advancement to maintain unity: all MPs realize that there comes a point where advancement is no longer forthcoming and once this point is reached, leaders must find other ways to elicit their MPs' loyalty. Discipline is an option, of course, but as the results of the previous chapter indicate, it is at most a stopgap measure. Certainly, those who take a sociological view of parliamentary politics argue that party leaders deal with these conditions instead by cultivating among their members a voluntary commitment to norms of loyalty and unity (e.g., Kornberg 1967, p. 134; Crowe 1986, p. 180; Jackson 1987, p. 55; Searing 1994). Thus over time MPs come to feel a sense of duty to the party and to internalize the costs of engaging in undesirable behaviour. In this chapter, I use data on British MPs' parliamentary careers and voting records to demonstrate in a quantitative fashion that socialization into norms of party loyalty limits MPs' propensity to dissent once their careers begin to decline. These results demonstrate that social norms and socialization reinforce party unity once appeals to MPs' career ambitions have lost their force.

Career trajectories in the British House of Commons

One of the advantages to studying parliamentary careers in the British House of Commons is the sheer size of the institution. With turnover averaging 21 per cent of a 650-seat House of Commons, incoming cohorts of British MPs are large enough (120–70 MPs) to withstand

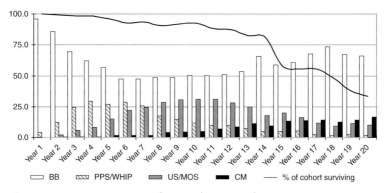

Figure 9.1 Career patterns in the British House of Commons*
*The sample encompasses all MPs elected between 1970 and 1983 and MPs from the 1964 and 1966 cohorts who stayed in office until at least 1992. Source: *Dod's Parliamentary Companion.*

attrition and leave enough data for statistical analysis. British parliamentary careers are also very stable, as Figure 9.1 indicates. Using data from Conservative and Labour MPs elected between 1964 and 1983, the graph traces the distribution of parliamentary ranks among a typical cohort of MPs over the course of their careers.[1] The data are aggregated by synchronizing the careers of each incoming cohort of MPs. For MPs elected to the House in 1970, for example, Year 1 corresponds to 1970; for MPs elected in 1983, Year 1 corresponds to 1983, and so on. Each year shows the percentage of MPs that hold positions as (1) backbenchers (BB) (including committee chairs), (2) parliamentary private secretaries (PPS) or whips, (3) under-secretaries (US) or ministers of state (MOS), or (4) cabinet or shadow cabinet ministers (CM). In an incoming cohort's first year in the House (Year 1), for example, 95 per cent of the new MPs are backbenchers, with only a small percentage holding a position as a PPS or a whip. The percentage of the cohort that survives

---

[1] The 1992 and 1983 cut-off dates may seem arbitrary, but reflect the availability of data. MPs' responses to the 1992 *British Candidate Study* furnish important data on MPs' social norms and ideological positions, and so it is important to have in the sample a large number of MPs who survived to contest the 1992 election and fill out the survey. The 1983 cut-off date is important because the redistribution preceding the 1983 election was especially far-reaching, making it difficult to obtain comprehensive data on parliamentary constituencies (especially in Scotland) prior to 1983.

in office is also shown on the graph so that one can tell how the base on which these percentages are calculated changes over time.[2]

There are three distinct stages in a cohort's parliamentary life cycle. Many MPs advance quickly up the parliamentary career ladder to intermediate positions during their first five years in office. The percentage of MPs on the back bench falls rapidly during this first term, but only during the second term (running from about Years 6–11) is it eclipsed by the percentage of MPs holding some higher rank. Indeed, between 25–30 per cent of a cohort's MPs will enjoy a spell on the party front bench as a junior minister or opposition spokesperson. After this point, however, the percentage of MPs holding these junior frontbench positions begins to decline. This is a direct result of a culling process. Most MPs return to the back bench, and from Year 12 onward (near the end of the MP's third term of office) the percentage of backbenchers plainly begins to increase again. Only a small stream of MPs, comprising about 15 per cent of the surviving members of the cohort, move on to the cabinet or shadow cabinet. These patterns and figures are not atypical, mirroring in many respects the results of previous work on British parliamentary careers (e.g., Willson 1959, 1970; King 1981; MacDonald 1987).

Figure 9.1 sets out in sharp relief the scope of the problem facing party leaders. Only a few MPs ever attain cabinet-level positions. Moreover, even if they enjoy spells as junior ministers, most MPs end their careers on the back benches. By Year 11, most MPs' career prospects are on the decline and future advancement is unlikely. Attrition through defeat, retirement, or death is hardly so high as to relieve leaders from having to deal with the logjam on the back benches. On the contrary, the limitations of relying exclusively on advancement to elicit loyalty are even more binding than Figure 9.1 suggests.

Table 9.1 shows the relationship between an early promotion (i.e., within four years of entering the Commons) and the highest rank subsequently achieved by the MP. The results are stark: almost a quarter of MPs who receive an early promotion make it into the cabinet

---

[2] The fact that the base reflects only those MPs remaining in the House from year to year is not a problem because these are precisely the MPs with whom the party leaderships must deal. Note that it is possible for the base to increase because MPs can enter the House via by-elections. Note also that the data run until 1996, so information on the 1983 cohort drops out after Year 14 creating a somewhat noisier series after that point.

Table 9.1. *Early promotion and career achievement in the British House of Commons, 1964–96**

Highest parliamentary rank subsequently achieved by MP

	Backbencher	Committee chair	Parliamentary private secretary	Whip	Under-secretary	Minister of state	Cabinet minister	N
Not promoted within four years	34.8 (90)	3.9 (10)	15.8 (41)	7.0 (18)	10.8 (28)	17.4 (45)	10.4 (27)	259
Promoted within four years	n/a	0 (0)	19.8 (37)	4.8 (9)	21.4 (40)	29.4 (55)	24.6 (46)	187
N	90	10	78	27	68	100	73	446

Cell entries are row percentages with raw numbers in parentheses.

* The sample encompasses all MPs elected between 1970 and 1983 and MPs from the 1964 and 1966 cohorts who stayed in office until at least 1992.

Source: *Dod's Parliamentary Companion.*

or the shadow cabinet.[3] In contrast, only one in ten MPs who did not receive early promotion achieved that high rank, and over a third of these MPs remained on the back benches throughout their careers. Thus, while Figure 9.1 gives the impression that MPs' careers typically stall late in their third term, Table 9.1 shows that for almost 60 per cent of MPs (259 of 446) the decline is visible by the start of their second term. For this large group of MPs the probability that they will enjoy high office – hence the expected utility that they attach to career advancement – is significantly diminished.

Several other factors compound the situation. Entering the Commons later in life, for example, severely handicaps a member's chances of achieving ministerial status (Buck 1963; King 1981, pp. 264–5), and demotion at any stage is, of course, damaging.[4] It is helpful conceptually to put these facts together by noting that at any given point in time, one can divide a parliamentary party into three equally sized groups, the first composed of new MPs starting their way up the parliamentary career ladder, the second firmly ensconced in frontbench positions, and the last sitting on the back benches after falling by the wayside. Only the first two groups can be expected to respond to career advancement incentives. In Britain, this would leave leaders of the two major parties without direct leverage over approximately 100 of their MPs on average, far too many to control via formal discipline.

Social norms, socialization, and dissent

If advancement and discipline were the only way to maintain unity, this large group of MPs who are beyond advancement and too numerous to discipline should be prone to dissent. Social norms, that is, shared expectations about appropriate behaviour (Kornberg 1967, p. 5), may nevertheless help leaders maintain control of the situation. Norms can help by imposing obligations on the MP toward the party and its leaders (Crowe 1986, p. 163). Leaders can then prevail on the MP's sense of duty to build unity. Over time, MPs may also come to see their leaders' expectations of loyalty and deference as legitimate and valuable goals

---

[3] This is not because these MPs rose straight to the cabinet. Figure 9.1 makes clear that these early promotions tend to be to the lower rungs of the parliamentary career ladder.

[4] The effects of age and early promotion are independent, however: even MPs who entered the House in their forties benefited substantially from an early promotion.

(Crowe 1986, p. 165). In both cases, social norms lower the cost to the leadership of maintaining unity and in so doing ease leaders' reliance on advancement and formal discipline. Thus, to the extent that socialization is effective, MPs may remain loyal even after their career prospects decline.

In saying that socialization is 'effective' one must distinguish between the process by which the MP acquires social norms and the norms themselves. Socialization refers to the process of exposure or learning through which MPs acquire certain norms. Membership in the parliamentary party is the most obvious avenue of socialization, and it is for this reason that statistical analyses of legislative socialization tend to use the MP's time in office as a proxy for socialization (e.g., Mughan *et al.* 1997).[5] The premise is that the longer an MP is in parliament, the more firmly norms of party loyalty become entrenched in the MP's mind, and hence the more strongly they should constrain the MP's actions. Knowing how long an MP has been in parliament does not, however, tell one what norms an MP values or how intensely they value them. First, as Asher (1973, p. 512) points out, MPs may come to office already well socialized. Indeed, extended membership in the extra-parliamentary party or party training programmes for prospective parliamentary candidates provide MPs with a means of learning about parliamentary and party norms before they actually arrive in parliament. Moreover, simply because the MP comes to know certain social norms does not mean that the MP sees them as a prescription for behaviour (Kirkpatrick and McLemore 1977). Thus, the MP's time in parliament is neither necessary nor sufficient for socialization to be effective. It is more precise to say that socialization is effective when MPs come to value the 'right' norms, to wit, loyalty, solidarity, and deference to leadership – and it is these norms rather than the amount of time the MP spends in parliament that constrain the MP's behaviour. This argument suggests the following hypothesis:

Hypothesis 1   (the direct effect of social norms). The greater the importance the MP attaches to norms of party loyalty, the less the MP dissents, *ceteris paribus* (including, importantly, the MP's career prospects).

---

[5] This can be contrasted with interpretive analyses of socialization (e.g., Crowe 1983; Searing 1994), which tend to use interview or survey data to measure social norms and roles.

The constant exposure to social norms and repetition of normatively appropriate behaviour that comes with time in parliament may, however, amplify the effect of social norms. This suggests a second hypothesis:

Hypothesis 2 (socialization). The constraining effect of party loyalty on dissent grows stronger the longer the MP is in parliament.

One might also wish to venture further and posit that the longer the MP remains in parliament, the less the MP dissents. This is a reasonable hypothesis to the extent that membership in the parliamentary party is the most obvious avenue of socialization. Even so, as I have pointed out above, lengthy parliamentary service is neither necessary nor sufficient for socialization. Moreover, there are many alternative hypotheses for why dissent might decline over the course of an MP's parliamentary tenure. It could well be, for example, that long-serving MPs stop dissenting because after twenty years they simply grow tired of jousting with party leaders or that they hope to translate their loyalty into a post-parliamentary sinecure. Thus, one cannot draw any inferences about socialization *per se* from a negative relationship between parliamentary tenure and dissent. This is not to say that evidence to this effect is irrelevant. On the contrary, data that show that MPs rein in their dissent over time signal that party leaders are, in some fashion or another, able to overcome the end-game problem inherent in advancement.

Data and methods

I test these hypotheses against data from a panel of British Conservative and Labour MPs elected between 1964 and 1983 who remained in the House as of the 1992 election. Data on these MPs' parliamentary careers and voting records are recorded on an annual basis from the time they entered the House until their defeat, death, or retirement.[6] (Those MPs who survived the 1992 election are followed until the next election in 1997.) To avoid limiting the sample to MPs who continuously contested and won elections, I also include all MPs from the 1970, 1974, 1979, and 1983 cohorts who survived to contest the 1983

---

[6] The dissent data employed in this chapter are from Norton and Cowley's data set, *Dissension in the House of Commons, 1979–92*, and *Dissension in the House of Commons, 1992–97*, ECSR Study Nos. 3929 and 4055, respectively. Dissent data for the 1964–79 period were taken from Norton (1975) and Norton (1980).

election.[7] This places in the sample a large number of MPs who either voluntarily retired or lost elections.

The statistical analysis of these data is not straightforward. The most serious problem is that MPs' voting behaviour is endogenous to their career prospects. All else equal (e.g., the MP's ideological position and electoral security), the MP toes the line when he or she is confident that promotion is forthcoming. Correspondingly, party leaders tend to promote MPs who toe the party line. I deal with this problem via two-stage least squares. A first-stage equation estimates the MP's parliamentary rank in a given year ($Rank_{it}$). $Rank$ is measured with the same seven-category scale used in Table 9.1. Thus, backbench MPs are scored 1, select committee chairs, 2, all the way up to cabinet or shadow cabinet ministers, who are scored 7. A second-stage equation estimates the number of dissenting votes the MP cast in that year ($Dissent_{it}$).

In light of the panel structure of the data set, the model is estimated as a random-effects model. The chief reason I employ a random-effects model as opposed to a fixed-effects model is that the former is able to incorporate information on the importance the MP attaches to party loyalty ($Loyalty_i$), while the latter cannot. The problem with the fixed-effects model is that $Loyalty$ is measured at one point in time (i.e., it is a fixed effect), so it drops out of fixed-effects models as a result of collinearity. Note, however, the random- and fixed-effects models return broadly similar coefficients for the other variables in the model and I report both sets of coefficients.

A third statistical complication is that the number of dissenting votes an MP casts is a count variable. Applying a least squares estimator to a count variable can result in inconsistent estimates (King 1988). Taking the natural logarithm of dissenting votes (as I do here) ensures that the model provides non-negative estimates, but it does not correct the underlying statistical problem. There is no easy solution to this problem. No standard instrumental variable estimator for count models exists, and yet instrumental methods are imperative here given the endogeneity between dissent and career advancement. My response to this problem is to bootstrap the coefficients and standard errors so that they do not depend on unmet distributional assumptions.

---

[7] Footnote 1 above explains why the 1992 and 1983 cut-off dates were chosen.

Modelling MPs' career prospects

The dependent variable in the first-stage career prospects model is the MP's rank in a given year, $Rank_{it}$. The MP's age (Age_{it}), first-term promotion ($Early\ promotion_i$), or demotion ($Demoted_{it}$) all provide relevant information on the MP's career prospects as per the discussion above. The MP's rank in the previous year ($Rank_{t-1}$) and the number of years the MP has spent in that rank ($Years\ in\ rank_{it}$) provide additional information on the MP's career trajectory. The longer the MP is in a given rank, the more likely he or she is to move to another rank, and if the MP is already at or near the top of the career ladder, the move (as the data in Figure 9.1 suggest) is likely to be downward. The MP's party's seat share ($Party\ seat\ \%_{it}$) provides a sense of the competition the MP faces for spots on the party front bench. The larger the party's seat share in a given Parliament, the more intense the competition for promotion. Finally, the model includes the logarithm of the number of dissenting votes the MP casts in that year ($ln\ Dissent_{it}$)and in the previous year ($ln\ Dissent_{it-1}$). Plainly, the first of these variables is endogenous to the MP's current rank, and hence it is instrumented.

Modelling MPs' dissent

The dependent variable in the second-stage dissent model is the natural logarithm of the number of dissenting votes the MP casts in a given year.[8] The central independent variables in this model are the MP's adherence to a norm of party loyalty ($Loyalty_i$) and the number of years the MP has served in the House ($Tenure_{it}$). The *Loyalty* variable was constructed using data from the 1992 *BCS*. The survey asked MPs the importance they placed on various aspects of an MP's job (e.g., constituency service, party activity, and the like). A factor analysis connected three items in this battery of questions to party loyalty: the importance that the MP attached to (a) voting the party line in Parliament, (b) defending party policy, and (c) supporting the party leader. MPs' scores on these three items were then used to construct a three-point loyalty scale identical to that used in Chapter 7 on the Canadian Liberals (see page 157).[9] Thus, high scores on the *Loyalty*

---

[8] A constant of .1 is added to ensure that the dependent variable is defined for MPs who cast no dissenting votes.

[9] See Appendix 2 for further details on this scale.

variable indicate that the MP places great importance on voting the party line, supporting the party leader, and defending party policy. In theory, the more importance an MP places on these norms, the less the MP should dissent. Interacting *Loyalty* with *Tenure* allows the constraining effect of *Loyalty* on dissent to vary over time. The expectation is, of course, that this constraining effect grows stronger the longer the MP serves in Parliament. This effect, especially, would seem to be prima-facie evidence of socialization.

The remaining variables in the model control for other factors that affect dissent. One set of variables controls for electoral incentives to dissent. The MP's majority at the previous election ($Majority_{it-1}$) provides a measure of the MP's own electoral security, whilst the party's mean level of popularity through the year ($Popularity_t$) and the change in that level from the previous year ($\Delta Popularity_t$) give one a sense of the electoral security of the party as a whole.[10] Finally, the percentage of strong party identifiers in the electorate (% *Strong party ID$_t$*) controls for the incentives to dissent that are generated by dealignment. This variable also picks up the generally increasing trend in the dissent data.

Ideological pressures to dissent are measured using the British left–right scale employed in Chapter 4. For every Parliament, I record the absolute deviation between the MP's ideological position and the party's mean ideological position (*Ideological position$_{it}$*). Thus while the MP's ideological position is measured just once (with data from the 1992 *BCS*), the MP's position vis-à-vis his or her party can still vary over time because of changes in the composition of the parliamentary party. Dummy variables control for the party's government status (*Government status$_t$*) and the MP's party affiliation (*Labour MP$_i$*). The last variable in the model is the MP's parliamentary rank in that year (*Rank$_{it}$*), or, more precisely, predicted parliamentary rank given its endogeneity to dissent.

Results

The results of the career prospects and dissent models are presented in Tables 9.2 and 9.3, respectively. Both tables report results for

---

[10] These data are obtained from the Gallup poll data recorded in Butler and Butler (1994), supplemented by data from MORI polls (www.ipsos-mori.com/polls/trends/voting-all-trends.shtml).

Table 9.2. *Two-stage least squares estimates of parliamentary career prospects in the British House of Commons*

Covariate	Random effects B	95% confidence interval[†] Lower	Upper	Fixed effects B	95% confidence interval Lower	Upper
Age_{it}	$-.01^{***}$	$-.02$	$-.01$	$-.02^{***}$	$-.03$	$-.02$
Early promotion$_{it}$	$.59^{***}$	$.47$	$.74$	1.03^{***}	$.91$	1.15
Demotion$_{it}$	$-.17^{**}$	$-.30$	$-.04$	$-.22^{***}$	$-.36$	$-.08$
Years in rank$_{it}$	$-.02^{***}$	$-.02$	$-.01$	$.00$	$-.02$	$.01$
Rank$_{t-1}$	$.76^{***}$	$.72$	$.79$	$.65^{***}$	$.62$	$.68$
Party seat %$_{it}$	$.00^{**}$	$-.01$	$.00$	$.00$	$.00$	$.01$
Dissent$_{it-1}$	$-.05^{***}$	$-.09$	$-.02$	$-.08^{**}$	$-.06$	$-.01$
Dissent$_{it}$	$.06$	$-.04$	$.16$	$-.03$	$-.19$	$.02$
Constant	1.46^{***}	1.21	1.72	1.45^{***}	1.03	1.86
R^2 within	$.57$			$.60$		
R^2 between	$.97$			$.88$		
R^2 overall	$.76$			$.74$		
N observations	$7,187$			$7,187$		
N MPs	445			445		

One-tailed *p*-values
[*]$p < .10$
[**]$p < .05$
[***]$p < .01$
p-values and confidence intervals are based on the bootstrapped standard errors.
[†] Percentile confidence intervals from 1,000 bootstrap samples.

random-effects and fixed-effects model, though I rely primarily on the former. The high R^2 statistics for the career prospects model indicate that it does a good job of predicting MPs' parliamentary ranks. Thus the model generates a high-quality instrument for the dissent model. The main result is the persistence of parliamentary career paths (as evidenced by the strong positive coefficient on the MP's lagged rank). Even so, the variables discussed above, early promotion, age, demotion, and the like, still have visible and expected effects on the MP's parliamentary career status. It is also clear from the results that dissent travels alongside poor career prospects, though it appears that lagged dissent rather than contemporaneous dissent is the better predictor of the MP's

Table 9.3. *Two-stage least squares estimates of backbench dissent in the British House of Commons*

Covariate	Random effects			Fixed effects		
		95% confidence interval[†]			95% confidence interval	
	B	Lower	Upper	B	Lower	Upper
Loyalty$_i$	$-.14^{**}$	$-.25$	$-.01$	–		
Tenure$_{it}$	$-.05^{***}$	$-.07$	$-.03$	$-.09^{***}$	$-.11$	$-.06$
Loyalty$_i$ × tenure$_{it}$	$-.01$	$-.01$	$.00$	$-.01$	$-.02$	$.00$
Majority$_{t-1}$	$-.01^{***}$	$-.01$	$.00$	$-.01^{***}$	$-.01$	$.00$
Party popularity$_t$	$.00$	$-.01$	$.00$	$-.01^{***}$	$-.01$	$.00$
Δ party popularity$_t$	$-.01$	$-.01$	$.00$	$.00$	$-.01$	$.00$
Percentage strong party ID$_t$	$-.07^{***}$	$-.08$	$-.06$	$-.11^{***}$	-013	$-.10$
Ideological position$_{it}$	$.06^{***}$	$.02$	$.09$	$.12^{**}$	$.02$	$.23$
Rank$_{it}$	$-.34^{***}$	$-.36$	$-.32$	$-.32^{***}$	$-.35$	$-.29$
Government status$_t$	$.02$	$-.08$	$.12$	$.12^{*}$	$.02$	$.23$
Labour MP$_i$	$.87^{***}$	$.77$	$.98$	–		
Constant	1.08^{***}	$.61$	1.52	3.35^{***}	2.76	3.94
R^2 within		$.13$			$.14$	
R^2 between		$.36$			$.09$	
R^2 overall		$.21$			$.12$	
N observations		$7,187$			$7,187$	
N MPs		445			445	

One-tailed p-values
$^{*}p<.10$
$^{**}p<.05$
$^{***}p<.01$
p-values and confidence intervals are based on the bootstrapped standard errors.
[†] Percentile confidence intervals from 1,000 bootstrap samples.

career prospects. This negative relationship between career prospects and dissent is not a surprising result, but it is a reassuring one, none the less. There are some minor differences between the random and fixed effects estimates, but nothing so serious as to suggest gross misspecification.

The career prospects results are included for interest and completeness; the dissent model in Table 9.3 is the centrepiece of the analysis. Career trajectory has a statistically significant impact on dissent, with every rank the MP climbs on the parliamentary ladder reducing the number of dissenting votes cast in a year by 0.34 votes. Now this marginal effect is not linear, but for an MP who cast 1.68 dissenting votes per year (the sample average), a promotion of one rank would suppress the MP's dissent by about 0.4 dissenting votes each year. This is not a massive reduction, but to the extent that it reflects the same pattern between dissent and career prospects that is observed in previous chapters it builds confidence in the results.

It is the relationship between the MP's dissent, party loyalty, and parliamentary tenure that is of primary interest here, however. The fixed-effects results are of limited utility in this regard because, as mentioned above, the *Loyalty* variable is itself a fixed effect across MPs. Still, the random-effects results show that the more normative importance the MP attached to party loyalty, the less the MP dissented. The negative sign on the interaction also indicates that this effect grew stronger over the course of the MP's tenure in the House. The marginal effects and statistical significance of these variables cannot be judged directly from these results, and so this is done graphically in Figure 9.2. The bold line in Figure 9.2 traces the marginal effect of party loyalty on dissent over the MP's tenure; the dashed lines bracketing the bold line delimit the boundaries of the corresponding 95 per cent confidence interval. Plainly, the marginal effect of loyalty on dissent becomes increasingly negative over time, and as the tight confidence bounds around this estimate suggest, the result is statistically significant.

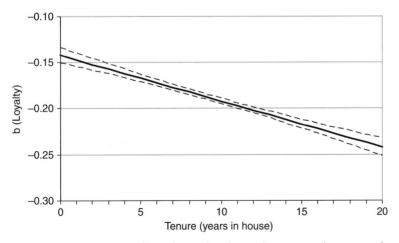

Figure 9.2 The marginal effect of party loyalty on dissent over the course of an MP's parliamentary tenure

Statistical and substantive significance are not equivalent, of course. A central substantive issue is the power of social norms and socialization relative to career self-interest in shaping parliamentary behaviour. The counterfactual question at hand is how does an MP with no sense of party loyalty behave after being demoted. To answer this question I construct a series of predicted voting records for a hypothetical MP using the random-effects coefficients in Table 9.3. The MP's career path for these scenarios is made close to that traced out in Figure 9.1: the MP sits on the back bench for the first three years in office, is promoted to PPS in the fourth year, and then again to under-secretary in the seventh year. The MP holds this rank until their eleventh year in office, when they are demoted to the back bench.[11] In a baseline scenario the MP is given a score of 1.5 on the three-point loyalty scale. This allows party loyalty some scope to restrain the MP's post-demotion dissent. In a second scenario the MP's party loyalty score is set to zero so that it cannot affect dissent. The knock-on effect of this constraint is that the interaction between *Loyalty* and *Tenure* is also set to zero, though the direct impact of tenure on dissent (which may or may not reflect socialization) is left unchanged. Thus, the second scenario gives one a sense of how the MP behaves when shorn of party loyalty norms.

The hypothetical voting records are shown in Figure 9.3. Promotion has a noticeable impact on dissent. Once the MP is promoted in the fourth year, dissent drops by 0.5 votes per year, and it drops a further 0.3 votes to near zero when the MP is promoted to under-secretary in the seventh year. Demotion produces exactly the opposite effect, with dissent jumping by about 0.5 votes in the twelfth year, when the MP returns to the back bench. (These figures may seem small, but one dissenting vote per year – so four to five per Parliament – would in fact mark a British MP as fairly rebellious.) The importance the MP attaches to norms of party loyalty also makes a difference, however, the absence of any sense of party loyalty increasing the MP's dissent by anywhere from 25–50 per cent over the course of the MP's career. In

---

[11] The remaining control variables in the model are set at values typical of the sample, the MP's majority to 10 per cent, party popularity to 40 per cent with an annual change of –0.5 per cent, ideological distance vis-à-vis the party to 2. Government status and Labour Party affiliation were also assumed. These values were all within the inter-quartile values of the sample.

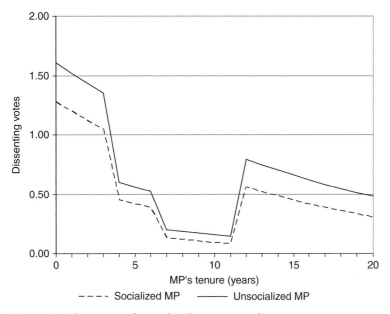

Figure 9.3 The impact of party loyalty norms on dissent

relative terms the impact of promotion and demotion is on average about twice as large as party loyalty. For example, following demotion, the socialized MP's dissent jumps by about 0.5 dissenting votes per year; for the unsocialized MP this post-demotion surge is closer to 0.75 dissenting votes per year. Thus, the lack of party loyalty accounts for an extra 0.25 dissenting votes relative to the 0.5 generated by demotion.

These are, it should be noted, conservative estimates. Should one count the effect of tenure on dissent as reflective of socialization, one would put the impact of social norms and socialization and progressive ambition on equal footing. This assumption is not without risk, however, because there are many alternative explanations for why MPs might rein in their dissent over time, and these need not be connected to social norms or socialization. That said, the dampening effect of tenure serves an important function in suppressing dissent at the end of the MP's career. Indeed, if the tenure effect is constrained to zero, the MP's post-demotion dissent increases far more than in the scenarios depicted in Figure 9.3 – and it continues to increase over time. Thus while the tenure effect may or may not reflect socialization, it limits end-game opportunism by MPs.

Conclusion

A succinct conclusion to this chapter would be that social norms matter. Certainly, social norms and socialization play an important role in intra-party politics. It is not possible for leaders to deliver advancement to all of their members, and once MPs know that they will not be promoted (at all or beyond some point in their careers), they have commensurately less incentive to toe the party line. Discipline, as the previous chapter suggested, is simply not sufficient to deal with the scope of the problem. It is critical, then, that party leaders can rely on social norms and socialization to constrain dissent once MPs' career prospects decline.

One should not, however, go beyond this and infer (as some scholars do) that norms drive self-interest out of intra-party politics (e.g., Searing 1994, p. 4). The evidence set out above shows that this is patently untrue. Even after one controls for the MP's sense of party loyalty and continued exposure to party norms, one finds that the MP's career prospects powerfully influence the MP's voting behaviour: those doing well under the rules of the game tend to toe the party line, whereas those who are faring poorly tend, on average, to dissent. This is not an artefact of endogeneity between the MP's career prospects and voting behaviour; the statistical models used here explicitly avoid that problem. Indeed, these results suggest that it is more accurate to see social norms as reinforcing, rather than displacing, the MP's self-interest. Equally, the importance the MP attaches to party loyalty is not simply a reflection of doing well under the rules of the game. Even with the MP's parliamentary rank held constant, the MP's sense of party loyalty constrains dissent.

10 | Conclusion

Summary

This book has been about the relationship between leaders of parliamentary parties and their MPs, how the two sides interact and sometimes clash. The LEADS model provides a comprehensive framework for understanding how the incentives and objectives of both leaders and MPs come together in a particular manner to produce either loyalty and unity or dissent and disunity. In the model ideological disagreements and electoral pressures (i.e., differences in electoral environments across constituencies) set the stage for dissent to occur. Leaders have several means of controlling their MPs' dissension, but I argue that in the main, leaders take advantage of their MPs' progressive ambitions and their control of parliamentary career channels to maintain unity. While this strategy is effective in the medium term, there comes a point when the MP can no longer be promoted, and the lure of advancement loses its capacity to constrain the MP's behaviour. Yet dissent does not necessarily surge at this point in MPs' careers. Why not? One reason is that party leaders turn to discipline to maintain unity. Discipline is costly, however, and hence I end by arguing that socialization fills the void. MPs internalize norms of party loyalty, and over time these norms help to constrain their behaviour, limiting their propensity to dissent even after their career prospects have declined.

This is an overtly synthetic model of intra-party politics, drawing on several theoretical approaches to legislative behaviour. In structuring the relationship between these approaches, I have tried to avoid a 'race of the variables' in which one approach is declared correct because its proxy variable is more strongly associated with dissent than variables representing other approaches. On the contrary, my argument has been that party unity is shaped by a variety of factors – electoral pressures, the availability or scarcity of advancement, social norms, and the like – coming together in a particular fashion. This does not imply that everything matters. First, not everything that might be relevant to intra-party politics (e.g., the structure of caucus policy committees or leadership selection rules) is in the model. While these factors may explain aspects of intra-party politics that I have not considered here, they are neither logically nor empirically required to explain MPs' decisions to toe the party line or dissent. Second, the empirical evidence from candidate surveys, national election studies, media reports, and personal interviews establishes that some factors have more or less impact on party unity than others. The data in Chapter 4, for example, show that neither the ideological diversity of the parliamentary party as a whole nor the MP's ideological position within the parliamentary party are strong predictors of the party's unity or the MP's loyalty. This suggests, in turn, that the screening mechanisms these parties employ at preselection are not crucial to party unity; other factors – notably electoral dealignment and availability of career advancement opportunities in the party – appear to be far more important determinants of party unity. These aspects of the model and the statistical results surrounding them deserve closer attention.

The impact of electoral dealignment on intra-party politics

One of the central results of Chapter 3 is the correlation in the cross-national data between electoral dealignment and aggregate measures of backbench dissent. What makes this result especially compelling, however, is the evidence from New Zealand that shows that non-partisan voters react positively to their MPs' dissent. It is no coincidence, then, that electoral dealignment and parliamentary dissent proceed in lock-step: as the party system dealigns, and as party identification weakens in the electorate, dissent becomes a more effective and worthwhile vote-winning strategy for MPs. The importance of this insight should not be understated. Though Alt (1984) had speculated early on that the partisan dealignment of the 1970s was behind the surge in parliamentary dissent in Britain, the consensus that emerged from the broader debate on dealignment (see, e.g., Dalton *et al.* 1984; Dalton 2000) was that dealignment primarily affected the party-in-the-electorate. The party-in-office, on the other hand, was seen to be insulated from these electoral changes by a variety of institutional forces (e.g., Thies 2000). This view provided no logical or empirical basis for connecting trends in backbench dissension to dealignment (Bowler 2000). The evidence set out in Chapters 3 and 5 certainly challenges that position. Indeed, there is a good deal of Cox's (1987) *Efficient Secret* in reverse here. For Cox, the development of a party-oriented electorate in Britain during the middle of the nineteenth century was a concomitant part of the rise of unified, programmatic political parties at Westminster. The modern corollary appears to be that as party identification in the electorate declines, the unity of parliamentary parties is slowly eroded.

This relationship comes about because dissent, like constituency service, is principally an electoral strategy intended to win the MP a personal vote, a fact that is reflected in the close connection between the MP's electoral security, constituency service efforts, and propensity to dissent in Parliament. This relationship is direct evidence that MPs' parliamentary and constituency worlds are *not* compartmentalized. Electoral dealignment is precisely what provides MPs with the incentive to link their parliamentary and constituency activities: as party identification weakens the affective connections that structure voters' ballot decisions break down, and the door opens for the MP to use dissent to win personal votes. Of course, the corresponding difficulty for party leaders is that electoral dealignment exacerbates the severity of the parties' collective action problem: even as MPs use dissent to win the votes of non-partisan electors in their constituencies, they undercut the party's ability to communicate its position to the party's core voters in the electorate at large.

Career advancement and party unity

The institutional feature that has the most visible and immediate impact on intra-party politics is the leadership's monopoly on the career advancement pathways that lead to the cabinet or shadow cabinet. The aggregate-level data in Chapter 3 reveal that the frequency and extent of backbench dissent in a party increase as the relative size of its front bench decreases. The results of Chapter 7, based on the Canadian Liberal Party's transition from opposition to government, corroborate this result, showing a tight causal relationship between a Liberal MP's demotion and his or her subsequent dissent.[1] The panel data on British

---

[1] The Canadian data are also noteworthy in that they show how the distribution of preferment in the party hinges on the internal politics of leadership selection, with Liberal MPs who failed to back Chrétien in the 1991 leadership contest suffering most in the 1993 reshuffle.

MPs' parliamentary career trajectories and voting records follow a similar pattern. In short, a variety of evidence identifies the leadership's monopoly on career advancement as the primary bulwark of party unity, and when leaders cannot meet their followers' demands on this front, or when MPs begin to discount the value of higher office, their propensity to dissent increases.

There are two important caveats to this relationship, however. First, party unity cannot be sustained solely by distribution of preferment. Once MPs' career prospects begin to decline, leaders must rely on discipline and socialization to maintain unity. The evidence set out in Chapter 8 suggests, first, that leaders do switch to discipline when advancement is no longer effective in eliciting an MP's loyalty and second, that doing so partly suppresses the MP's propensity to dissent. That said, a long-run process of socialization into norms of party loyalty appears far more effective than discipline in eliciting loyalty once the MP's career prospects have declined. This in turn suggests a second caveat to the career advancement thesis, to wit, that MPs' loyalty to their parties is not solely a function of doing well under the rules of the game.

Policy compromise, agenda control, and party unity

This book makes clear how important electoral dealignment and career advancement are to party unity; its commentary on the impact of policy compromise and agenda control is far more implicit. Indeed, the book does not explicitly test the extent to which party unity hinges on leaders' willingness to compromise on policy or their ability to set the agenda. Still, the many incidents of dissent cited throughout the book offer two lessons on this front. First, in many cases, party leaders' capacity to set the policy agenda is highly constrained – and this is true even of prime ministers at the head of majority governments. The British Labour Party's revolt over Iraq stands as the best example of this lesson. Caught between the Bush administration's belligerence toward Iraq on one hand and French diplomatic intransigence on the other, Blair was denied the flexibility he required to find a policy position that all Labour MPs could support. International actors were not the only constraints on Blair, however. Blair was not constitutionally obliged to seek parliamentary approval before committing the country to war, but several of his cabinet ministers would not allow him to bypass the House of Commons (Seldon 2004, p. 595). There are similarities here to the positions in which John Major, Jean Chrétien, and John Howard found themselves: John Major was hemmed in by his precommitment to the terms of the Maastricht Treaty; Jean Chrétien's flexibility on economic policy was limited by the country's near-bankruptcy; and John Howard was constrained by a powerful Senate that was beyond his direct control.

Still, it would be incorrect to see constraints on policy as making backbench dissent inevitable. (Indeed, the formal model directly cautions against making such an inference.) If Chrétien lacked the flexibility to compromise with left-wing Liberal MPs over economic policy, he had plenty of room to manoeuvre on social policy – yet he persisted in pushing forward with a series of social policies (on gun control, hate crimes, and same-sex spousal benefits) that overtly antagonized the more right-wing, rural section of the Liberal parliamentary party. Similarly, John Howard brokered a deal with an independent senator over Native Title to get a bill through the Senate, even though doing so ran directly against the political interests and preferences of the more conservative and rural elements of his Liberal–National Coalition. Both Chrétien and Howard evidently preferred to rely on discipline rather than policy compromise to limit internal dissent – just as the formal version of the LEADS model predicted. A second lesson, then, is that party leaders are sometimes willing to sacrifice party unity to secure their policy goals. This is not to deny the importance of agenda control in parliamentary and intra-party politics, but certainly any argument that control of the policy agenda is sufficient on its own to secure party unity needs to be tempered: party leaders' control over the policy agenda is often limited, and even when it is not, party leaders may willingly trade-off party unity to secure their policy objectives.

Generalizing beyond Westminster

The central role of advancement in maintaining intra-party unity springs from the double monopoly of power that characterizes Westminster parliamentary government – a single party's monopoly on cabinet and the cabinet's monopoly on office perks and policy influence. The first element of this double monopoly provides party leaders (on the government side, especially) with control over the career channels that lead to the cabinet. The second element enhances the value of a cabinet office by ensuring that it appeals to office- and policy-seeking MPs alike. This raises a provocative counterfactual: what happens to party unity if leaders do not control advancement, or alternatively, if advancement is systematically less valuable to MPs?

Looking at the level of party unity in parliamentary systems where leaders' control over the distribution of office perks and policy influence is not as complete as at Westminster would seem to provide a direct answer to this question. Parliaments in Sweden and Italy, for example, have strong committee systems that are fairly autonomous of party control (Döring 1995; Powell 2000, p. 34). In theory, MPs who are motivated by policy influence rather than the office perks of ministerial office can operate in relative freedom from the party line, secure in the knowledge that they can develop their careers in the committee system. To some extent the fissiparous incentives inherent in these arrangements have materialized in Italy (Hine 1993; Mershon and Heller 2005). In contrast, Swedish parties remain highly cohesive (Jensen 2000).

This sort of cross-national comparison is limited by the fact that it rests on the assumption that dissent results whenever leaders do not control parliamentary career channels. However, the more general message of the LEADS model is that party leaders switch from costly or ineffective means of controlling their MPs to less costly and more effective methods. Thus, while the distribution of preferment is crucial to the unity of parliamentary parties in Westminster systems, theory and evidence also show that party leaders switch to discipline and social pressure once preferment loses its hold over the MP. From a comparative perspective, then, institutional rules that weaken party control of advancement or diminish the value of ministerial office to MPs need not produce higher aggregate levels of intra-party dissent because party leaders may resort to (and have access to) methods of control that are more effective in that particular institutional context. Scandinavian parties, for example, appear to rely heavily on agenda control and policy compromise to limit internal dissension (Aylott 2002). What changes across institutional settings, then, is not necessarily the level of intra-party dissent but the mixture of strategies that leaders use to maintain unity. The more precise theoretical prediction is, therefore, that leaders should select the most cost-effective strategies available to them given the institutional environment in which they find themselves. The broader message is that the equilibrium level of dissent in a party, whether it is in a Westminster or multi-party parliamentary environment, is determined by the effectiveness of the leaders' loyalty-eliciting strategies relative to the strength of MPs' incentives to dissent.

Appendix 1
Comparative statics and proofs

This appendix provides a formal and complete treatment of the game theoretic model described in Chapter 2. The discussion here is technical and shorn of much of the narrative that is provided in Chapter 2, and hence readers may find it easier to read Chapter 2 closely before engaging with the material that follows below.

Players, strategies, and utility functions

The game is predicated on a policy disagreement between the party leader (L) and the MP, the leader wishing to secure the MP's support for her most preferred policy, and the MP hoping to avoid the electoral consequences of any uncongenial party policy. To structure this policy disagreement, the players have ideal points on the unit interval, such that MP $= 0$ and L $= 1$.[1] The leader has the privilege of defining a party policy, $x \in [0, 1]$, but can also offer advancement, $a \geq 0$, or apply disciplinary sanctions, $s \geq 0$, to the MP to induce the MP to support x. In extending advancement or applying sanctions L incurs costs of a^2 and s^2, respectively. The MP can support or dissent from x, with $r \in [0, 1]$ denoting the extent of the MP's dissension. The MP's dissent imposes a direct cost of r^2 on the leader and dilutes the policy gains that L obtains by moving x toward her ideal point; i.e., L's utility from party policy is $(1 - r)x$.

On the MP's side, dissent protects the MP from the electoral impact of x. Specifically, the MP's re-election prospects (and utility) decline linearly in x, but only to the extent that the MP supports the policy, i.e., the MP's re-election prospects equal $-x(1 - r)$. A direct cost of dissent to the MP of r^2 ensures that the electoral return to dissension is diminishing and possibly negative – as might be expected if voters view dissent

---

[1] The game is symmetric in the players' positions, and in so far as any policy distance between the MP and leader can be normalized to the unit interval, this structure involves no loss of generality.

beyond a certain point as a sign of the MP's unreliability or opportunism. Dissent also exposes the MP to disciplinary sanctions and closes
off advancement in the party in proportion to the MP's dissension, the
MP suffering a disciplinary penalty $-rs$ for opposing x, and enjoying
office rewards of $(1 - r)a$ for supporting x.

The path of play involves just two steps: (1) L sets party policy,
advancement, and sanctions, $\{x, a, s\}$, and (2) the MP responds with
some level of dissent (r) to x. The outcome of the game is a Nash
equilibrium, with the leader's payoff defined by the utility function,

$$U_L = (1 - r)x - r^2 - a^2 - s^2,$$

and the MP's payoff by the utility function,

$$U_{MP} = -x + xr - r^2 - rs + (1 - r)a.$$

Baseline equilibrium result

In equilibrium, L plays $\{x^*, a^*, s^*\} = \{1, {}^1/_3, {}^1/_3\}$, and the MP responds
with $r^* = (x - a - s)/2 = {}^1/_6$ (see Proposition 1 below). The comparative
statics of this baseline result follow directly from the MP's strategy: all
else equal, moving policy further away from the MP (i.e., increasing x),
or decreasing advancement (a) or sanctions (s), increases the MP's
resistance (r).

Altering the electoral returns to dissent

What is the impact on the game of increasing or decreasing the electoral
return of dissent to the MP? This question can be answered by altering
the MP's utility function from $xr - r^2$ to $xdr - r^2$, $d \geq 0$. The alteration
changes the MP's optimal level of dissension to the leader's policies. At
$d = 0$ there is no incentive to dissent; the action imposes costs $(-r^2)$
without providing offsetting benefits. As d increases, however, the
optimal level of dissent increases. Figure A1.1 shows this pattern for
three different levels of d, the MP's maximum gain from dissent (i.e.,
$dr - r^2$) occurring at increasingly higher levels of dissension.

In the initial formulation, setting $a = s = {}^1/_3$ allowed the leader to obtain
her most preferred policy $(x = 1)$ with $r = {}^1/_6$. This outcome disappears
once the MP's incentive to dissent is allowed to vary (see Proposition 2
below). Figure A1.2 shows the players' equilibrium strategies given

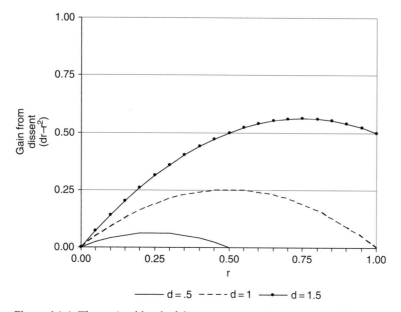

Figure A1.1 The optimal level of dissent given varying returns to dissent

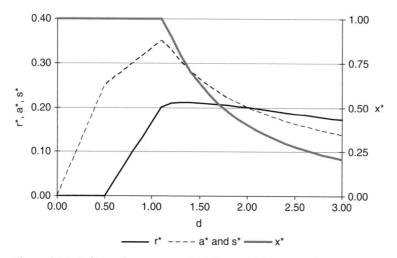

Figure A1.2 Policy, advancement, discipline, and dissent with varying returns to dissent

various levels of d. When $d < \frac{1}{2}$, the MP does not dissent, and the leader can obtain $x = 1$ with fewer resources than in the baseline model, i.e., a and $s < \frac{1}{3}$. Party unity disappears abruptly at $d = \frac{1}{2}$, however. The leader still obtains her most preferred policy, but now has to tolerate the MP's dissent in equilibrium. The leader's initial response to the MP's dissension is confined to increased advancement and discipline. Only when $d = (\frac{3}{2}\sqrt{2}) - 1$ (the point at which dissent peaks) does the leader begin to compromise on policy, moving x toward the MP's policy position. This policy compromise reduces the MP's dissension and lowers the leader's office and disciplinary costs.[2] The main point, then, is twofold. First, the electoral returns to dissent must hit a threshold $(d = \frac{1}{2})$ before the MP dissents. Second, policy compromise occurs only when the returns to dissent to the MP are quite high.

Increasing office costs

How leaders react to increasing advancement costs is explored by altering the cost of advancement to the leader from a^2 to ka^2 so that for $k > 1$ advancement becomes more costly than sanctions or dissent (see Proposition 3 below). Figure A1.3 shows the impact of this change on the leader's strategy. With $k < 1$, office is less costly to the leader than discipline, and as a result the leader relies almost exclusively on office to secure the MP's loyalty. As k increases, the leader relies steadily more on discipline to control the MP. However, because there are increasing marginal costs to imposing discipline, the substitution effect is not complete, and the leader delivers less advancement and discipline in total to the MP as k increases. Thus, the substitution does not proceed in a manner that leaves the aggregate level of advancement and discipline intact. Note also that the shift from advancement to discipline operates quite independently of policy, which remains largely unaffected by increasing office costs until k hits very high levels.

With the leader delivering less advancement and discipline in total to the MP, and policy largely unresponsive to rising office costs, one might expect dissent to increase. Indeed, it does. Figure A1.4 maps the MP's

---

[2] Eventually, for very large values of d (not shown in Figure A1.2) the leader places policy at the MP's ideal point, offers no advancement or discipline, and (in the limit) incurs no dissent. Of course, such a scenario implies such a complete disconnection between the MP and the party that it is merely an abstraction.

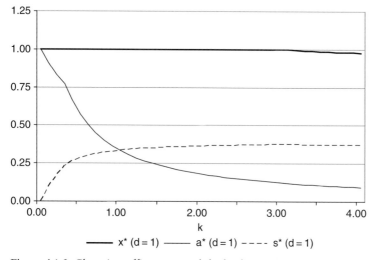

Figure A1.3 Changing office costs and the leader's strategy

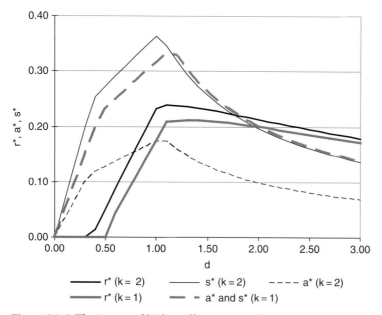

Figure A1.4 The impact of higher office costs on dissent

response to the leader's advancement and disciplinary strategies under higher office costs alongside changes in d. To assist comparison the advancement and discipline and dissent strategies from Figure A1.2 (where $k = 1$, i.e., advancement, discipline, and dissent are equally weighted) are superimposed on Figure A1.4. Higher office costs do indeed increase dissent, pushing the peak of dissent close to $r = .25$. The other visible effect of higher office costs is to make dissent appear at lower values of d. In other words, the knock-on effect of higher office costs to the leader is to sharpen the MP's incentive to dissent.

Note also that because advancement and disciplinary sanctions are interchangeable variables in the model:

1. Higher office costs are directly equivalent to lower disciplinary costs. It follows that exactly the same conditions characterize decreases in the cost of imposing discipline. Thus, should the cost to the leader of imposing discipline fall, the model predicts leaders to rely more heavily on discipline rather than advancement to rein in MPs.
2. The discounting of office benefits has an impact on the game similar to that of higher office costs for the leader: if MPs discount advancement, every unit of advancement has a smaller marginal impact on the MP's behaviour, and the leader has to offer the MP more preferment to secure a given outcome.[3] It follows that the discounting of office benefits by the MP will induce the leader to rely more heavily on discipline to elicit the MP's support.

Policy constraints

What happens when policy is exogenously constrained so that the leader cannot offer the MP policy concessions? In answering this question the most illuminating case to consider is one in which policy is held

---

[3] If the MP does not discount a, then $\partial U_{MP}/\partial a = (1 - r)$ and L's ratio of office costs to this marginal effect is $a^2/(1 - r)$. If, on the other hand, the MP discounts office by $\delta \in (0, 1]$, then $\partial U_{MP}/\partial a = (1 - r)\delta$, and L's ratio of office costs to $\partial U_{MP}/\partial a$ becomes $a^2/(1 - r)\delta$. In general, L can always find some $a' > a$ that makes up for the MP's discounting. For example, if L set $a' = a/\delta$, L's office costs would rise to a^2/δ^2, but the marginal effect of advancement on the MP would return to $(1-r)$. Alternatively, L could set $a' = a/\sqrt{\delta}$. This would push L's office costs to a^2/δ, but would take the ratio of office costs to marginal effects back to $a^2/(1 - r)\delta$. These examples show the close relationship between discounting and higher office costs.

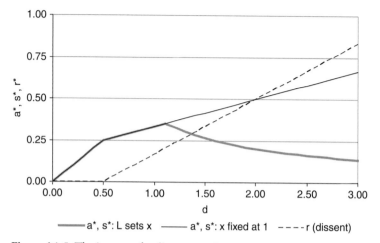

Figure A1.5 The impact of policy constraints

at L's ideal point (i.e., $x = 1$).[4] Up until $d = {}^3/_2\sqrt{2} - 1$ L's strategy follows exactly the path illustrated in Figure A1.2, i.e., $a^* = s^* = d/2$ if $d < \frac{1}{2}$ and $a^* = s^* = (1 + d)/6$ if $d \geq \frac{1}{2}$ (see Proposition 2 below). In other words, until the MP's incentive to dissent grows sharp enough, policy constraints have no discernable impact on intra-party politics.

This is not so beyond $d = {}^3/_2\sqrt{2} - 1$. At this point, L would prefer to shift policy toward the MP and rein in advancement and discipline (again, just as in Figure A1.2). This strategy dampens dissent and maximizes L's utility. If policy is fixed, however, L must rely more heavily on advancement and discipline to maintain control of the party. Thus, the first effect of policy rigidity is to increase the level of advancement and discipline needed to keep dissent in check – and these levels increase alongside the MP's incentive to dissent (i.e., d). Figure A1.5 illustrates this relationship. The thick grey line traces the levels of a and s that L would play if she were free to set policy.[5] With policy constrained, however, L must continue to play $a^* = s^* = (1 + d/6$ (the solid line), and plainly this latter strategy imposes higher office and disciplinary costs on L. Dissent (the dashed line), nevertheless, continues to climb as d increases, the higher levels of a and s unable to make

---

[4] If policy were fixed at the MP's ideal point, there would be no need for L to offer advancement or impose discipline to secure the MP's support.

[5] The strategy is $a^* = s^* = (1 + d)/(2d^2 + 4d - 1)$. See the proof of Proposition 2.

up for L's lack of control over policy. The second effect of policy constraints, then, is to amplify dissent.

Proofs

All of the proofs below involve solving a rather mechanical constrained optimization problem: the relevant Kuhn-Tucker conditions are set out and solved, and then inspected to ensure that they respect the restrictions on the game's parameters.

Proposition 1: Absent constraints on x, a, and s, L plays $\{x^*, a^*, s^*\} = \{1, {}^1/_3, {}^1/_3\}$, and the MP responds with $r^* = (x - a - s)/2 = {}^1/_6$.

Proof: Maximizing $U_{MP} = -x + xr - r^2 + (1 - r)a - rs$ requires,

$$\partial U_{MP}/\partial r = x - 2r - a - s = 0. \qquad [1]$$

The solution is $r^* = (x - a - s)/2$, and the quadratic nature of U_{MP} ensures that it is the MP's optimal response to L's strategy.

L's maximization problem is, therefore,

$$argmax(x, a, s)U_L = (1 - r^*)x - r^{*2} - a^2 - s^2$$

subject to the constraint, $r^* \in [0, 1]$. (The lower bound is the real issue here as L's incentive is to minimize the MP's opposition.) The Lagrangian for this problem is,

$$L(x, s, a)(1 - r^*)x - r^{*2} - a^2 - s^2 - \lambda(w^2 - r^*), \qquad [2]$$

where w is the slack variable. Substituting for r^* provides,

$$L(x, s, a)(1 - (x - a - s)/2)x - [(x - a - s)/2]^2 - a^2 - s^2 \\ - \lambda(w^2 - (x - a - s)/2),$$

which, in turn, provides the following first order conditions:

$$\partial U_L/\partial x = 1 - 3/2x + s + a + \lambda/2 = 0 \qquad [2a]$$

$$\partial U_L/\partial a = x - (5a - s - \lambda)/2 = 0 \qquad [2b]$$

$$\partial U_L/\partial s = x - (5s - a - \lambda)/2 = 0 \qquad [2c]$$

$$\partial U_L/\partial \lambda = (x - a - s)/2 - w^2 = 0 \qquad [2d]$$

$$\partial U_L/\partial w = -2w\lambda = 0 \qquad [2e]$$

If the constraint is passive (i.e., $\lambda = 0$), the solution (from Equations 2a, 2b, and 2c), is $x = 6/5$, $a = 2/5$, $s = 2/5$. This solution violates the additional constraint that $x \in [0, 1]$, and only the solution to the binding constraint (i.e., $w = 0$) is acceptable: $x = 1$, $a = \frac{1}{2}$, $s = \frac{1}{2}$. Convexity of the leader's utility function obviates the need to inspect the second-order conditions.

There is, however, another strategy to check, namely one in which the leader sets $x = 1$ but $a < \frac{1}{2}$ and $s < \frac{1}{2}$ such that $r^* > 0$. Thus, rather than playing $x = 1$, $a = \frac{1}{2}$, $s = \frac{1}{2}$, a strategy that respects constraints on both x and r, the leader may be better off playing a strategy that is bound only by the constraints on x and which tolerates $r^* > 0$. To solve this problem, repeat the exercise above, substituting $x = 1$ into the MP's utility function and differentiate with respect to r:

$$\partial U_{MP}/\partial r = 1 - 2r - a - s = 0. \tag{1b}$$

The solution is $r^* = (1 - a - s)/2$. L's maximization problem is, therefore,

$$argmax(a, s)U_L = (1 - r^*) - r^{*2} - a^2 - s^2$$

subject to the constraint, $r^* \in [0, 1]$. The corresponding Lagrangian is,

$$L(s, a)(1 - r^*) - r^{*2} - a^2 - s^2 - \lambda(w^2 - r^*), \tag{2f}$$

Substituting for r^* provides,

$$L(s, a)(1 + a + s)/2 - [(1 - a - s)/2]^2 - a^2 - s^2 \\ - \lambda[w^2 - (1 - a - s)/2],$$

which, in turn, provides the following first-order conditions:

$$\partial U_L/\partial a = 1 - (5a - s - \lambda)/2 = 0 \tag{2g}$$

$$\partial U_L/\partial s = 1 - (5s - a - \lambda)/2 = 0 \tag{2h}$$

$$\partial U_L/\partial \lambda = (1 - a - s)/2 - w^2 = 0 \tag{2i}$$

$$\partial U_L/\partial w = -2w\lambda = 0 \tag{2j}$$

Only the solution when the constraint is passive (i.e., $\lambda = 0$) is in play here. (The solution when the constraint binds is, of course, $x = 1$, $a = \frac{1}{2}$, $s = \frac{1}{2}$.) With $\lambda = 0$ Equation 2h returns $s = 2/5 - 1/5a$, $a = 1/3$ (via Equation 2g), and hence $s = 1/3$. L's strategy is therefore $\{x^*, a^*, s^*\} = \{1, \frac{1}{3}, \frac{1}{3}\}$. This strategy elicits $r^* = (1 - \frac{2}{3})/2 = 1/6$ from the MP, an admissible solution.

The issue, then, is whether the leader is better off playing $\{x^*, a^*, s^*\} = \{1, \frac{1}{2}, \frac{1}{2}\}$ or $\{x^*, a^*, s^*\} = \{1, \frac{1}{3}, \frac{1}{3}\}$. Simple algebra shows that the leader's utility from the first strategy is $\frac{1}{2}$ as compared to 7/12 from the second strategy. It follows that the leader's best response is $\{x^*, a^*, s^*\} = \{1, \frac{1}{3}, \frac{1}{3}\}$. The Nash equilibrium to the game is therefore:

$$\sigma_L^*(\sigma_{MP}(.)) = \{1, 1/3, 1/3\}$$

$$\sigma_{MP}^*(\sigma_L(.)) = (x - a - s)/2$$

Proposition 2: If $U_{MP} = -x + dxr - r^2 + (1 - r)a - rs$, where $d \geq 0$, L plays,

$$\{x^*, a^*, s^*\} = \begin{cases} \{1, d/2, d/2\} \text{ if } d < 1/2 \\ \{1, (1+d)/6, (1+d)/6\} \text{ if } d \in [1/2, (3/2\sqrt{2}) - 1] \\ \{6/(2d^2 + 4d - 1), (1+d)/(2d^2 + 4d - 1), \\ (1+d)/(2d^2 + 4d - 1)\} \text{ if } d \geq [3/2\sqrt{2}) - 1] \end{cases}$$

and the MP responds with $r^* = (dx - a - s)/2$.

Proof: The solution is almost identical to that for Proposition 1. Maximizing $U_{MP} = -x + dxr - r^2 + (1 - r)a - rs$ requires,

$$\partial U_{MP}/\partial r = dx - 2r - a - s = 0. \qquad [1c]$$

This has the solution $r^* = (dx - a - s)/2$. Substituting this solution into Equation 2 from Proposition 1 provides the Lagrangian,

$$L(x, s, a)(1 - (dx - a - s)/2)x - [(dx - a - s)/2]^2 - a^2 - s^2$$
$$- \lambda(w^2 - (dx - a - s)/2). \qquad [3]$$

The first-order conditions are:

$$\partial U_L/\partial x = 1 - dx + (s + a + d\lambda)/2 - d[(dx - s - a)/2] = 0 \qquad [3a]$$

$$\partial U_L/\partial a = (x + dx - 5a - s - \lambda)/2 = 0 \qquad [3b]$$

$$\partial U_L/\partial s = (x + dx - 5s - a - \lambda)/2 = 0 \qquad [3c]$$

$$\partial U_L/\partial \lambda = (dx - a - s)/2 - w^2 = 0 \qquad [3d]$$

$$\partial U_L/\partial w = -2w\lambda = 0 \qquad [3e]$$

When the constraint is passive (i.e., $\lambda = 0$), Equations 3a, 3b, and 3c return $x = 6/(2d^2 + 4d - 1)$, $a = s = (1 + d)/(2d^2 + 4d - 1)$. When the constraint binds (i.e., $w = 0$), $x = (a + s)/d$, $\lambda = (a + s - 2)/d$, $a = s = 1/(2d)$ is the solution. Replacing a and s in $x = (a + s)/d$ then provides $x = 1/d^2$.

This is not the end of the matter, however. The constrained solution must respect $r^* \geq 0$, and both solutions must also ensure that x does not exceed its upper bound of 1. These additional constraints imply that the unconstrained solution is feasible iff $d \geq \frac{1}{2}$ (to ensure $r^* \geq 0$) and $d \geq (^3/_2\sqrt{2}) - 1$ (to ensure $x \leq 1$), the latter condition being the more stringent one. Similarly, the constrained solution requires $d \geq 1$ to guarantee $x \leq 1$.

Short of these boundaries (i.e., $d < (^3/_2\sqrt{2}) - 1$ or $d < 1$ as the case may be), L can do no better than to set x^* to its upper bound of 1. The players' strategies are now solved by repeating the exercise above with $x = 1$. The MP's strategy is now,

$$argmax(r)U_{MP} = -1 + dr - r^2 + (1 - r)a - rs :$$
$$\partial U_{MP}/\partial r = d - 2r - a - s = 0. \qquad [1d]$$
$$\therefore r^* = (d - a - s)/2.$$

The leader's problem is therefore:

$$argmax(a, s)U_L = (1 - r^*) - r^{*2} - a^2 - s^2$$

subject to $r \in [0, 1]$. The Lagrangian is,

$$L(a, s)1 - (d - a - s)/2 - [(d - a - s)/2]^2 - a^2 - s^2$$
$$- \lambda(w^2 - (d - a - s)/2), \qquad [3f]$$

and the first-order conditions are:

$$\partial U_L/\partial a = (1 + d - 5a - s - \lambda)/2 = 0 \qquad [3g]$$

$$\partial U_L/\partial s = (1 + d - 5s - a - \lambda)/2 = 0 \qquad [3h]$$

$$\partial U_L/\partial \lambda = (d - a - s)/2 - w^2 = 0 \qquad [3i]$$

$$\partial U_L/\partial w = -2w\lambda = 0 \qquad [3j]$$

Given $\lambda = 0$ (i.e., the constraint does not bind), one obtains $a = s = (1 + d)/6$. Given $w = 0$ (i.e., the constraint binds), one obtains $s = d - a$ (by Equation 3i), $\lambda = 1 - 4d - 4a$ (by Equation 3h), and $a = d/2$ (on substitution into Equation 3g). The solution is therefore, $a = s = d/2$.

For $d < \frac{1}{2}$, the unconstrained strategy $a = s = (1 + d)/6$ still has $r^* < 0$, and L can do no better than to play the constrained solution under these conditions.[6] Thus, part of L's strategy is $\{x^*, a^*, s^*\} = \{1, d/2, d/2\}$ if $d < \frac{1}{2}$.

The remainder of L's strategy is determined by examining U_L in the intervals $d \in [\frac{1}{2}, 1]$, $d \in [1, {}^3/_2\sqrt{2} - 1)$ and $d \geq (^3/_2\sqrt{2}) - 1$. In the

---

[6] This must be the case because the optimal a and s defined by the unconstrained strategy (i.e., $a = s = (1 + d)/6$) exceed the optimal a and s defined by the constrained strategy (i.e., $d/2$) for $d < \frac{1}{2}$ – but these extra costs to L generate no benefits because r^* cannot fall below 0.

interval $d \in [\frac{1}{2}, 1]$ L's utility from the unconstrained strategy (i.e., $\{x^*, a^*, s^*\} = \{1, (1+d)/6, (1+d)/6\}$) is, $^{13}/_{12} - d/3 - d^2/6$, whereas the constrained strategy (i.e., $\{x^*, a^*, s^*\} = \{1, d/2, d/2\}$) returns $1 - d^2/2$. Simple algebra shows that $^{13}/_{12} - d/3 - d^2/6 > 1 - d^2/2$ holds for $d > \frac{1}{2}$. Thus, for $d \in [\frac{1}{2}, 1]$ L's strategy is $\{x^*, a^*, s^*\} = \{1, (1+d)/6, (1+d)/6\}$.

In the third interval, $d \in [1, \,^{3}/_{2}\sqrt{2} - 1)$, the unconstrained strategy still provides L with $^{13}/_{12} - d/3 - d^2/6$, but the utility from unconstrained strategy changes to $1/(2d^2)$. In the interval, the former is always greater than the latter. In the last interval, $d \geq (^{3}/_{2}\sqrt{2}) - 1$, the constrained strategy again provides $1/(2d^2)$ whilst the unconstrained strategy returns $3/(2d^2 + 4d - 1)$. Again, simple algebra shows that $3/(2d^2 + 4d - 1) > 1/2d^2 \,\forall\, d > 0$.

L's complete strategy can then be stated as,

$$\{x^*, a^*, s^*\} = \begin{cases} \{1, d/2, d/2\} \text{ if } d < 1/2 \\ \{1, (1+d)/6, (1+d)/6\} \text{ if } d \in [1/2, (3/2\sqrt{2}) - 1) \\ \{6/(2d^2 + 4d - 1), (1+d)/(2d^2 + 4d - 1), \\ \quad (1+d)/(2d^2 + 4d - 1)\} \text{ if } d \geq [3/2\sqrt{2}) - 1] \end{cases}$$

The Nash equilibrium to the game is thus,

$$\sigma_L^*(\sigma_{MP}(.)) = \begin{cases} \{1, d/2, d/2\} \text{ if } d < 1/2 \\ \{1, (1+d)/6, (1+d)/6\} \text{ if } d \in [1/2, (3/2\sqrt{2}) - 1)] \\ \{6/(2d^2 + 4d - 1), (1+d)/(2d^2 + 4d - 1), \\ \quad (1+d)/(2d^2 + 4d - 1)\} \text{ if } d \geq [3/2\sqrt{2}) - 1] \end{cases}$$

$$\sigma_{MP}^*(\sigma_L(.)) = (dx - a - s)/2$$

Proposition 3: If the cost to L of offering advancement to the MP is ka^2 with $k \geq 0$, L plays,

$$\{x^*, a^*, s^*\} = \begin{cases} \{1, d/(1+k), dk/(1+k)\} \text{ if } k < 1/(4d-1), d \in (0,2) \\ \{1, (1+d)/(1+5k), k(1+d)/(1+5k)\} \\ \quad \text{if } k \in [1/(4d-1), 3/(4d^2 + 8d - 11)), d \in \{(1/4, 2) \\ \{2(1+5k)/(4d^2k + 8dk - k - 1), \\ \quad 2(1+d)/(4d^2k + 8dk - k - 1), \\ \quad 2k(1+d)/(4d^2k + 8dk - k - 1)\} \\ \quad \text{if } k \geq 3/(4d^2 + 8d - 11), d < 1/2\sqrt{15} - 1 \end{cases}$$

and the MP responds with $r^* = (dx - a - s)/2$.

Proof: This formulation of the problem leaves the MP's strategy intact:

$$r^* = (dx - a - s)/2.$$

L's utility function is now,

$$U_L = (1 - r)x - r^2 - ka^2 - s^2,$$

and substituting r^* into Equation 4 and maximizing it subject to the constraint $r^* \geq 0$, one obtains:

$$L(x, s, a)(1 - (dx - a - s)/2)x - [(dx - a - s)/2]^2 - ka^2 - s^2 \\ - \lambda(w^2 - (dx - a - s)/2). \qquad [4]$$

The first-order conditions are:

$$\partial U_L/\partial x = 1 - dx + (a + s + \lambda d)/2 - d(dx - a - s)/2 = 0 \qquad [4a]$$

$$\partial U_L/\partial a = (x + dx - s - a - \lambda)/2 - 2ka = 0 \qquad [4b]$$

$$\partial U_L/\partial s = (x + dx - 5s - a - \lambda)/2 = 0 \qquad [4c]$$

$$\partial U_L/\partial \lambda = (dx - a - s)/2 - w^2 = 0 \qquad [4d]$$

$$\partial U_L/\partial w = -2w\lambda = 0 \qquad [4e]$$

The unconstrained solution ($\lambda = 0$) from this system of equations is: $x = 2(1 + 5k)/(4d^2k + 8dk - k - 1)$, $a = 2(1 + d)/(4d^2k + 8dk - k - 1)$, $s = 2k(1 + d)/(4d^2k + 8dk - k - 1)$. The constrained solution ($w = 0$) from this system of equations is: $x = (1 + k)/(2d^2k)$, $a = 1/2dk$, $s = 1/2d$. The unconstrained solution is viable only in so far as it generates $r^* \in [0, 1]$, and as in the proof for Proposition 2 above, both solutions also have to respect $x \in [0, 1]$. These conditions imply that the unconstrained solution is feasible iff:

i. $k \geq 1/(4d - 1)$
ii. $k \geq 1/(4d^2 + 8d - 1)$
iii. $k \geq 3/(4d^2 + 8d - 11)$

The first condition ensures that $r^* > 0$, the second condition, that x, a, and $s \geq 0$, and the third condition, that $x \leq 1$. The first condition can be met iff $d > \frac{1}{4}$ (i.e., if $d \leq \frac{1}{4} \Rightarrow \sim \exists\, k > 0$ such that $k \geq 1/(4d - 1)$). The third condition is more demanding of k than the second, and it can be met iff $d > \frac{1}{2}\sqrt{15} - 1$ (i.e., if $d \leq \frac{1}{2}\sqrt{15} - 1 \Rightarrow \sim\exists\ k > 0$ such that $k \geq 3/(4d^2 + 8d - 11)$). The first and third conditions are equivalent at $d = 2$; prior to this point $k \geq 3/(4d^2 + 8d - 11)$ is more demanding of k. Thus, the strategy $\{x^*, a^*, s^*\} = \{2(1 + 5k)/(4d^2k + 8dk - k - 1), 2(1 + d)/(4d^2k + 8dk - k - 1), 2k(1 + d)/(4d^2k + 8dk - k - 1)\}$ is admissible iff $k \geq 3/(4d^2 + 8d - 11)$ for $d \geq \frac{1}{2}\sqrt{15} - 1$.

By construction the constrained solution ensures $r^* > 0$, but $x^* = (1 + k)/(2d^2k)$ implies that the strategy is viable iff $k > 0$ and $k \geq 1/(2d^2 - 1)$; the latter condition is the more exacting, and it can be met iff $d > \sqrt{\frac{1}{2}}$. Thus, $\{x^*, a^*, s^*\} = \{(1 + k)/(2d^2k), 1/2dk, 1/2d\}$ is a viable strategy iff $d > \sqrt{\frac{1}{2}}$ and $k \geq 1/(2d^2 - 1)$. Outside these intervals, L can do no better than to play $x = 1$. As in Proposition 2 above, the MP's strategy conditional on $x = 1$ is $r^* = (d - a - s)/2$. The leader's problem is therefore:

$$arg\,max(a, s)U_L = (1 - r^*) - r^{*2} - ka^2 - s^2$$

subject to $r \in [0, 1]$. The Lagrangian is,

$$L(a, s)1 - (d - a - s)/2 - [(d - a - s)/2]^2 - ka^2 - s^2$$
$$- \lambda(w^2 - (d - a - s)/2), \tag{4f}$$

and the first-order conditions are:

$$\partial U_L/\partial a = (1 + d - a - s - \lambda)/2 - 2ka = 0 \tag{4g}$$

$$\partial U_L/\partial s = (1 + d - 5s - a - \lambda)/2 = 0 \tag{4h}$$

$$\partial U_L/\partial \lambda = (d - a - s)/2 - w^2 = 0 \tag{4i}$$

$$\partial U_L/\partial w = -2w\lambda = 0 \tag{4j}$$

With a binding constraint on r^* (i.e., $w = 0$), the solution is $a = d/(1+k)$, $s = dk/(1 + k)$. When the constraint is passive (i.e., $\lambda = 0$), however, the solution follows directly from Equations 4g and 4h: $a = (1+d)/(1 + 5k)$, $s = k(1 + d)/(1 + 5k)$. This solution provides $r^* \geq 0$ iff $k \geq 1/(4d - 1)$.

L therefore has four possible strategies at hand:

1. $\{x, a, s\} = \{1, d/(1 + k), dk/(1 + k)\}$
2. $\{x, a, s\} = \{1, (1 + d)/(1 + 5k), k(1 + d)/(1 + 5k)\}$
3. $\{x, a, s\} = \{(1 + k)/(2d^2k), 1/2dk, 1/2d\}$
4. $\{x, a, s\} = \{2(1 + 5k)/(4d^2k + 8dk - k - 1), 2(1 + d)/(4d^2k + 8dk - k - 1), 2k(1 + d)/(4d^2k + 8dk - k - 1)\}$

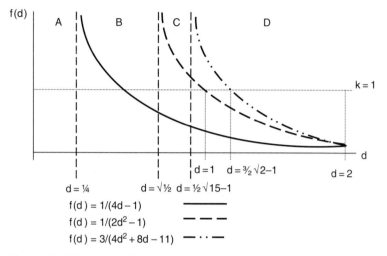

Figure A1.6 Limits on L's strategies

Values of k and d render some of these strategies inadmissible (i.e., given k and/or d, a strategy may return $r^* < 0$ and/or $x > 1$), however, and among admissible strategies, one may dominate the others. The limits on L's strategies can be set out as in Figure A1.6. In area A only the first strategy listed above is admissible; in area B, the first two strategies listed above are admissible, and so on.

In area A, defined by $k < 1/(4d-1)$, $d \in [0, 2)$, the constrained strategy $\{x, a, s\} = \{1, d/(1+k), dk/(1+k)\}$ is the only admissible strategy, returning $U_L = (1+k-kd^2)/(1+k)$. Thus, part of L's strategy is $\{x^*, a^*, s^*\} = \{1, d/(1+k), dk/(1+k)\}$ if $k < 1/(4d-1)$.

In area B, defined by $k \in [1/(4d-1), 1/(2d^2-1))$, $d \in (\tfrac{1}{4}, 2)$, L has the option of playing $\{x, a, s\} = \{1, (1+d)/(1+5k), k(1+d)/(1+5k)\}$. This strategy returns $U_L = (5 + 21k - 4kd^2 - 8kd)/4(1+5k)$, and as $(5 + 21k - 4kd^2 - 8kd)/4(1+5k) \geq (1+k-kd^2)/(1+k) \; \forall \; k \geq 1/(4d-1)$, L plays $\{x^*, a^*, s^*\} = \{1, (1+d)/(1+5k), k(1+d)/(1+5k)\}$ in area B.

Area C, defined by $k \in [1/(2d^2-1), 3/(4d^2+8d-11))$, $d \in (\sqrt{\tfrac{1}{2}}, 2)$, opens up a third strategy: $\{x, a, s\} = \{(1+k)/(2d^2k), 1/2dk, 1/2d\}$. This strategy provides $U_L = (1+k)/(4kd^2)$. Basic algebra shows that $(1+k)/(4kd^2) > (1+k-kd^2)/(1+k) \; \forall \; k \geq 1/(2d^2-1)$, hence this third strategy dominates the first in area C. (Comparison of the second and third strategies is less direct, and I bypass it momentarily.)

In area D, defined by $k \geq 3/(4d^2 + 8d - 11)$, $k \geq 1/(4d - 1)$, $d \geq \frac{1}{2}\sqrt{15} - 1$, L can play $\{x, a, s\} = \{2(1 + 5k)/(4d^2k + 8dk - k - 1), 2(1 + d)/(4d^2k + 8dk - k - 1), 2k(1 + d)/(4d^2k + 8dk - k - 1)\}$. This strategy returns $U_L = (1 + 5k)/(4d^2k + 8dk - k - 1)$. Within area D the utility provided by this strategy exceeds that provided by any of the other strategies. Thus L plays $\{x^*, a^*, s^*\} = \{2(1 + 5k)/(4d^2k + 8dk - k - 1), 2(1 + d)/(4d^2k + 8dk - k - 1), 2k(1 + d)/(4d^2k + 8dk - k - 1)\}$ if $k \geq 3/(4d^2 + 8d - 11)$, $d \geq \frac{1}{2}\sqrt{15} - 1$.

This leaves a single question unresolved: Should L play $\{x, a, s\} = \{1, (1 + d)/(1 + 5k), k(1 + d)/(1 + 5k)\}$ or $\{x, a, s\} = \{(1 + k)/(2d^2k), 1/2dk, 1/2d\}$ in area C? The first of these strategies returns:

$$U_L = (5 + 21k - 4kd^2 - 8kd)/4(1 + 5k)$$

The other returns:

$$U_L = (1 + k)/(4kd^2)$$

These two utilities are equal when, in the interval $d \in (\sqrt{\frac{1}{2}}, 2]$ (where both strategies are admissible),

$$k = min\left\{ \frac{5d^2 - 6 - \left[(9d^2 + 4d + 4)(d - 2)^2\right]^{\frac{1}{2}}}{2[5 + d^2(2d + 7)(2d - 3)]} \\ \frac{5d^2 - 6 - \left[(9d^2 + 4d + 4)(d - 2)^2\right]^{\frac{1}{2}}}{2[5 + d^2(2d + 7)(2d - 3)]} \right\}$$

When k exceeds this minimum value, $\{x, a, s\} = \{1, (1 + d)/(1 + 5k), k(1 + d)/(1 + 5k)\}$) dominates $\{x, a, s\} = \{(1 + k)/(2d^2k), 1/2dk, 1/2d\}$. Note, in addition, that this second strategy is admissible iff $k > 1/(2d^2 - 1)$. However, $1/(2d^2 - 1) > (1 + k)/(4kd^2) \ \forall \ d > \sqrt{\frac{1}{2}}$. This means that the k at which the strategy $\{x, a, s\} = \{1, (1 + d)/(1 + 5k), k(1 + d)/(1 + 5k)\}$ begins to return a higher utility than $\{x, a, s\} = \{(1 + k)/(2d^2k), 1/2dk, 1/2d\}$ is reached before the boundary marking off area C. It follows that $\{x^*, a^*, s^*\} = \{1, (1 + d)/(1 + 5k), k(1 + d)/(1 + 5k)\}$) dominates $\{x, a, s\} = \{(1 + k)/(2d^2k), 1/2dk, 1/2d\}$ throughout area C.

L's strategy can therefore be summarized as:

$$\{x^*, a^*, s^*\} = \begin{cases} \{1, d/(1+k), dk/(1+k)\} \text{if} k < 1/(4d-1), d \in (0,2) \\ \{1, (1+d)/(1+5k), k(1+d)/(1+5k)\} \text{if } k \in \\ [1/(4d-1), 3/(4d^2+8d-11)), d \in (1/4,2) \\ 2(1+5k)/(4d^2k+8dk-k-1), 2(1+d)/ \\ (4d^2k+8dk-k-1), 2k(1+d)/(4d^2k+8dk-k-1) \\ \text{if } k \geq 3/(4d^2+8d-11), d \geq 1/2\sqrt{15}-1 \end{cases}$$

The Nash equilibrium of the game is thus:

$$\sigma_L^*(\sigma_{MP}(.)) = \begin{cases} \{1, d/(1+k), dk/(1+k)\} \text{if} k < 1/(4d-1), d \in (0,2) \\ \{1, (1+d)/(1+5k), k(1+d)/(1+5k)\} \text{ if } k \in \\ [1/(4d-1), 3/(4d^2+8d-11)), d \in \{(1/4,2) \\ \{2(1+5k)/(4d^2k+8dk-k-1), 2(1+d)/ \\ (4d^2k+8dk-k-1), 2k(1+d)/(4d^2k+8dk-k-1)\} \\ \text{if } k \geq 3/(4d^2+8d-11), d < 1/2\sqrt{15}-1 \end{cases}$$

$$\sigma_{MP}^*(\sigma_L(.)) = (dx - a - s)/2$$

Appendix 2
Content and construction
of ideological scales

This appendix describes the how the ideological and party loyalty scales used in Chapters 4–8 were constructed. Tables A2.1–A2.9 list the survey items that are used to create the scales used in this paper, their response categories (e.g., strongly agree, agree, neutral, disagree, strongly disagree), and the factor solutions that were used to identify the scales.

Data sources

A series of candidate surveys conducted at roughly the same time in each country provided the basic data with which to construct the ideological scales. These surveys were:

1. Jones, R., I. McAllister, and D. G. Gow. 1996. *Australian Candidate Study, 1996* (SSDA Study No. 944). Canberra: Social Science Data Archives, The Australian National University.
2. Erickson, Lynda. 1993. *Canadian Candidate Study, 1993*. Burnaby, BC: Simon Fraser University.
3. Norris, Pippa and Joni Lovenduski. 1992. *British Candidate Study, 1992*. Available online at: http://ksghome.harvard.edu/~pnorris/Data/data.htm.
4. McAllister, I., Jones, R., D. Denemark, and D. G. Gow. 1994. *Australian Candidate Study, 1993* (SSDA Study No. 764). Canberra: Social Science Data Archives, The Australian National University.
5. Norris, Pippa and Joni Lovenduski. 1997. *British Representation Study, 1997*. Available online at: http://ksghome.harvard.edu/~pnorris/Data/data.htm.

As many of the policy-related questions contained in the 1996 *ACS* were included in the 1993 *ACS*, I was able to use the latter surveys to obtain responses for some of the Australian MPs who did not respond to the 1996 *ACS*. The 1997 *BRS* was used in a similar fashion, providing data on some British MPs who did not respond to the 1992 *BCS*.

228

Table A2.1. *Survey items used to construct the British left–right ideological scale*

	1992 BCS survey item	Question wording	Response categories
1.	G42A	Do you think the government should or should not spend more money to get rid of poverty? (a) Definitely should … (e) Definitely should not.	5
2.	G42B	Do you think the government should or should not encourage the growth of private medicine? (a) Definitely should … (e) Definitely should not.	5
3.	G42D	Do you think the government should or should not introduce stricter laws to regulate trade unions?	5
4.	G46	Do you think that trade unions in this country have far too much power, too much power, etc. …?	5
5.	G47	And do you think that business and industry have far too much power, too much power, etc. …?	5
6.	G52J	There is one law for the rich and one for the poor (Agree / Disagree).	5
7.	G52K	There is no need for strong unions to protect employees' working conditions and wages (Agree / Disagree).	5
8.	G52L	Private enterprise is the best way to solve Britain's economic problems (Agree / Disagree).	5
9.	G52M	Major public services and industries ought to be in state ownership (Agree / Disagree).	5
10.	G52N	It is government's responsibility to provide a job for everyone who wants one (Agree / Disagree).	5

Methods

Scales were identified (and survey items selected) using an approach very similar to the 'vanilla' method used by Gabel and Huber (2000): factor analyse all issue items (the source here being candidate surveys, not party manifestos) via principal components and take the factor that

Table A2.2. *Survey items used to construct the British devolution scale*

1992 BCS survey item	Question wording	Response categories
1. G49	On the whole do you think the UK's interests are better served by closer links with Western Europe, America, or both equally?	3
2. G50	How would you like to see the EC develop: (a) A fully integrated Europe with most major decisions taken by a European government ... (d) Complete British withdrawal from the EC?	4
3. G53A	Which of these statements comes closest to your view: (a) Scotland should become independent, separate from the UK and the EC ... (d) There should be no change from the present system?	4
4. G53B	Which of these statements comes closest to your view: (a) Wales should become independent, separate from the UK and the EC ... (d) There should be no change from the present system?	4
5. G48	Which, if any, of these statements comes closest to your own opinion on British nuclear weapons? (a) Britain should keep her own nuclear weapons , independent of other countries ... (c) Having nothing to do with nuclear weapons under any circumstances.	3

explains the most variance in the data as the left–right dimension. The difference between my method and Gabel and Huber's is that I do not constrain the factor analysis to return just one factor. The rotated factor solutions (Tables A4.3 and A4.6) and notes relevant to them are shown below.

Additive scales were then created based on the factor solutions by adding together respondents' scores on a factor's constituent items. Additive scales were used in place of factor scores because it is not realistic to assume that exactly the same factor scores would have emerged had the survey response been 100 per cent. However, one might still expect the same factors to emerge had the response been 100 per cent. Scale items were normalized to range between 0 and 1 from left to right before being added together. Thus an item with five response categories

Table A2.3. *The British factor solution*

1992 BCS survey item	Factor 1 (class cleavage, economic left–right)	Factor 2 (European Union, devolution)
G42A	–.61	.49
G42B	.74	–.46
G42D	.80	–.23
G46	.82	–.16
G47	–.69	.32
G52K	.67	–.18
G52L	.83	–.25
G52M	–.80	.31
G52N	–.73	.26
G48	.68	–.49
G49	–.36	.60
G50	–.03	.76
G53B	–.39	.80
G53A	–.38	.79
Eigenvalue	7.97	1.24
Percentage of variance explained	56.9	8.8

Note: G54B (Have Welfare benefits that are available to people today gone too far ... not nearly far enough?) or G54D (Have attempts to give equal opportunities to black people and Asians in Britain gone too far ... not nearly far enough?) might have been added to the first factor, but given the factor's strong focus on the 'old' class cleavage (i.e., on the conflict between trade unions and workers and capitalists and the state), I omitted them from the left–right scale. When these and similar items were included they tended to form a third factor centred on the extent of the welfare state. However, the first factor identified here, which is firmly focused on the class cleavage and trade union power, is far more powerful. Questions on abortion similarly tended to load on their own factor, but again had relatively weak eigenvalues. In view of this fact, and the greater substantive interest in the role of Euroscepticism in the 1992–7 British Parliament, I decided to keep the anti-devolution dimension as the second ideological dimension. G48 is included in factor 2 for the substantive reason that it is the one item that taps into the Eurosceptic left. This ideological strain has historically been expressed within the Labour Party alongside an aversion to a British nuclear arsenal and advocacy of a Bevanite foreign policy. The factor solution corroborates this interpretation: candidates opposed to a British nuclear arsenal are also anti-devolution and anti-Europe.

Table A2.4. *Survey items used to construct the Canadian left–right ideological scale*

	1993 CCS survey item	Question wording	Response categories
1.	VD3	Do you think government should see to it that everyone has a job or leave people to get ahead on their own?	3
2.	VD6D	Capital punishment is never justified no matter what the crime. (a) Strongly agree … (e) Strongly disagree.	5
3.	VD6H	The welfare state makes people nowadays less willing to look after themselves. (a) Strongly agree … (e) Strongly disagree.	5
4.	VD6M	We have gone too far in pushing equal rights in this country. (a) Strongly agree … (e) Strongly disagree.	5
5.	VD9	Which of these statements comes closest to your view: (a) We can only be sure everyone's needs are met if the government provides the same services to all; (b) The government should not provide services to those who can afford them.	2
6.	VD10	Which of these statements comes closest to your view: (a) Government should control inflation even if it means higher unemployment; (b) Government should control unemployment even if it means higher inflation?	2
7.	VD6B	The government must do more to reduce the income gap between poor and rich Canadians. (a) Strongly agree … (e) Strongly disagree.	5
8.	VD6K	We must crack down on crime, even if it means that criminals lose their rights. (a) Strongly agree … (e) Strongly disagree.	5
9.	VC6B	Do you approve or disapprove of party quotas and affirmative action for women candidates? (a) Strongly approve … (d) Strongly disapprove.	4
10.	VC6C	Do you approve or disapprove of special financial support for women candidates? (a) Strongly approve … (d) Strongly disapprove.	4

Table A2.5. *Survey items used to construct the Canadian social conservatism scale*

1993 CCS survey item	Question wording	Response categories
1. VD4	Which of the following positions on abortion is closest to your own: (a) Never permitted ... (c) A woman's personal choice.	3
2. VD6A	People today don't have enough respect for traditional values. (a) Strongly agree ... (e) Strongly disagree.	5
3. VD6C	The banning of pornographic films and magazines is necessary to uphold moral standards? (a) Strongly agree ... (e) Strongly disagree.	5
4. VD6E	Society would be better off if more women stayed home with their children. (a) Strongly agree ... (e) Strongly disagree.	5
5. VD6G	Homosexual couples should be allowed to get legally married? (a) Strongly agree ... (e) Strongly disagree.	5
6. VD6I	Only people who are legally married should be having children. (a) Strongly agree ... (e) Strongly disagree.	5
7. VD6J	Respect for authority is one of the most important things that children should learn? (a) Strongly agree ... (e) Strongly disagree.	5
8. VD8	Gender equality	2

was, for example, coded (0, .25, .5, .75, 1) while an item with three response categories was coded (0, .5, 1).

A chief advantage of this construction is that it is possible to say in a concrete fashion that MP_i answered 'agree' or 'strongly agree' to more rightist policy items than MP_j. Moreover, if one also considers the high degree of ideological constraint (Converse 1964) exhibited by MPs and their shared political culture, comparisons across individuals on these scales (but not countries) would seem to be meaningful. A high degree of ideological constraint, after all, implies that MPs are not answering questions randomly, and a shared political culture, that they are placing similar weights on similar policy items. Thus, there is a sound basis for taking the

Table A2.6. *The Canadian factor solution*

1993 CCS survey item	Factor 1 (economic left–right)	Factor 2 (social conservatism)
VC6BR	.73	.26
VC6CR	.70	.33
VD3	–.82	–.18
VD6B	–.78	–.26
VD6D	–.56	–.44
VD6H	.53	.50
VD6M	.60	.45
VD9	–.69	–.10
VD10	.75	.10
VD4	.19	.57
VD6A	.25	.66
VD6C	–.18	.65
VD6E	.34	.54
VD6G	–.41	–.63
VD6K	.38	.61
VD6I	.28	.59
VD6J	.21	.72
VD8	–.29	–.30
Eigenvalue	7.55	1.62
Percentage of variance explained	41.9	9.0

difference in the number of rightist responses given by any two MPs as indicative of the true ideological distance between these individuals.

Missing data and multiple imputation

Missing data generated by survey non-response were imputed using multiple imputation methods. I used *NORM 2.2 for Windows* to generate five British, five Canadian, and five Australian data sets.[1] The percentages of data missing in the data sets were 11.0 per cent for Britain, 8.2 per cent for Canada, and 6.9 per cent for Australia. The

---

[1] *NORM 2.2 for Windows* is written by Joseph Schafer and is available online at www.stat.psu.edu/~jsl/.

Table A2.7. *Survey items used to construct the Australian left–right scale*

1996 ACS survey item	Question wording	Response categories
1. C2TAX	High income tax makes people less willing to work (Agree / Disagree).	5
2. C2STRICT	There should be stricter laws to regulate the activities of trade unions (Agree / Disagree).	5
3. C2EQUAL	Income and wealth should be redistributed toward ordinary working people (Agree / Disagree).	5
4. C3	If the government had a choice between reducing taxes or spending more on social services, which do you think that it should do?	5
5. D1EQUOP	Do you think that equal opportunities for women have gone much too far (too far, about right, not far enough, not nearly far enough)?	5
6. D1ABOR	Do you think that government help for Aborigines has gone much too far (too far, about right, not far enough, not nearly far enough)?	5
7. D2LAWBRK	People who break the law should be given stiffer sentences (Agree / Disagree).	5
8. D4	Do you think that the government should spend more or spend less on defence?	5
9. C2TUPOW	The trade unions in this country have too much power (Agree / Disagree).	5
10. E3	How important do you feel the Queen and the Royal Family are to Australia?	3

percentage of missing data should not be confused with the response rates of the surveys (on which see page 78) or the rate of missing information in any particular variable (on which see Rubin 1987). To conceive of the percentage of missing data the reader should imagine the data set as a matrix of n cases by k variables. For every one of the nk cells in the matrix a datum is observed (i.e., the cell contains some realization of the kth variable for the nth case) or missing, in which

Table A2.8. *The Australian factor solution*

1996 ACS survey item	Factor 1 (class cleavage, economic left–right)
C2TAX	.73
C2STRICT	.78
C2EQUAL	.73
C3	.83
D1EQUOP	.69
D1ABOR	.77
D2LAWBRK	.64
D4	.72
C2TUPOW	.83
E3	.52
Eigenvalue	5.32
Percentage of variance explained	53.2

Note: Solution is unrotated because only one factor was extracted. It was possible to construct another issue dimension centred on republicanism, but even when the factor analysis was constrained to produce this second dimension, the items listed above still loaded on the main left–right dimension, even item E3.

Table A2.9. *Survey items used to construct the party loyalty scale* *

Wording of survey question: In your view, how important are the following aspects of an MP's job?	Response categories
1. Supporting the party leadership (Very important / Not at all important)	4
2. Voting with the party in Parliament	4
3. Defending party policy	4

* The following survey items were used to construct the party loyalty scale:
  items C2SupPl, C2Vot, and C2DefPol in 1993 ACS;
  items vc2g, vc2i, and vc2n in 1993 CCS;
  items Q26g, Q26i, and Q26n in 1992 BCS.

case the cell is empty. The percentage of missing data is just the percentage of the *nk* cells that are empty.

There are two reasons why the percentage of missing data is far lower than the response rates of the candidate surveys might lead one to expect. First, some variables such as the MP's age, educational background, party affiliation, parliamentary rank, date of first election, and the like were available from public sources such as the *Canadian Parliamentary Guide* or *Dod's Parliamentary Companion*. In these cases, a missing cell could be filled with the observed datum. The second reason is technical, but put *very* simply, the more observed data one has on hand, the better one does at estimating values for the missing data. This does not occur because of a larger sample size (though that helps), but because the addition of fully observed background variables makes it more likely that one has accounted for unobserved differences in the survey responses of respondents and non-respondents (Rubin 1977, p. 540). The aim, then, is to include in the matrix vectors of observed data that are thought to be related to the missing data (see Rubin 1996, pp. 478–9). As the number of fully observed vectors is added to the matrix, the percentage of cells with missing data necessarily shrinks. I used three sources of information to help impute survey responses for non-responding MPs:

1. Survey responses from all other major party candidates, with a dummy variable to identify winners (i.e., MPs) and losers (as per Meng 1994, p. 541). With the addition of these cases non-responding MPs comprise 19.8 per cent of available British observations and 21.5 per cent of available Canadian observations.
2. Socio-economic profiles of every constituency garnered from recent census data.
3. The electoral histories (i.e., party vote shares) of every constituency over the past three elections in each country.

Once these data are included in the data matrix, the percentage of missing data as a result of non-responding MPs is quite small.

Appendix 3
Sampling and coding of media dissent and discipline

This appendix describes how I sampled and coded reports of media dissent and party discipline employed in Chapters 5 and 8.

Sample selection

I tracked media dissent and party discipline through several major dailies in Canada, Australia, and New Zealand, trying to balance the needs for regional coverage and quality reporting.

- Reports of media dissent and party discipline in Australia were tracked in three sources: (1) *Sydney Morning Herald* – the major source; (2) *The Age* (Melbourne) – for Victorian MPs and Senators; (3) *West Australian* (for West Australian MPs and Senators). MPs' names were used as search terms in each database. Newspaper stories appearing between 1 May 1996 and 30 September 1998 were coded for dissent and duplicates weeded out.

- Canadian media dissent and party discipline reports were tracked in the following sources: (1) Southam Newspapers (*Vancouver Sun, Calgary Herald, Winnipeg Free Press, Toronto Star, Ottawa Citizen, Montreal Gazette,* and *Halifax Daily News*); (2) *Globe and Mail*; (3) *La Presse*. As in the Australian case, MPs' names were used as search terms in the above databases. The Canadian sampling frame dated from 5 November 1993 to 30 April 1997. The Canadian media databases were more flexible than the Australian databases (primarily because Southam owns newspapers in a number of urban centres) and permitted more geographically sensitive searches. I could, for example, search for a Quebec MP's name in the *Montreal Gazette* or *La Presse* instead of relying solely on the *Globe and Mail* (essentially the Canadian counterpart to the *Sydney Morning Herald*).

- The New Zealand media dissent data were collected from New Zealand's two major newspapers, the Auckland-based

New Zealand Herald and the Wellington-based *Dominion*. The sampling frame encompassed the 1990–3 term of Jim Bolger's National Party government. The media archives of the Department of Politics of the University of Auckland provided the material.

Coding rules

Media dissent

I employ two categories of dissent, explicit dissent and veiled dissent. I define explicit dissent as a direct or indirect quotation from an identified MP in which that MP categorically criticizes party leaders, attacks a policy endorsed by the party leader(s), or threatens to vote or speak against party policy. This definition excludes anonymous threats or complaints of cross-voting or discontent and reports of critical speeches or remarks without direct or indirect quotation. Veiled dissent occurs when backbenchers express concerns or misgivings about the party's policies or leaders. Again, anonymous threats or complaints of cross-voting or discontent and reports of critical speeches or remarks that cannot be linked to a specific MP are excluded. For greater clarification, I list several examples below.

Explicit dissent by direct quotation
Describing the [National] Government's economic policy as 'a fraud upon the electorate' after its election pledges of balanced policies, Mr Peters [a National MP] urged a shift from 'this failed experiment' to a proved middle way. Source: 'Peters Slates Quality of Policymaking Advice', *New Zealand Herald*, 10 October 1991.

Explicit dissent by indirect quotation
Mr Peters and Mr Campion [National Party MPs] said they opposed the Income Tax Bill No 6 because it contained an element of taxing capital gains, which the National Party had opposed since 1936. Source: 'Nat MPs Cross Floor to Oppose Tax Bill', *New Zealand Herald*, 28 February 1991.

Explicit versus veiled dissent (direct quotation)
'If it's the same legislation that Kim Campbell [justice minister in the previous Canadian Conservative government] brought forward, I could drive a Mac truck through it – and I certainly intend to,' Mr. Wappel said in an interview. Source: *Globe and Mail*, 18 May 1994, A4.

Some same-sex advocates are concerned that even Mr. Rock's [the Liberal justice minister] rights amendment, which is intended merely as a government catch-up with past court rulings, could get caught up in the fallout from the [strongly Conservative] Ontario vote. 'Bearing in mind that every MP but two from Ontario is a Liberal, one would presume that the Liberal MPs federally have taken some sort of message from this provincial vote,' said Tom Wappel, MP for Scarborough West in Toronto. Source: *Globe and Mail*, 11 June 1994, A4.

In both quotations Tom Wappel, a Canadian Liberal backbencher, warns the justice minister about potential opposition to Bill C-41, the bill referred to in Chapter 4. Only the first quotation is taken as an instance of explicit dissent; Wappel explicitly warns the minister that he intends to undermine the government's legislation. In the second quotation, however, Wappel merely implies that Ontario Liberal backbenchers will approach the government's bill warily because of provincial election results in which the Conservatives did well. These sorts of quotations are coded as instances of *veiled dissent*, not explicit dissent.

Explicit versus veiled dissent (indirect quotation)

In other developments, a Victorian Liberal MP, Mr. Peter Nugent, slammed the Government's record on indigenous issues in an interview with the Uniting Church's monthly newspaper, *Crosslight*. Mr. Nugent told the newspaper the 10-point Wik plan added up to extinguishment in all but name. He said that in a country that espoused adherence to the rule of law, governments should not be extinguishing citizens' rights. Source: *The Age*, 4 September 1997, 7.

In other developments, a Liberal backbencher, Mr. Peter Nugent, broke ranks during debate on the bill in the House of Representatives late on Tuesday night, saying he had serious concerns about the impact on the reconciliation process. He told Parliament that despite his concerns he would vote for the legislation to avoid his view being used for political purposes as a sign of Government disunity. Mr. Nugent said other Government members had privately expressed their doubts about the bill to him after his speech but none were also prepared to go on the public record. Source: *The Age*, 23 October 1997, 9.

The ten-point Wik plan was Prime Minister Howard's personal response to a Supreme Court ruling on Aboriginal land claims. Nugent's remarks in the first excerpt, therefore, directly indict the prime minister's policy and so count as an act of explicit dissent. The second excerpt, on the other hand, states only that Nugent had 'serious concerns' about the (Native Title) bill. The second report is therefore not counted as explicit dissent, but provides a good example of veiled dissent.

Uncodable statement (unidentified quotation)

'We are just sick to heavens of some ministers falling into holes, not doing their jobs properly and producing problems for the rest of us to solve,' one [National Party MP] said. Source: 'Reshuffle Rejection Irks MPs', *New Zealand Herald*, 23 March 1993.

Uncodable statement (second-hand report without quotation)

Backbench MPs have also been irritated by ministers announcing key policy changes before the full caucus, and not just a caucus committee, has been briefed. Source: 'A Government in Need of Management and Discipline', *Dominion*, 26 August 1991.

Discipline

Coding rules for reports of party discipline had to be more flexible because many acts of discipline occur behind the closed doors of party rooms. However, as with dissent, I coded gradations of discipline, differentiating, in particular, between formal and informal discipline. Informal discipline occurs when an MP is publicly rebuked or threatened by a superior member of the party (e.g., the prime minister, a cabinet minister, or the chairman of the extra-parliamentary party). Formal discipline involves the application of formal sanctions such as demotion or deselection. Again, examples make these coding rules a little clearer.

Formal discipline:

The Prime Minister forced Liberal backbencher Mr. Don Randall to apologise publicly to Ms Cheryl Kernot yesterday for telling Parliament she had 'the morals of an alley cat in heat'.

Mr Randall was told not to attend the Liberal Party's national convention in Brisbane, where his extraordinary attack on Ms Kernot overshadowed yesterday's opening and the party's women's conference. Source: *Sydney Morning Herald*, 14 March 1998, 7.

Informal discipline

Jeanes was in trouble again this week when she stood and told Howard in the party room that she intended to reserve her right to vote against the Prime

Minister's beloved work-for-the-dole legislation. Howard was not impressed. He insisted the scheme was popular in the community, that Jeanes withdraw her remarks and, if she wouldn't, he wanted to see her privately after the party meeting. Jeanes stood her ground.

Last December, Sue Jeanes was one of two Liberal MPs who abstained from voting for the Government's rankly political Hindmarsh Island Bridge legislation. The other was Victoria's Peter Nugent. That earned them both a terse 'please explain' rebuke. The thought that this time Jeanes might actually cross the floor and vote against the Government is something, John Howard made clear in the privacy of the party room this week, he will not tolerate. Source: *Sydney Morning Herald*, 22 March 1997, 43.

The first excerpt is an example of formal discipline: Randall is banned by the party from attending its annual conference. The second excerpt is example of informal discipline. Howard does not strip Jeanes of any position; he just rebukes and threatens her in the party room for her dissent. Note that the coding rules for discipline, unlike those for dissent, count this second excerpt even though it is based on an anonymous and perhaps second-hand source.

Appendix 4
Demotion and the parliamentary careers of Canadian MPs

This appendix examines the impact of demotion on an MP's parliamentary career. I estimate a model of ministerial career prospects with data from the 1972 cohort of Canadian Liberal and Conservative MPs. The sampling frame spans 1972 to 1995, the year by which the last MP elected in 1972 left the Commons. The dependent variable is a dummy variable that notes whether an MP enjoyed some time as a junior or senior minister or opposition critic. The key independent variable is a demotion variable that measures the number of ranks (if any) that an MP was demoted during their career. (If MPs were demoted twice, the data were based on their careers up until that first demotion.)

MacDonald's (1987) work on parliamentary careers stressed that MPs' professional ambition was the single best predictor of upward mobility, and it is quite reasonable to imagine that ambitious MPs are more likely to shrug off a setback and start a second climb up the parliamentary career ladder than their less ambitious colleagues. If ambition is a critical control variable, it is also a difficult one to measure. MacDonald used surveys to assess how professionally ambitious British MPs were, but I do not have the luxury of these sorts of data. Instead, I use the MP's career trajectory to construct a proxy for ambition. I ask whether an MP has been able to come back from a professional setback, and I assume that MPs who have managed to do this are more ambitious and driven (and luckier) than their colleagues.

I describe MPs who have come back from a setback – either a demotion, an electoral defeat, or spell of retirement – as having 'multi-peaked' careers. This terminology and my coding of ministerial careers and demotion are made clearer with an illustration. Figure A4.1 depicts the careers trajectories of four MPs. Each trajectory can be assessed on three dimensions telling one whether the MP: (a) enjoyed a ministerial career – or not; (b) was demoted at some point (and by how many ranks) – or not; and (c) had a multi-peaked career – or not.

Key: 0 = not in house, 1 = backbencher, 2 = committee chair, 3 = parliamentary
secretary, 4 = whip, 5 = junior minister, 6 = cabinet minister, 7 = prime minister

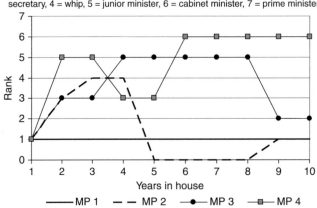

Figure A4.1 Four hypothetical parliamentary career trajectories

There are six possible combinations here (if one momentarily thinks of demotion in dichotomous terms), but the four shown give one a good idea of how I have coded MPs' careers. MP_1 is a career backbencher. He was never promoted, and hence never held a post, ministerial or otherwise, from which he might have been demoted. MP_2 started out as a backbencher, rose to the whips' office, but then suffered an electoral defeat. MP_2 returned to the House subsequently, but never moved beyond the back bench in her second stint. Thus MP_2's career was not ministerial but was multi-peaked: even though MP_2 was never demoted, she came back from an electoral defeat. MP_3 became a junior minister late in her career and served a few years in that capacity before being demoted to a committee chairmanship, a position which she held for a few years before retiring. MP_3's career was marked by a demotion (of three ranks by my coding), but as she was unable to move beyond her committee chairmanship after the demotion, her career is not categorized as multi-peaked. Nor, for coding purposes, is MP_3's career considered ministerial, because she never *reattained a ministerial position after demotion*. Remember, the main objective here is to identify the *after-effects* of demotion on an MP's career. MP_4's career provides a useful contrast to MP_3's. MP_4 rose quickly to the junior ministry, only to be demoted shortly afterwards to the somewhat lesser position of parliamentary secretary. Unlike MP_3, however, MP_4 overcame this demotion to become a cabinet minister. MP_4's career is therefore coded as having been ministerial, multi-peaked, and marked by demotion.

Table A4.1. *The effect of demotion on MPs' chances of becoming ministers*

Pr(MP$_i$ became a minister)	B	z values[†]
Demoted during career	−1.10	−1.84*
Multi-peaked career	7.15	3.28***
University-educated	−.03	−.02
Age entered Commons	−.15	−2.12**
Promoted by third year	6.39	2.86***
Electoral margin	.09	2.34**
Conservative	5.19	3.11***
Conservative × university-educated	−1.23	−1.59
Constant	−2.56	−1.04
Pseudo R^2	.67	
χ^2	25.95	
Log likelihood	−16.93	
N	76	

*$p < .10$
**$p < .05$
***$p < .01$
[†] Calculated using Huber-White standard errors.

I also include in the model the MP's age of entry into the Commons, a dummy indicating that the MP had received a promotion by the third year in the House, the MP's margin of victory in his or her first election, post-secondary education, and party affiliation. A university education, youthful entry into the Commons, electoral security, and early promotion are all hallmarks of upward mobility in Parliament. Party affiliation is important because the Progressive Conservatives were in opposition for much of the sampling frame. It may be harder to start a political career in opposition (the party's status connotes electoral vulnerability), but should one secure a safe seat, the opportunity for advancement is actually quite good. The situation is similar to promotion in the army during wartime: the young lieutenant who manages to survive moves quickly up the ranks.

The results of the model are shown in Table A4.1. Almost all the variables are statistically significant and in the expected direction. Younger MPs from safe seats who have secured promotions by their third year in the House are more likely than their colleagues to be junior

Table A4.2. *The probability of a ministerial career conditional on demotion*

Ranks demoted	Promoted by third year	Not promoted by third year
	99.8	47.8
1	99.5	23.4
2	99.3	19.9
3	95.3	3.3
4	86.9	1.1
5	69.0	0.4

Cell entries are the MP's probability (percentages) of attaining a ministerial post. MPs are assumed to be forty-three-year-old Liberals with 15 per cent electoral margins and university educations.

or senior frontbenchers at some point in their careers. These results suggest that the model is fairly well specified at least. The key variable here is demotion. Given the small sample and reasonable grounds for using a one-tailed test (how can demotion help a career?), the coefficient's *p*-value of .07 can be taken as evidence of statistical significance. To get a sense of how demotion affects an MP's career, imagine two equally ambitious Liberal MPs. These MPs arrive in the Commons at forty-three years of age, university-educated, representing constituencies in which they secured majorities of 15 per cent, and received promotion before three years were up.[1] Let the only difference between these MPs be the fact that one is promoted by her third year in the Commons, while the other has to wait four or more years for promotion.

Table A4.2 summarizes the results of this simulation. The MP who received early promotion was almost certain to attain a ministerial post, and minor demotions of up to two ranks (e.g., moving from the junior ministry to a whip's job) have little effect. Beyond this, however, the impact was more serious. Drop four ranks from the junior ministry to the back bench, for example, and the MP's chances at returning to the ministry decline by about 15 per cent, drop five ranks, and the MP's chances decline a further 15 per cent. More striking is how heavily the

[1] *NORM* 2.2 *for Windows* is written by Joseph Schafer and is available online at www.stat.psu.edu/~jsl/.

MP's prospects depend on securing promotion in the first three years of office. Indeed, it hard to overstate how great an impact this event has on an MP's career prospects. Without such a promotion, an MP's chances of a ministerial career under these conditions top out at just under 50 per cent. Even a slight demotion in these circumstances virtually dooms the MP to a career on the back bench. Being demoted from a parliamentary secretaryship to the back bench, a drop of three ranks, leaves the MP with just a 3.3 per cent chance of ever becoming a minister.

Demotion – particularly from the ministry to the back bench – is not automatically lethal to an MP's ministerial ambitions, but it is a serious setback. These results are, of course, based on a small sample of MPs, and this suggests caution when trying to make generalizations based on these data. The results are a long way from being *sui generis*, however: they jibe with much previous work on British parliamentary careers (e.g., Buck 1963; MacDonald 1987) and correspond closely to some of the professional dynamics that appeared in British MPs' careers (compare, for example, Table A4.2 with Table 8.2).

References

Newspaper sources

Daily Telegraph. 2 November 2002. 'Tory Leader Gives MPs "Free Vote" on Gay Adoption', 17.

The Economist. 7 November 2002. 'Where Did It All Go Wrong?', 59.

The Economist. 18 March 2003. 'Blair Sticks to His Guns', www.economist. com/agenda/displaystory.cfm?story_id=E1_TGQSQVN.

Globe and Mail. 24 November 1994. 'Internal Party Fight over Bill Sputters. Solidarity Reigns', A6.

Guardian. 10 November 2005. 'Blair Defeated on Terror Bill', www.guardian. co.uk/politics/2005/nov/09/uksecurity.terrorism.

Sydney Morning Herald. 11 May 1996. 'Iron-bar Makes PM Blink', 37.

Sydney Morning Herald. 22 May 1996. 'PM Cuts Deal on Native Title', 3.

Sydney Morning Herald. 14 June 1996. 'Tuckey Takes an Iron-bar to "Executive Arrogance"', 4.

Sydney Morning Herald. 11 July 1996. 'Howard Stands Firm against Gun Crimping', 1.

Sydney Morning Herald. 6 March 1997. 'Howard Faces Revolt over Cut to Sugar Tariff', 6.

Sydney Morning Herald. 20 March 1997. 'Howard Faces Coalition Revolt over Wik Compromise Plan', 3.

Sydney Morning Herald. 27 March 1997. 'Dissatisfaction Mounts on the Back Benches', 43.

Sydney Morning Herald. 23 October 1997. 'A Show of Hands – And Then Another Liberal Rebels on Wik', 8.

Sydney Morning Herald. 29 October 1997. 'Libs Move to Avoid NP Split on Wik', 3.

Sydney Morning Herald. 30 October 1997. 'Blow to Coalition as Renegades Cross Floor over Wik', 3.

Sydney Morning Herald. 2 December 1997. 'Sunset Clause beyond Pale, Says Harradine', 4.

Sydney Morning Herald. 18 June 1998. 'Moderates Push for Wik Compromise', 7.

Sydney Morning Herald. 4 July 1998. 'The Dust Settles: The Painful Journey to a Deal', 29.

The Times. 5 November 2002. 'Challenge to Rebels Was the Mark of a Vulnerable Leader, Not a Strong One'.

Toronto Star. 6 February 1995. 'Liberals Face Rough Ride in House. Explosive Issues Top Agenda as MPs Return to Ottawa', A9.

Vancouver Sun. 13 June 1995. 'Liberals Expected to Pass 3 Thorny Bills within a Week: "The Longer They Let Things Drag On the More Difficult It Would Be to Control their Backbenchers"', A7.

Winnipeg Free Press. 15 June 1995. 'Iftody to Rebel Again', A1.

Data sets and computer programs

Clarke, H., D. Sanders, M. Stewart, and P. Whiteley. *British General Election Study, 2001; Cross-Section Survey* [computer file]. Colchester, Essex: UK Data Archive [distributor], March 2003. SN: 4619.

British Election Study, 2005: Internet Rolling Campaign Panel Data and British Parliamentary Constituency Database [computer file]. Colchester, Essex: UK Data Archive [distributor], November 2006. SN: 5496.

Erickson, Lynda. 1993. *Canadian Candidate Study, 1993*. Burnaby, BC: Simon Fraser University.

Heath, A., R. Jowell, and J. K. Curtice. *British General Election Study, 1983; Cross-Section Survey* [computer file]. Colchester, Essex: UK Data Archive [distributor], 1983. SN: 2005.

British General Election Study, 1987; Cross-Section Survey, 2nd edn [computer file]. Colchester, Essex: UK Data Archive [distributor], April 1993. SN: 2568.

British Election Panel Study, 1992–1997 [computer file]. Colchester, Essex: UK Data Archive [distributor], July 1998. SN: 3888.

Heath, Anthony F., Roger M. Jowell, John K. Curtice, and Pippa Norris. 1999. *British General Election Cross-Section Survey, 1997* [computer file]. ICPSR version (ICPSR 2615). London: Social and Community Planning Research [producer], 1998. Colchester, Essex: ESRC Data Archive/Ann Arbor, MI: Interuniversity Consortium for Political and Social Research [distributors], 1999.

Jones, R., I. McAllister, and D. G. Gow. 1996. *Australian Candidate Study, 1996* (SSDA Study No. 944). Canberra: Social Science Data Archives, The Australian National University.

McAllister, I., R. Jones, D. Denemark, and D. G. Gow. 1994. *Australian Candidate Study, 1993* (SSDA Study No. 764). Canberra: Social Science Data Archives, The Australian National University.

Norris, Pippa and Joni Lovenduski. 1992. *British Candidate Study, 1992*. Available online at: http://ksghome.harvard.edu/~pnorris/Data/data.htm. 1997. *British Representation Study, 1997*. Available online at: http://ksghome.harvard.edu/~pnorris/Data/data.htm.

Norton, Philip and Philip Cowley. 1999. *Dissension in the House of Commons 1992–1997 Codebook*. UK Data Archive. SN: 4055

Tomz, Michael, Jason Wittenberg, and Gary King. 2001. '*CLARIFY: Software for Interpreting and Presenting Statistical Results*', version 2.0. Cambridge, MA: Harvard University, 1 June, http://gking.harvard.edu.

Vowles, Jack, Peter Aimer, Helena Catt, Raymond Miller, and Jim Lamare. 1994. *1992 New Zealand Election Survey* [computer file]. Auckland: Department of Political Science, University of Auckland. Available online at www.nzes.org/exec/show/1993.

Parliamentary sources

Parliamentary Debates of the Commonwealth of Australia (House of Representatives). Various volumes. Canberra: The House of Representatives of the Commonwealth of Australia.

Parliamentary Debates of the Commonwealth of Australia (Senate). Various volumes. Canberra: The Senate of the Commonwealth of Australia.

Annotated Standing Orders of the House of Commons. 1989. Ottawa: The House of Commons of Canada.

Parliamentary Debates of the House of Commons of Canada. Ottawa: Queen's Printer. Available online at www.parl.gc.ca/cgi-bin/hansard/e_hansard_master.pl.

Parliamentary Debates (Hansard). Various Volumes. Wellington, NZ: House of Representatives.

Standing Orders of the House of Representatives. 2005. Wellington, NZ: House of Representatives.

Parliamentary Debates of the House of Commons (Hansard). Sixth series. Various volumes. London: HMSO.

Monographs and journal articles

Aldrich, John H. 1995. *Why Parties? The Origin and Transformation of Political Parties in America*. University of Chicago Press.

Alt, James E. 1984. 'Dealignment and the Dynamics of Partisanship in Britain', in Russell Dalton, Scott Flanagan, and Paul Allen Beck (eds.), *Electoral Change in Advanced Industrial Democracies*. Princeton University Press, 298–329.

Anagnoson, J. Theodore. 1987. 'Does Constituency Work Have an Electoral Impact? The Case of New Zealand MPs', *Political Science*, 39: 105–18.

Asher, Herbert B. 1973. 'The Learning of Legislative Norms', *American Political Science Review*, 67: 499–513.

Aylott, Nicholas. 2002. 'Let's Discuss This Later: Party Responses to Euro-Division in Scandinavia', *Party Politics*, 8: 441–61.

Benedetto, Giacomo and Simon Hix. 2007. 'The Rejected, Dejected, and the Ejected: Explaining Government Rebels in the 2001–05 British House of Commons', *Comparative Political Studies*, 40: 755–81.

Bean, Clive. 1990. 'The Personal Vote in Australian Elections', *Political Studies*, 38: 253–68.

Beck, Nathaniel and Jonathan N. Katz. 1995. 'What to Do (and Not to Do) with Time-Series Cross-Section Data', *American Political Science Review*, 89: 634–47.

2001. 'Throwing Out the Baby with the Bathwater: A Comment on Green, Yoon, and Kim', *International Organizations*, 55: 487–95.

Beer, Samuel H. 1965. *Modern British Politics*. London: Faber and Faber.

Berkeley, Humphrey. 1972. *Crossing the Floor*. London: Allen and Unwin.

Bowler, Shaun. 2000. 'Parties in Legislatures: Two Competing Explanations', in Russell Dalton and Martin Wattenberg (eds.), *Parties without Partisans*. Oxford University Press, 157–79.

Bown, Francis. 1990. 'The Defeat of the Shops Bill, 1986', in Michael Rush (ed.), *Parliament and Pressure Politics*. Oxford University Press, 213–33.

Brambor, Thomas, William R. Clark and Matthew Golder. 2005. 'Understanding Interaction Models: Improving Empirical Analyses', *Political Analysis*, 14: 63–82.

Buck, Philip. 1963. 'The Early Start toward Cabinet Office, 1918–55', *Western Political Quarterly*, 16: 624–32.

Butler, David and Gareth Butler. 1994. *British Political Facts, 1900–1994*. New York: St. Martin's Press.

Butler, David and Denis Kavanagh. 1997. *The British General Election of 1997*. New York: St. Martin's Press.

Butler, David and Donald E. Stokes. 1969. *Political Change in Britain: Forces Shaping Electoral Choice*. London: Macmillan.

Butt, Ronald. 1967. *The Power of Parliament*. London: Constable.

Cain, Bruce E., John A. Ferejohn, and Morris P. Fiorina. 1987. *The Personal Vote: Constituency Service and Electoral Independence*. Cambridge, MA: Harvard University Press.

Campbell, Angus, Philip E. Converse, Warren E. Miller, and Donald E. Stokes. 1960. *The American Voter*. University of Chicago Press.

Carty, R. Kenneth. 2002. 'Canada's 19th Century Cadre Parties at the Millennium', in Paul Webb, David Farrell, and Ian Holliday (eds.), *Political Parties in Advanced Industrial Democracies*. Oxford University Press, 345–79.

Clarke, Harold D., Karl Ho, and Marianne C. Stewart. 2000. 'Major's Lesser (Not Minor) Effects: Prime Ministerial Approval and Governing Party Support in Britain Since 1979', *Electoral Studies*, 18: 255–74.

Clarke, Harold D., David Sanders, Marianne C. Stewart, and Paul F. Whiteley. 2004. *Political Choice in Britain*. Oxford University Press.

Converse, Philip. 1964. 'The Nature of Belief Systems in Mass Publics', in David E. Apter (ed.), *Ideology and Discontent*. New York: The Free Press, 206–61.

Cook, Robin. 2003. *The Point of Departure*. London: Simon & Schuster.

Cowley, Philip. 1999. 'Rebels and Rebellions: Conservative MPs in the 1992 Parliament', *British Journal of Politics and International Relations*, 1: 84–105.

 2002. *Revolts and Rebellions: Parliamentary Voting under Blair*. London: Politico's.

 2005. *The Rebels: How Blair Mislaid His Majority*. London: Politico's.

Cowley, Philip and Philip Norton. 1996. 'Are Conservative MPs Revolting?', Research Paper in Legislative Studies, 2/96. Hull: Centre for Legislative Studies, University of Hull.

Cowley, Philip and Philip Norton, with Mark Stuart and Matthew Bailey. 1996. 'Blair's Bastards: Discontent within the Parliamentary Labour Party', Research Paper in Legislative Studies, 1/96. Hull: Centre for Legislative Studies, University of Hull.

Cowley, Philip and Mark Stuart. 2004. 'Still Causing Trouble: The Conservative Parliamentary Party', *Political Quarterly* 75: 356–61.

 2005. 'Government Defeated Twice on Terrorism Bill', briefing paper. Available online at www.revolts.co.uk/Blair%20defeated%20twice% 20on%20Terrorism%20Bill.pdf.

Cox, Gary W. 1987. *The Efficient Secret: The Cabinet and the Development of Parties in Victorian England*. Cambridge University Press.

 1999. *Making Votes Count: Strategic Coordination in the World's Electoral Systems*. Cambridge University Press.

 2000. 'On the Effects of Legislative Rules', *Legislative Studies Quarterly*, 25: 169–92.

Cox, Gary W. and Matthew McCubbins. 2005. *Setting the Agenda: Responsible Party Government in the US House of Representatives*. Cambridge University Press.

Crewe, Ivor and Anthony King. 1994. 'Did Major Win? Did Kinnock Lose? Leadership Effects in the 1992 Election', in Anthony Heath, Roger Jowell, and John Curtice (eds.), *Labour's Last Chance? The 1992 Election and Beyond*. Aldershot: Dartmouth, 125–48.

Crewe, Ivor, Bo Sarlvik, and James E. Alt. 1977. 'Partisan Dealignment in Britain, 1964–1974', *British Journal of Political Science*, 7: 129–90.

Crowe, Edward W. 1983. 'Consensus and Structure in Legislative Norms: Party Discipline in the House of Commons', *Journal of Politics*, 45: 487–510.

1986. 'The Web of Authority: Party Loyalty and Social Control in the British House of Commons', *Legislative Studies Quarterly*, 11: 161–85.

Dalton, Russell J. 1993. *Politics in Germany*. New York: HarperCollins.

2000. 'The Decline of Party Identification', in Russell J. Dalton and Martin P. Wattenberg (eds.), *Parties without Partisans: Political Change in Advanced Industrial Democracies*. Oxford University Press, 19–36.

Dalton, Russell J., Scott C. Flanagan, and Paul Allen Beck. 1984. *Electoral Change in Advanced Industrial Democracies: Realignment or Dealignment*. Princeton University Press.

Denemark, David. 2000. 'Partisan Pork Barrel in Parliamentary Systems: Australian Constituency-level Grants', *Journal of Politics*, 62: 896–915.

Diermeier, Daniel and Timothy J. Feddersen. 1998. 'Cohesion in Legislatures and the Vote of Confidence Procedure', *American Political Science Review*, 92: 611–22.

Docherty, David. 1997. *Mr. Smith Goes to Ottawa: Life in the House of Commons*. Vancouver: University of British Columbia Press.

Döring, Herbert (ed.). 1995. *Parliaments and Majority Rule in Western Europe*. New York: St. Martin's Press.

Downs, Anthony. 1957. *An Economic Theory of Democracy*. New York: Harper-Row.

Duverger, Maurice. 1962. *Political Parties*, trans. Barbara and Robert North. New York: Wiley.

Epstein, David, David Brady, Sadafumi Kawato, and Sharyn O'Halloran. 1997. 'A Comparative Approach to Legislative Organization: Careerism and Seniority in the United States and Japan', *American Journal of Political Science*, 41: 965–98.

Erickson, Lynda. 1997. 'Might More Women Make a Difference? Gender, Party and Ideology among Parliamentary Candidates', *Canadian Journal of Political Science*, 30: 663–88.

Fenno, Richard F. Jr. 1973. *Congressmen in Committees*. Boston: Little, Brown.

Ferejohn, John A. and Brian Gaines. 1991. 'The Personal Vote in Canada', in Herman Bakvis (ed.), *Representation, Integration, and Political Parties in Canada*. Toronto: Dundurn Press, 275–302.

Franklin, Mark, Alison Baxter, and Margaret Jordan. 1986. 'Who Were the Rebels? Dissent in the House of Commons, 1970–1974', *Legislative Studies Quarterly*, **11**: 143–59.

Franks, C. E. S. 1987. *The Parliament of Canada*. University of Toronto Press.

Friedrich, Robert J. 1982. 'In Defense of Multiplicative Terms in Multiple Regression Equations', *American Political Science Review*, **26**: 797–833.

Gabel, Matthew J. and John Huber. 2000. 'Putting Parties in Their Place: Inferring Party Left–Right Ideological Positions from Party Manifestos Data', *American Journal of Political Science*, **44**: 94–103.

Gaines, Brian J. and Geoffrey Garrett. 1993. 'The Calculus of Dissent: Party Discipline in the British Labour Government, 1974–79', *Political Behavior*, **15**: 113–35.

Golder, Matt. 2003. 'Electoral Institutions, Unemployment and Extreme Right Parties: A Correction', *British Journal of Political Science*, **33**: 525–34.

Green, Donald P., Soo Yeon Kim, and David H. Yoon. 2001. 'Dirty Pool', *International Organization*, **55**: 441–468.

Hager, Gregory and Jeffery C. Talbert. 2000. 'Look for the Party Label: Party Influences on Voting in the U.S. House', *Legislative Studies Quarterly*, **15**: 75–99.

Heath, Anthony F., Roger M. Jowell, and John K. Curtice. 1985. *How Britain Votes*. Oxford: Pergamon.

  2001. *The Rise of New Labour: Party Policies and Voter Choices*. Oxford University Press.

Heitshusen, Valerie, Garry Young, and David M. Wood. 2005. 'Electoral Context and MP Constituency Focus in Australia, Canada, Ireland, New Zealand, and the United Kingdom', *American Journal of Political Science*, **49**: 32–45.

Hine, David. 1993. *Governing Italy: The Politics of Bargained Pluralism*. Oxford University Press.

Hirschman, Albert O. 1970. *Exit, Voice, Loyalty: Response to Decline in Firms, Organizations, and States*. Cambridge, MA: Harvard University Press.

Hixon, William and Aaron E. Wicks. 2000. 'Measuring Congressional Support for the President: Evaluating the NOMINATE Scores', *Presidential Studies Quarterly*, **30**: 186–93.

Hobby, M. 1987. '*The Crack of the Whips, Party Cohesion and Institutional Consensus in the New Zealand Parliament, 1936–85*', unpublished MA thesis, University of Canterbury, Christchurch.

Huber, John D. 1996a. *Rationalizing Parliament: Legislative Institutions and Party Politics in France*. New York: Cambridge University Press.

1996b. 'The Vote of Confidence in Parliamentary Democracies', *American Political Science Review*, 90: 269–82.

Huber, John D. and Ronald Inglehart. 1995. 'Expert Interpretations of Party Space and Party Locations in 42 Societies', *Party Politics*, 1: 73–111.

Irvine, W. P. 1982. 'Does the Candidate Make a Difference? The Macro-politics and Micro-politics of Getting Elected', *Canadian Journal of Political Science*, 15: 755–82.

Jackson, John and John W. Kingdon. 1992. 'Ideology, Interest Group Scores, and Legislative Votes', *American Journal of Political Science*, 36: 805–23.

Jackson, K. 1987. *The Dilemma of Parliament*. Auckland: Allen and Unwin.

Jackson, R. 1968. *Rebels and Whips: An Analysis of Dissension, Discipline, and Cohesion in British Political Parties*. New York: St. Martin's Press.

Jaensch, Dean. 1992. *The Politics of Australia*. Melbourne: Macmillan Australia.

Jensen, Torben K. 2000. 'Party Cohesion', in Peter Esaiasson and Knut Heider (eds.), *Beyond Westminster and Congress: The Nordic Experience*. Columbus: Ohio State University Press, 210–36.

Kam, Christopher. 2002. '*Parliaments, Parties, and MPs: A Comparative Perspective on Backbench Dissent, Party Discipline, and Intra-party Politics*', unpublished PhD dissertation, University of Rochester.

Kam, Christopher and Indridi Indridason. 2005. 'The Timing of Cabinet Reshuffles in Five Westminster Parliamentary Systems', *Legislative Studies Quarterly*, 30: 327–63.

Katz, Richard S. 2001. 'The Problem of Candidate Selection', *Party Politics*, 7: 277–96.

King, Anthony. 1981. 'The Rise of the Career Politician in Britain – And Its Consequences', *British Journal of Political Science*, 11: 249–285.

King, Gary. 1988. 'Statistical Models for Political Science Event Counts: Bias in Conventional Procedures and Evidence for the Exponential Poisson Regression Model', *American Journal of Political Science*, 32: 838–63.

Kirkpatrick, Samuel A. and Lelan McLemore. 1977. 'Perceptual and Affective Components of Legislative Norms: A Social-Psychological Analysis of Congruity', *Journal of Politics*, 39: 685–711.

Kornberg, Alan. 1967. *Canadian Legislative Behaviour: A Study of the 25th Parliament*. New York: Holt, Rinehart and Winston.

Krehbiel, Keith. 1993. 'Where's the Party?', *British Journal of Political Science*, 23: 235–66.

1999. 'Paradoxes of Parties in Congress', *Legislative Studies Quarterly*, **14**: 31–64.

Laakso, M. and R. Taagepera. 1979. '"Effective" Number of Parties: A Measure with Application to West Europe', *Comparative Political Studies*, **23**: 3–27.

Laver, Michael. 1999. 'Divided Parties, Divided Government', *Legislative Studies Quarterly*, **14**: 5–30.

Laver, Michael and Ben Hunt. 1992. *Policy and Party Competition*. London: Routledge.

Laver, Michael and Norman Schofield. 1990. *Multiparty Government: The Politics of Coalition in Western Europe*. Oxford University Press.

Laws, Michael. 1998. *The Demon Profession*. Auckland: HarperCollins.

Lijphart, Arend. 1975. 'The Comparable-Cases Strategy in Comparative Research', *Comparative Political Studies*, **8**: 158–77.

Londregan, John. 1999. 'Estimating Legislators' Ideal Points', *Political Analysis*, **8**: 38–56.

Lucy, Richard. 1985. *The Australian Form of Government*. Melbourne: Macmillan.

McAllister, Ian. 1992. 'Australia: Changing Social Structure, Stable Politics', in Mark Franklin, Thomas T. Mackie, and Henry Valen (eds.), *Electoral Change: Responses to Evolving Social and Attitudinal Structures in Fifteen Countries*. Cambridge University Press, 61–82.

2006. 'Political Parties in Australia: Party Stability in a Utilitarian Society', in Paul Webb, David Farrell, and Ian Holliday (eds.), *Political Parties at the Millennium: Adaptation and Decline in Democratic Societies*. Oxford University Press, 379–408.

McAllister, Ian and Donley T. Studlar. 2000. 'Conservative Euroscepticism and the Referendum Party in the 1997 British General Election', *Party Politics*, **6**: 359–71.

MacDonald, Stuart Elaine. 1987. 'Political Ambition and Attainment: A Dynamic Analysis of Parliamentary Careers', unpublished PhD dissertation, University of Michigan.

McSmith, Andy. 1996. *Faces of Labour: The Inside Story*. New York: Verso.

Major, John. 1999. *John Major: The Autobiography*. New York: HarperCollins.

Matland, Richard E. and Donley T. Studlar. 2004. 'Determinants of Legislative Turnover: A Cross-National Analysis', *British Journal of Political Science*, **34**: 87–108.

Meng, Xiao-Li. 1994. 'Multiple Imputation Inferences with Uncongenial Sources of Input', *Statistical Science*, **9**: 538–73.

Mershon, Carol and William Heller. 2005. 'Party Switching in the Italian Chamber of Deputies, 1996–2001', *Journal of Politics*, **67**: 536–59.

Mezey, Michael L. 1993. 'Legislatures: Individual Purpose and Institutional Performance', in Ada Finifter (ed.), *The State of the Discipline II*. Washington, DC: American Political Science Association.

Morgenstern, Scott. 2004. *Patterns of Legislative Politics: Roll Call Voting in the United States and Latin America's Southern Cone*. Cambridge University Press.

Mughan, Anthony. 1990. 'Midterm Popularity and Governing Party Dissension in the House of Commons, 1959–79', *Legislative Studies Quarterly*, **15**: 341–58.

Mughan, Anthony, Janet Box-Steffensmeier, and Roger Scully. 1997. 'Mapping Legislative Socialisation', *European Journal of Political Research*, **32**: 93–106.

Müller, Wolfgang C. and Kaare Strøm. 1999. 'Political Parties and Hard Choices', in Wolfgang C. Müller and Kaare Strøm (eds.), *Policy, Office, or Votes? How Political Parties in Western Europe Make Hard Choices*. New York: Cambridge University Press.

Nevitte, Neal, André Blais, Elisabeth Gidengil, and Richard Nadeau. 2000. *Unsteady State: The 1997 Canadian Federal Election*. Oxford University Press.

Norris, Pippa and Joni Lovenduski. 1994. *Political Recruitment: Gender, Race and Class in the British Parliament*. Cambridge University Press.

Norris, Pippa, Elizabeth Vallance, and Joni Lovenduski. 1992. 'Do Candidates Make a Difference? Gender, Race, Ideology and Incumbency', *Parliamentary Affairs*, **45**: 497–517.

Norton, Philip. 1975. *Dissension in the House of Commons: Intra-Party Dissent in the House of Commons Division Lobbies, 1945–1974*. London: MacMillan.

1978. *Conservative Dissidents*. London: Temple Smith.

1980. *Dissension in the House of Commons, 1974–1979*. New York: Oxford University Press.

1981. *The Commons in Perspective*. New York: Longman.

1985. 'Behavioural Changes. Backbench Independence in the 1980s', in Philip Norton (ed.), *Parliament in the 1980s*. Oxford: Basil Blackwell.

1987. 'Dissent in the British House of Commons: Rejoinder to Franklin, Baxter, Jordan', *Legislative Studies Quarterly*, **12**: 143–52.

2000. 'The Individual Member in the British House of Commons: Facing Both Ways and Marching Forward', in Lawrence D. Longley and Reuven Y. Hazan (eds.), *The Uneasy Relationships between Parliamentary Members and Leaders*. London: Frank Cass, 53–74.

Norton, Philip and David M. Wood. 1993. *Back from Westminster: British Members of Parliament and Their Constituents*. Lexington: University of Kentucky Press.

Ozbudun, Ergun. 1970. *Party Cohesion in Western Democracies: A Causal Analysis.* Beverly Hills, CA: Sage Books.

Palmer, Matthew S. R. 1995. 'Toward an Economics of Comparative Political Organization: Examining Ministerial Responsibility', *Journal of Law, Economics and Organization,* 11: 164–88.

Paltzelt, W. 2000. 'What Can an Individual MP Do in German Parliamentary Politics?', in L. Longley and R. Hazan (eds.), *The Uneasy Relationship between Parliamentary Members and Leaders.* London: Frank Cass, 23–52.

Patterson, Samuel. 1989. 'Understanding the British Parliament', *Political Studies,* 37: 449–62.

Pattie, Charles, Edward Fieldhouse, and R. J. Johnston. 1994. 'The Price of Conscience: The Electoral Correlates and Consequences of Free Votes and Rebellions in the British House of Commons, 1987–92', *British Journal of Political Science,* 24: 359–80.

Piper, J. Richard. 1991. 'British Backbench Rebellion and Government Appointments, 1945–87', *Legislative Studies Quarterly,* 16: 219–238.

Poole, Keith T. and Howard Rosenthal. 1997. *Congress: A Political-Economic History of Roll Call Voting.* New York: Oxford University Press.

Popkin, Samuel L. 1994. *The Reasoning Voter: Communication and Persuasion in Presidential Campaigns.* University of Chicago Press.

Powell, G. Bingham. 2000. *Elections as Instruments of Democracy: Majoritarian and Proportional Visions.* New Haven: Yale University Press.

Powell, G. Bingham and Guy D. Whitten. 1993. 'A Cross-National Analysis of Economic Voting: Taking Account of the Political Context', *American Journal of Political Science,* 37: 391–414.

Przeworski, Adam and Henry Teune. 1970. *The Logic of Comparative Inquiry.* Malabar, FL: R. E. Krieger.

Rasch, Bjørn Erik. 2000. 'Parliamentary Floor Voting Procedures and Agenda Setting in Europe', *Legislative Studies Quarterly,* 25: 3–23.

Rice, Stuart A. 1925. 'The Behavior of Legislative Groups', *Political Science Quarterly,* 40: 60–72.

Rubin, Donald B. 1977. 'Formalizing Subjective Notions about the Effect of Nonrespondents in Sample Surveys', *Journal of the American Statistical Association,* 72: 538–43.

⸻ 1987. *Multiple Imputation for Nonresponse in Surveys.* New York: Wiley and Sons.

⸻ 1996. 'Multiple Imputation after 18+ Years', *Journal of the American Statistical Association,* 91: 473–89.

Saalfeld, Thomas. 1986. 'On Dogs and Whips: Recorded Votes', in *International Centre for Parliamentary Documentation, Parliaments of the World: A Comparative Reference Compendium*. New York: Facts on File.

Sartori, Giovanni. 1991. 'Comparing and Miscomparing', *Journal of Theoretical Politics*, 3: 243–57.

Sayers, Anthony M. 1999. *Parties, Candidates, and Constituency Campaigns in Canadian Elections*. Vancouver: University of British Columbia Press.

Schafer, J.L. 1997. *Analysis of Incomplete Multivariate Data*. London: Chapman & Hall.

Schlesinger, Joseph A. 1961. *Ambition and Politics*. Chicago: Rand McNally.

Schwarz, John E. 1980. 'Exploring a New Role in Policy Making: The British House of Commons in the 1970s', *American Political Science Review*, 74: 23–37.

Searing, Donald D. 1994. *Westminster's World: Understanding Political Roles*. Cambridge, MA: Harvard University Press.

Searing, Donald D. and Chris Game. 1977. 'Horses for Courses: The Recruitment of Whips in the British House of Commons', *British Journal of Political Science*, 7: 361–85.

Seldon, Anthony. 2004. *Blair*. London: The Free Press.

Silk, Paul and Rhodri Walters. 1987. *How Parliament Works*. London and New York: Longman.

Snyder, James M. and Tim Groseclose. 2000. 'Estimating Party Influence in Congressional Roll-Call Voting', *American Journal of Political Science*, 44: 193–211.

Sowemimo, Matthew. 1996. 'The Conservative Party and European Integration, 1988–95', *Party Politics*, 2: 77–97.

Spirling, Arthur and Ian McLean. 2007. 'UK OC OK? Interpreting Optimal Classification Scores for the UK House of Commons', *Political Analysis*, 15: 85–96.

Stanbury, William T. 1993. 'Financing Federal Politics in Canada in an Era of Reform', in Arthur B. Gunlicks (ed.), *Campaign and Party Finance in North America and Western Europe*. Boulder, CO: Westview Press, 68–120.

Stimson. James A. 1985. 'Regression in Space and Time: A Statistical Essay', *American Journal of Political Science*, 29: 914–47.

Strøm, Kaare. 1986. 'Deferred Gratification and Minority Governments in Scandinavia', *Legislative Studies Quarterly*, 10: 583–605.

Thies, Michael F. 2000. 'On the Primacy of Party in Government: Why Legislative Parties Can Survive Party Decline in the Electorate', in Russell J. Dalton and Martin P. Wattenberg (eds.), *Parties without Partisans*. New York: Oxford University Press, 238–57.

Tocqueville, Alexis de. 1848/1965. *Democracy in America*. Garden City, New York: Doubleday.

Tsebelis, George. 2002. *Veto Players. How Political Institutions Work*. Princeton University Press.

Vandoren, Peter M. 1990. 'Can We Learn the Causes of Congressional Decisions from Roll-Call Data?', *Legislative Studies Quarterly*, **15**: 311–39.

Vowles, Jack and Peter Aimer. 1992. *The Voters' Vengeance: The 1990 Election in New Zealand and the Fate of the Fourth Labour Government*. Auckland University Press.

Ward, Norman. 1987. *Dawson's The Government of Canada*, 6th edn. University of Toronto Press.

Wearing, Joseph. 1998. 'Guns, Gays, and Gadflies: Party Dissent in the House of Commons under Mulroney and Chrétien', paper presented at the Annual Meeting of the Canadian Political Science Association, University of Ottawa, 31 May–2 June 1998.

Webb, Paul D. 1994. 'Centralized Parties and Decentralized Selection', in Richard S. Katz and Peter Mair (eds.), *How Parties Organize: Change and Adaptation in Party Organizations in Western Democracies*. Thousand Oaks, CA: Sage Publications.

Willson, F. M. G. 1959. 'The Routes of Entry of New Members of the British Cabinet 1868–1958', *Political Studies*, 7: 222–32.

    1970. 'Entry to the Cabinet, 1959–68', *Political Studies*, **18**: 236–38.

Index